Speech Stories

Speech Stories

How Free Can Speech Be?

Randall P. Bezanson

NEW YORK UNIVERSITY PRESS

New York and London

NEW YORK UNIVERSITY PRESS
New York and London

Library of Congress Cataloging-in-Publication Data
Bezanson, Randall P.
Speech stories : how free can speech be? /
Randall P. Bezanson.   p.   cm.
Includes bibliographical references and index.
ISBN 0-8147-1320-3 (clothbound: acid-free paper). — ISBN
0-8147-1321-1 (paperback: acid-free paper)
1. Freedom of speech—United States.   I. Title.
KF4770.B49   1998
342.73'0853—dc21   97-33821
                                                    CIP

New York University Press books are printed on acid-free paper,
and their binding materials are chosen for strength and durability.

Manufactured in the United States of America

10 9 8 7 6 5 4 3 2 1

Contents

Preface and Acknowledgments

I have now taught the First Amendment for more than two decades. I began teaching law in 1973, and, with the exception of occasional administrative assignments that took me from the classroom for brief periods, I have taught a course on constitutional law, communication law, law and journalism, or (in the best of years) a free speech seminar each year.

When I reflect on teaching the First Amendment over that period of time, I am most struck by the fact that certain cases seem never to grow old; they remain alive and intellectually challenging even as the Supreme Court's free speech doctrine changes. When I began teaching, *Cohen v. California*, the subject of the first story, was just two years old. By 1998, twenty-five years had passed since Justice Harlan crafted his most famous opinion in that seemingly "inconsequential" case, as he described it, of the jacket with a "scurrilous epithet" painted on the back, but I still use the opinion as the starting point in my free speech seminar, for it brings all of the nettlesome questions surrounding free speech straight to the surface for the students' examination.

The *Jenkins v. Georgia* case, involving the decision of a jury in Albany, Georgia, that the film *Carnal Knowledge* was obscene, would be decided shortly after I began teaching in 1973. But it is a remarkable and resilient case, drawing us back to the civil rights era and the culture of the rural South, and in doing so forcing students to come to understand how the communication process really works, how meaning, like "obscene," becomes associated with a text or film, and then pulling us forward to 1995 and the feminist critique of pornography, which represents an alternative battle over the power to interpret and give meaning to speech.

Other cases that have arisen more recently seem also to have a persistent quality, serving as vessels, if you will, for unlocking the fundamental mysteries of the First Amendment. Only time will tell, of course, whether the cross-burning case, *R.A.V. v. St. Paul* ("The Burning Cross"), or the flag-burning case, *Texas v. Johnson* ("The Medium and the Message"), or *McIntyre v. Ohio Elections Commission*, the petty vendetta against Margaret McIntyre and her leaflet that should never have gotten to court ("The Author"), will continue to inspire understanding over the years. My guess is that they will.

I have always believed that the wonderful mysteries of the First Amendment—the peculiar byways and the intellectual puzzles of free speech—should be made available to any interested "student" of the First Amendment, and not be reserved only for law students. It is with that object in mind that I undertook to write this book. In my fairly long academic career, nothing has proved more enjoyable to write than these stories. They have animated students from the fields of law, communication studies, journalism, and English in my First Amendment seminars, often leading to interesting and passionate disagreements. They have likewise animated faculty seminars at Washington & Lee University and the University of Iowa, and have enlivened conversations with colleagues in law teaching, in the fields of communication and journalism, and in the practice of journalism, throughout the country. More important, they have captured the interest and engaged the attention of many more friends who do not carry around an academic rank or professional pedigree but who instead are simply bright women and men who enjoy being intellectually engaged in questions that know no certain answers, where the pursuit is more fruitful than the prey.

By publishing these stories in book form I hope that many other people will find themselves engaged in the deep and challenging mysteries of the First Amendment, and that many after-dinner conversations, accompanied by fresh coffee and good wine, might result.

There are many people whose contributions to this book should be acknowledged. First and foremost is my wife, Elaine, who encouraged me to write about the First Amendment in a more readable and accessible way than legal academics ordinarily do, and who patiently introduced me to the art of writing in the active voice, an art I have only begun to master. My colleagues at the Washington & Lee University School of Law and the University of Iowa College of Law were generous enough to read selected stories and offer their opinions, often critical but always helpful, in faculty colloquia. And a number of colleagues, students, and friends in the legal academy and outside it undertook the more arduous task of reading stories and offering their editorial advice and substantive comments. These persons, to whom I am greatly indebted, are Sam Becker, Arthur Bonfield, Bill Buss, Gil Cranberg, Louise Halper, Gwen Handleman, Linda Hirshman, Kathryn Ingle (to whom I am also grateful for the Beckett quote), Vaishali Javeri, John Jennings, Nick Johnson, Sheldon Kurtz, Lewis LaRue, Robert Post, Mark and Sandy Schantz, Joan Shaughnessy, John Soloski, David and Rhoda Vernon, Allan and Brenda Vestal, and Jerry Wetlaufer. It goes without saying that none of these people bear any responsibility for any views that I express or errors that I have made. But I hope that they will find the final product improved as a result of their advice and counsel.

Clam Lake, Wisconsin
Iowa City, Iowa

Introduction

When we talk about what "freedom of speech" means in America, the discussion almost always centers on "freedom," not on "speech." "Speech" is something we know and can easily recognize. Our arguments therefore concern how much freedom it should enjoy. But is this a correct way of thinking about free speech? Are we wrong in simply taking the speech part of the equation for granted?

When a group of boys in St. Paul, Minnesota, sets fire to a cross on the front yard of a black family, our arguments about the extent to which the First Amendment should immunize their behavior from punishment tend to revolve around the extent of the "freedom" that the boys should enjoy; we take it for granted that "speech" was involved in the boys' act. When a campaign committee broadcasts an advertisement for a candidate, we likewise assume that the ad possesses status as "speech" protected by the First Amendment, and proceed to argue about the ability of government to regulate political campaigns only in terms of the "freedom" speech enjoys. And when Mobil publishes one of its "public service advertisements" addressing an important public issue, we don't question for a minute that what Mobil is saying is "speech," though we may disagree about Mobil's "freedom" to purchase the space to disseminate it.

We are wrong to so limit our focus to questions of "freedom" that we often ignore questions of "speech." The First Amendment protects "speech," and "speech" is an inherently ambiguous thing. And it is becoming more ambiguous every day as changing habits of discourse combined with new technologies of distribution alter the idea of "speech" at its very foundations.

The American idea of free speech grew out of the individual act of dissent and belief. Freedom of speech sheltered acts of personal conviction, uncommon acts of bravery undertaken in the face of significant risk. The heroes of free speech included Patrick Henry, Elizabeth Cady Stanton,

Henry David Thoreau, Martin Luther King, Jr., and countless others, both famous and anonymous, who felt strongly enough about their beliefs to attempt to convince others of their merit.

Today, speaking is a complex act. It rarely consists of an individual's act of belief or dissent. Instead, speech is now largely group oriented, money dependent, and medium driven. Speech in today's "marketplace" increasingly involves ideas collectively arrived at and assembled by organized, planned effort. Its medium is increasingly monetary because solicitation of the funds that must then be expended for space and time in the distribution system has necessarily become a dominant occupation of anyone interested in "legitimate" and "public" expression. And the impact of speech is often inseparable from—indeed, it is sometimes *exclusively based on*—medium and market rather than the strength of an idea.

The nature of "speech" is changing, in other words, and arguments based on "freedom" alone are no longer capable of bearing most of the burden under the First Amendment. It is time, therefore, to undertake a new and serious reexamination of the largely forgotten half of the free speech question: Is this speech? More specifically, it is time to reexamine a number of apparently simple but in fact profoundly important and unsettling questions: Is anything—any word, any image, any act—that can be said to have meaning, speech? Must speech possess a speaker—must it be the product of someone's intention and will? Is "speech" the idea communicated or the medium of its communication—or both?

That these are fundamental questions under the First Amendment may be more obvious to the uninitiated than to the initiated. The questions have largely been ignored (or, to put it more accurately, *assumed*) by the Supreme Court until recently. They are hardly mentioned in the legal academy. That they have been ignored says more about the comfort with which we could rely on speech always to have a speaker—just like babies, who, until lately, have always had a mother—than about any failure of the Court or academy. But these matters can no longer be ignored. As the following pages will disclose, speech does not always, in this "modern" world, have a speaker. Meaning can be more a function of method or form (medium, audience) than of substance. And the "medium" of exchange in which speech now transpires is not so much persuasion as purchasing power; not words but money. Where does this leave the old-fashioned idea of speech?

My purpose is not to define "speech" as the term is used in the First Amendment or even to outline *how* we should go about doing so. It is instead to argue that we must begin to think anew, free of ideological trappings and intellectual habits, about speech itself, instead of just its freedom. My argument, such as it is, rests on a selected group of "stories" about speech, each of which is an outgrowth of a case presented to the Supreme Court. In each we are confronted with unavoidable questions about the meaning of what we call "speech" protected by the First Amendment.

Freedom of speech is, in a real sense, both the beginning and the end of American liberty. It is, as James Madison said, essential to the working of democratic self-government. And without our idea of individual liberty — of individualism, itself — democracy would be little more than a cruel hoax. So we safeguard the individual's ability to speak freely and without censorship by government in order to make "we, the people" an operative principle of democracy, and we assure freedom of conscience and belief for each member of society out of the conviction that moral agency belongs to all humans, individually. In this way we might describe the "uncontroversial core" of the First Amendment's freedom of speech; we can safely assert that with few exceptions most people agree about these core purposes and the need for a degree of freedom of speech that accomplishes them.

But if the core of freedom of speech is clear and coherent, the same cannot be said about the periphery. What about speech that does not serve these self-governing and liberty purposes but, instead, serves other ends, such as efficient commercial markets? What about speech that serves self-governing or liberty ends but in peculiar ways (as with pornography), or only idiosyncratically (as with flag burning), or with other costs (as with racist insults)? What about speech whose contribution to liberty and democracy depends on its regulation (such as medical advice, legal advice, and perhaps campaign "advice")? What about speech that takes new and different forms, such as money (campaign contributions), or medium (cable TV), or words that occur inadvertently or mechanically (such as automated telemarketing)?

My interest is with these and other "peripheries" of free speech. It turns out that little is understood about the peripheries of speech. The cases arising in the peripheries are often little known. It turns out, also, that the "peripheries" are not, really, peripheral but central. The most fundamental free speech questions lie there. More strikingly, the principles of free speech that apply to them are astoundingly uncertain.

There is, of course, the question whether ignorance of the peripheries of speech is useful. Perhaps, as the late professor Alexander Bickel, drawing upon Edmund Burke, once suggested—and here I paraphrase—"Liberty defined is liberty lost." Perhaps, in other words, some degree of ambiguity and intellectual incoherence at the periphery of freedom of speech is desirable, at least in the sense that awareness of all of the corners and edges of the free speech landscape, and their consequent submission to our insatiable appetite to define the amount of liberty to be enjoyed there, would turn out to be destructive of liberty and democracy. Perhaps liberty and democracy—and human freedom itself—are too organic to be reduced to clearer definition.

I am sympathetic with this general view, as I am with much that Burke might be understood to suggest. My purpose is therefore not to dispute the conclusion (nor to argue for it) but instead to explore the periphery without reducing it to formulae in the belief that the intellectual curiosities it poses are useful and important even if they should not lead us to more specific definitions of the boundaries of free speech. I am confident, in other words, that knowledge is useful in itself, even if the uses we make of it often are not.

PART I

Speakers

The First Amendment reads: "Congress shall make no law . . . abridging the freedom of speech." The guarantee is brief and to the point. But its brevity bristles with ambiguity.

What is the significance of its application to Congress alone? As it turns out, the word Congress is to be read broadly to include all parts of the national government, legislative, executive, and even judicial, and state governments as well.

What does the term "law" mean, and for that matter, the term "no" law? The Supreme Court has never suggested, for example, that fraud accomplished through words cannot be prohibited. As we will see, "no law" does not mean "*No* law."

And what about the terms "abridge" and "freedom"? On their face these are terms with uncertain meaning that imply relativity. The First Amendment does not prohibit laws that "in any way interfere with" the "immunity" of speech from regulation. Whether the "freedom" to be accorded speech is "abridged," then, must depend in part on how great the restriction on speech is, and how pressing the competing interest supporting the restriction might be. Making extortion by speech a crime surely restricts speech, but the restriction is not an abridgment and freedom does not extend that far.

We will confront these ambiguities throughout this book. But the most important ambiguity that will occupy most of our attention in part I is the term "speech." "Speech" is the most important term in the First Amendment, for the term "speech," alone, contains the substance of the guarantee, with all of the other terms outlining the degree and kind of protection accorded "speech."

What is this thing called "speech" that the First Amendment protects? Is the First Amendment to be read to guarantee freedom for speech itself—the words, pictures, images, and actions through which messages are conveyed to us? Or does "freedom" belong to the person doing the communicating—the speaker—with protection of the speech an inevitable, though perhaps not necessary, by-product of the speaker's freedom?

The role of the speaker in the First Amendment's freedom of speech is the question that will occupy us in part 1. The question is an age-old one, though surprisingly the Supreme Court has only recently begun to give it much attention. Through the three stories that will be told, we will come to discover that the speaker plays a deceptively subtle and complex role in the First Amendment drama.

The first story, "The Jacket," will force us, initially, to confront the many possible meanings of the term "speech" as they might be applied to the "brutish" lettering placed on a jacket. The story will transport us into the murky depths of First Amendment speech, and then lead us out, happily, by shifting our focus away from the jacket and its painted lettering and toward the young man who wore it, thus defining speech by reference to a speaker, not words alone.

Fittingly, the second story, "The Author," starts where the first ends. It will make us think anew, perhaps, about one specific kind of First Amendment speaker: an author. Is the person who creates a text the author, or are the readers also authors? When the author's identity is missing, as with anonymous texts, does the author likewise disappear, leaving the text behind as a mere artifact — speech — that possesses no freedom of its own?

The third story, "The Corporation and the Candidate," will lead us to the next and final question: What about speech that has *no* author at all? Here we will explore, in the settings of speech by General Motors, Donald Trump, the NAACP, the ACLU, and the Michigan State Chamber of Commerce, the relationship of mind to speaking. If, for purposes of the First Amendment, speech must have a speaker, must speakers have a mind, a will of their own that, like the civil rights marcher, is being purposefully communicated to others? Do corporations and other forms of collective organizations have minds of their own, and if not, is their expression speech under the First Amendment?

These are the paths down which the three stories will carry us. Each story, in its own way, will invite us to think about issues that are foundational to the very idea of freedom of speech.

The Jacket
(Cohen v. California, 403 U.S. 15 (1971))

Was it because of the chill in the air that Paul Robert Cohen wore the jacket or was it because of the words "Fuck the Draft" painted on the back? As he put his jacket on and left his home on that fateful spring morning in 1968, Cohen did not realize that his destination, the Los Angeles County Courthouse, would be only the first stop on a much larger journey. He would enter the courthouse of his own volition. He would leave it under arrest. Thus began a journey that would shake the legal world, reshape the meaning of speech protected by the First Amendment to the United States Constitution, and end with a remarkable opinion by the Supreme Court of the United States.

But Paul Cohen, then a young man, was not aware of the journey that lay ahead as he left his home with his jacket on the morning of April 26, 1968. He was scheduled to testify as a witness in a misdemeanor trial at the Los Angeles County Courthouse, a majestic, imposing, and authoritative building whose sheer mass dominated part of the downtown Los Angeles landscape.

The Vietnam War loomed heavily on the consciousness of the American people in April of 1968. Lyndon Johnson had recently eliminated most college draft deferments. He would not be running for reelection in the fall. Richard Nixon would soon be elected president on a platform of a prompt, but honorable, end to the war. It was a volatile era during which peace symbols and antiwar slogans littered the landscape.

Paul Cohen's jacket expressed his depth of feeling about the war. Painted in white on the dark material were several peace symbols, the message "Stop the War," and, emblazoned on the back, the words "Fuck the Draft." Today we might treat such words on a jacket or T-shirt with indifference, even if with a certain disdain, for we have become acclimated to them . . . in movies, in humor, indeed in relatively polite conversation. But Cohen did not use the word "Fuck" in 1995;

he used it, in public, in 1968; in the waning years of a more innocent time, before our senses went numb in the face of pervasive sex, violence, and rock and roll.

Paul Cohen did not go out that morning to participate in a protest against the Vietnam War but, instead, to testify as a witness for the defense in a case that had no bearing on the draft or the war. In fact, no judges heard draft cases at the Los Angeles County Courthouse since it was a state, not a federal, courthouse. But it was by any standards a large — indeed by most standards monstrous — courthouse, nine stories high, with around one hundred courtrooms.

After entering the courthouse building Cohen walked down a long corridor, perhaps a half block in length, to a bank of elevators. He rode an elevator to the seventh floor, where Division 20 was located. The courthouse was busy that morning and the potential audience for the jacket's message numbered in the hundreds, including women and children. This was particularly the case on the seventh floor, for Division 20 was the main master calendar for all misdemeanors. Virtually all misdemeanors in the city, from traffic violations to loitering to petty theft and trespass and disturbing the peace, were tried there. According to Michael Sauer, the deputy city attorney for the City of Los Angeles who would handle Cohen's case, "On a normal day, at any hour, there were probably 200 people there."

Three police officers, Sergeant Shore, Sergeant Swan, and officer Alexander, spotted Cohen as he emerged from the elevator and walked down the wide corridor flanked by courtrooms. All of them noticed the jacket and its painted slogan "Fuck the Draft." But before they could approach him, Cohen turned toward one of the courtrooms, removed his jacket, folded it over his arm so that the lettering was hidden from view, and then entered the courtroom in which he was to testify. One of the officers followed him into the courtroom. The officer approached the bench and, in hushed tones, told the judge about Cohen's jacket, pointed him out, and asked the judge to hold Cohen in contempt of court. The judge refused.

When his business was completed, Cohen rose to leave. As he emerged through the doors of the courtroom into the busy corridor, the officers were awaiting him. They approached him immediately, confirmed that he had the jacket, and then arrested him for disturbing the peace by engaging in tumultuous and offensive behavior. We do not know whether he had put the jacket back on.

*

What Paul Cohen did on that April morning in 1968 had a profound but unanticipated influence on freedom of speech in the United States, an influence that would transcend his actions and even the antiwar protests of the Vietnam era, reaching forward nearly three decades to shape the way we think about free speech in today's climate of hate speech, campus speech codes, and pornography—indeed, to alter the very meaning of "speech" protected by the First Amendment. But to fully understand these implications and their importance, we must turn to Cohen's legal battle and the opinions of the courts in which it was waged.

Paul Cohen is someone about whom we learn virtually nothing in the course of the legal proceedings that followed his arrest. The further his case progressed, it seems, the less important he became to it. We know him only as "a young man." We can assume, also, that he was deeply opposed to the Vietnam War and the draft . . . deeply enough, at least, to paint "Fuck the Draft" in bold letters on the back of his jacket and thus to display his passion to all who would see it. This, at least, was his claim from the very beginning: that in displaying the message in all its brutal frankness he was exercising his freedom of speech protected by the First Amendment. He wore the jacket, his lawyer asserted, to express the depth of his feelings about the war. But he wore it also because "he was somewhat chilly. . . . he wasn't there [in the Los Angeles Court-house] to demonstrate or parade."

Cohen's trial was held in the Los Angeles County Courthouse, in a courtroom entered from the same corridor down which he had walked, displaying his jacket's message. He was charged with disturbing the peace by offensive and tumultuous conduct, a misdemeanor punishable by a fine of up to $200 or imprisonment in the county jail for no more than ninety days. At the trial, the three police officers who arrested Cohen testified that they had seen him walking in the corridor of the courthouse wearing the jacket with the words "Fuck the Draft" promi-nently displayed on his back. No one else who had seen Cohen walking in the corridor that morning was called to the witness stand, and there-fore no one else testified that he or she had seen the jacket or was offended by it. But the law Cohen violated, originally enacted in 1872, did not require such firsthand evidence of actual offense. His crime was violating the generally accepted standards of decency maintained by rea-sonable persons, whether any such persons were in fact present or, for that matter, offended.

Based essentially on these facts alone, and in the face of his claim that the jacket's message was speech protected by the First Amendment, Cohen was convicted. The presiding judge, James Harvey Brown of the Municipal Court of Los Angeles, sentenced him to thirty days in the Los Angeles County Jail. Judge Brown, it seems, had little time for Cohen's free speech claim, perhaps viewing Cohen's act of wearing the jacket as mostly conduct and little speech. We cannot know Judge Brown's views for certain because he wrote no opinion in the case, but the characterization of Cohen's action as conduct and not speech was to haunt the case all the way to the Supreme Court.

Judge Brown, however, was not to have the last word, for Cohen was not prepared to accept his conviction, serve his sentence, and resume his life. Instead, he appealed his case to the California Court of Appeal, challenging the constitutionality of the California law under which he had been convicted. In visiting its restriction on speech that is "offensive and tumultuous," he argued, the law punished speech simply because it was offensive and violated common standards of decency. Speech cannot be free under such a suffocating regime of government-imposed standards of taste and decency.

The appeals court, however, saw the case very differently. Cohen's conduct, the court said, "consisted of more than a quiet and peaceful dissertation of his convictions about the draft." In choosing "a courthouse corridor containing women and children" as a forum for his views, his purpose was not "to espouse a philosophy or a personal conviction" but to "shock," to "attract[] the attention of others to his views by the sheer vulgarity of his expression," and to "vex and annoy a substantial portion of his unwilling 'audience.'" If there were limits to government's authority to enforce standards of decency on speech, Cohen's conduct did not exceed them. With Cohen's free speech claim thus unceremoniously rejected, the appeals court affirmed his conviction. When Cohen thereafter appealed the Court of Appeal decision to the California Supreme Court, a court known for its active protection of First Amendment rights, that court declined even to review the case (though on a divided vote).

Cohen's only remaining option was an appeal to the United States Supreme Court. His chances were slim; of the nearly 5,000 cases filed with the Supreme Court each year, the Court accepts only 150 to 200 for review. But even though the odds were heavily against him, and notwithstanding the sweeping rejection of his free speech claim in the California courts, he took his case to the United States Supreme Court. And there fortune turned in his favor. In an order that must have surprised even Cohen, the Court accepted the case for review and set it down for oral argument on February 22, 1971.

At first blush Cohen's case seemed straightforward: a simple, if controversial, claim that his highly charged and offensive rhetoric could not be prohibited because the Constitution guaranteed his freedom to use it. But when his case came up for oral argument before the full Court, it became clear that Cohen's apparently inconsequential and straightforward case was, in fact, very complicated. The complexities emerged in the drama of the oral argument that took place in the Supreme Court Building in Washington, D.C.

Oral argument before the Supreme Court is a bracing experience for a lawyer. Walking up the dozens of steps leading to the grand entrance of the building—a building dubbed, by some, the marble palace—entering through the huge doors, proceeding down the wide and long marble corridor flanked by marble statues and columns rising nearly fifty feet to the ornate ceiling, the lawyer feels the seriousness and high politics that the majestic building signifies. Inside voices and footsteps reverberate in and around the damp chill of the white marble corridor as the lawyer walks toward the dark wood doors of the courtroom.

The courtroom imposes its authority even before the oral argument begins, encouraging the lawyer to reevaluate his or her sense of worth. The room is nearly three stories high, ringed with marble columns, and the ceiling is painted with frescos and bordered with friezes. The raised *banc*, behind which the justices sit, looms high and dominates the front of the courtroom. The lawyer's podium beneath it seems to be a miniature representation by comparison. It is from this podium, looking up at the justices, that the lawyer pleads the client's case, knowing that each argument may be interrupted with lightning-quick questions posed by the justices. In midsentence of a lawyer's well-prepared argument the relentless questions will come, sometimes in no particular order, often with apparent serendipity, but always, the lawyer knows, with a purpose that pierces to the heart of the case. The physical effect is chilling; the psychological effect is unnerving.

On the day that Cohen's case was argued, the nine black-robed justices who occupied the high-backed leather chairs behind the *banc* still matched the description "Nine Old Men." None of the justices was under fifty years of age, and most were in their sixties and seventies. In terms of years of service on the Court this was a particularly experienced and wise group. Only Justice Harry Blackmun and Chief Justice Warren Burger were new to the Court.

Chief Justice Earl Warren, who had led the Supreme Court through a remarkable period of judicial activism in the 1950s and 1960s, had resigned two years earlier. But in most respects the Court remained the "Warren Court," its membership still dominated by those justices who had served under Warren. These Warren Court justices included William O. Douglas and Hugo Black, both widely recognized as First Amendment absolutists. When the First Amendment says, "Congress shall make no law . . . abridging the freedom of speech," Hugo Black had said, it means "*No* Law!"

William Brennan and Thurgood Marshall were Warren Court liberals as well. Brennan was a strong proponent of free speech but not an absolutist. He had authored a famous decision that narrowed the definition of obscenity that could be prohibited, yet stated unequivocally that "obscenity is not protected by the freedoms of speech and press" because it is "utterly without redeeming social importance."

Thurgood Marshall, the Court's first African-American justice, had yet fully to establish his First Amendment credentials. This was only his fourth year on the Court, and new justices tend to be cautious in their opinion writing at the start. But Marshall and Brennan were rarely in disagreement, for they held similar views about the values that animated the Constitution and, particularly, the Bill of Rights.

The remaining three Warren Court justices, Byron White, Potter Stewart, and John Marshall Harlan, entertained the view that "no Law" does *not* mean no law, notwithstanding Justice Black's views to the contrary. Byron White was a Kennedy appointee, a former football star, a Rhodes scholar. He was intellectually inclined toward the pragmatic: to decisions grounded firmly on the facts, to gradualism, and to results that were practical.

Potter Stewart had been a member of the Court since the 1950s, having been appointed by President Eisenhower. He had gained a certain amount of fame, perhaps infamy, for stating in an opinion that, while he couldn't define obscenity, "I know it when I see it," and it isn't speech protected by the First Amendment. The statement expressed his frustration at the seemingly endless stream of allegedly obscene materials the Court obliged itself to review each year, but it also posed a simple truth.

Justice John Marshall Harlan, who would write the opinion for the Court in Cohen's case, was perhaps the most widely respected member of the Court. His diminutive appearance belied his notable pedigree and credentials. He bore the name of the greatest justice in the history of the Supreme Court, Chief Justice John Marshall, who served from 1801 to 1835 and who shaped the fundamental structure of our constitutional democracy in opinions that are still regularly relied upon and studied. Justice Harlan's grandfather, known as the Elder Harlan, had served on the Supreme Court during the post-Reconstruction period in the late nineteenth century and early twentieth, and was widely respected as one of the truly great justices in the history of the Court.

John Marshall Harlan, known as the Younger Harlan, had been educated in all the "right" places, had practiced law in New York City with one of the nation's most distinguished corporate firms, and over the course of his sixteen years on the Court had gained a deserved reputation for his keen intellect, his powerful and exacting analytical skills, and the clarity and intellectual honesty of his opinions.

Justice Harlan would retire at the end of the 1970 Term of the Court (which began in October of 1970 and ended in July of 1971), just five months after oral argument in *Cohen*. By the 1970 term he had become nearly blind and was assisted in his work by his staff, who would read briefs and opinions to him. But if anything, his loss of sight had enhanced his analytical skills and his fine sense of judgment. In the view of many constitutional scholars, *Cohen v. California* would be his most famous opinion.

So it was that the lawyers who would argue Paul Cohen's case faced a Supreme Court as imposing as the building in which it sat. The lawyers were well prepared for the intellectually demanding ritual of oral argument. Supreme Court cases are not simply an exercise in discovering the law but are, instead, exercises in *making* the law. What has happened in the past is important but not decisive. And the perspectives the Court brings to the facts of a case—the interpretation of the facts, and the imputation of meaning to them—are often new, just as the legal questions are without precise precedent. For this the lawyers would need their wits as well as their books.

At one o'clock in the afternoon of Monday, February 22, 1971, the two lawyers who would argue Cohen's case rose as the justices in their black robes entered the courtroom through the large curtain that draped the

wall behind the *banc*, coming single file in order of seniority and proceeding directly to their own chair, arranged by order of seniority.
Cohen's lawyer, who would argue first, was Melville Nimmer, a professor of law and one of the nation's leading authorities on freedom of
speech. Michael T. Sauer, deputy city attorney for the City of Los Angeles, was the lawyer for the State of California.

As Chief Justice Burger struck the gavel to bring the proceedings to
order and called Nimmer to the podium to present Cohen's case, it was
clear that the oral argument would focus very little on earlier precedents
or even on the Constitution's text or history. If it did, Cohen's case
would be open and shut and he would probably lose. In agreeing to hear
the case, the justices had signaled an intention to delve more deeply into
the First Amendment's meaning, perhaps making new law to replace the
old. Accordingly, Nimmer was given only a brief time in which to make
a formal presentation of the case and the legal theory underlying
Cohen's claimed right of free speech. This was not what interested the
justices. The existing law was well known to them. They and their pre-
decessors had, after all, made it. The justices were interested, instead, in
the new questions that Cohen's actions raised. Nimmer was therefore
quickly interrupted by a flurry of questions from the justices, questions
that homed in quickly on ambiguities in the factual record, on previously
little noticed aspects of Cohen's behavior and motivations, on the state's
justifications for the criminal conviction, and, most important, on defining the precise issue the case presented.

The first question had to do with why Cohen had removed his jacket
upon entering the Los Angeles County Courtroom in 1968. The issue
underlying the question was Cohen's motive and intent: How, if at all,
were they relevant to his claimed act of "speaking"?

> *Justice Stewart:* When he took off the jacket, did he put it in a place
> where it was prominently in view?
> *Mr. Nimmer:* No, Mr. Justice Stewart, he held it folded over his arm
> and it was not on view there. Furthermore, the policeman who
> observed him walking through the corridor before he went into the
> courtroom . . . requested the judge in the courtroom to hold the
> young man in contempt. The judge refused to hold the young man
> in contempt because there was nothing to be seen in the court-
> room—I shouldn't say that. I don't know what he would have
> done if he did see anything, but there was nothing to be seen. And
> then he left and at that point he was arrested.

The subject arose once again at a later point in the oral argument in response to Nimmer's claim that the words used on the jacket communicated Cohen's "depth of feeling that was evidenced by this word."

Mr. Nimmer: [T]he mere fact that this young man chose to use a word which many people would no doubt find disagreeable . . . is important data for the self-governing people to know — to know that he feels this deeply about this subject. If he had used the more laundered form of expression: 'I hate the draft,' they would have been ignorant to a degree.

Justice Marshall: Why did he take the jacket off when he entered the courtroom?

Mr. Nimmer: He took the jacket off because he was wearing the jacket as one would ordinarily wear a jacket: he was somewhat chilly. He knew that the sign was on there and he knew that this showed the depth of feeling of young men, but he wasn't there to demonstrate or parade. . . .

Justice Marshall: I think you missed the import of my question.

Mr. Nimmer: I'm sorry, Your Honor.

Justice Marshall: He was willing to do all this demonstrating but he wasn't willing to do it in the courtroom?

Mr. Nimmer: Well, Your Honor, he was not . . .

Justice Marshall: Does that lead me to believe he knew exactly what he was doing?

Mr. Nimmer: Your Honor he . . .

Justice Marshall: That he knew better than to wear it in the courtroom?

Mr. Nimmer: That he knew . . . ?

Justice Marshall: That he knew better than to wear it in the courtroom?

Mr. Nimmer: Perhaps he knew it would be improper to wear it in the courtroom. I have never questioned him on that. . . . I don't know.

Justice Marshall: Well, it should put emphasis [on the fact] that he folded it up.

Mr. Nimmer: Yes, indeed.

Justice Marshall: But he still has the right to parade around the courthouse halls, knowing that that building had nothing to do with the draft in any form or fashion, am I right?

Mr. Nimmer: You are quite right, Your Honor.

Justice Marshall: And you emphasize that?

Mr. Nimmer: Yes, Your Honor.

Justice Marshall: And my question is: why?

Mr. Nimmer: Because . . . I want to make the point that this does not get into the area of possible contempt of court. This is an ordinary . . . exercise in freedom of expression. . . .

Justice Marshall: Well, could he have stood in the court hallways and yelled those words?

Mr. Nimmer: Certainly not. That would have been highly improper, Your Honor.

Justice Marshall: Well, the fact that he has it emblazoned on his jacket, we can't tell whether that's loud or quiet. Can you?

Mr. Nimmer: Well, Your Honor, it was on his jacket, which meant that a person, if he wish[ed] to, could see it . . . and a person was not forced to continue to observe that as in terms of a loud voice . . .

Justice Marshall: Well, [a person] walking up the halls directly behind him couldn't help . . . seeing it.

Mr. Nimmer: For the moment. But obviously . . .

Justice Marshall: Obviously that's why he did it. [Do] you mean he didn't want people to see it?

Mr. Nimmer: No; I'm certainly not saying that at all. Quite definitely he did want to pass that message, but it's a somewhat different question . . . what his motive was in wearing it. And in part it was to convey this message, although he was not parading or picketing or anything of the sort. He was making his way to the courtroom and then made his way back. But he did want people to see this. On the other hand, it's a different question . . . whether or not people had to see it for any considerable period of time, and we would respectfully suggest that was not necessary under the circumstances. It is true that some people momentarily probably couldn't avoid seeing it, but there was no continuing requirement. . . .

The exchange about Cohen's folding his jacket when he entered the courtroom focuses on two aspects of the case that were important to the justices but were clouded in ambiguity. First, what does the act reveal about Cohen, who is an otherwise largely anonymous actor in an unfolding drama? His removing the jacket and carefully folding it to hide the message has the appearance of a well-mannered act, one of deference to place and occasion and authority of the court. His lawyer had implied as much: Paul Cohen was a young man with deeply held beliefs but also with a sense of the limits of propriety and manners, a young man who came to the courthouse to testify, not to protest, and who wore a jacket because of the chill in the air. Folding the jacket could, of course, have been a more calculated act taken in recognition that his behavior in the courtroom could affect the fate of the person for whom he was to testify. In either case, the act of removing his jacket in the courtroom is certainly not consistent with a picture of a trenchant, hard-bitten, ideologically committed antiwar protester whose mission was to disturb, disrupt, and impose his "truth" on others without sensitivity to time, place, or manner.

The second aspect of the case that was surrounded with considerable ambiguity even at the point of oral argument before the Court concerned Cohen's motives. The justices' questions probed Cohen's purpose in walking through the busy courtroom corridors with the message "Fuck the Draft" emblazoned on his jacket. Did he intend to convey an undeniably shocking and offensive message to all the people gathered there — men, women, and children who were no doubt preoccupied with their own pressing problems and not the least bit interested in Cohen's views on the war and the draft? Or did Cohen wear his jacket simply to warm himself in the chill of the morning air? Was he even specifically aware of the message on the jacket as he walked the corridors and rode the elevator to the seventh floor? Was wearing the jacket so second nature to him that he didn't even think about its lettering until he reached the courtroom, where, suddenly made conscious of it by the attention he was drawing, he contritely removed and folded it? Can we really say that he was "speaking" for purposes of the First Amendment, or was the "speech" on the jacket disembodied, much like a billboard at the side of a road?

Cohen's motives became all the more important, even if inscrutable, as the Court further parsed the facts in an effort to bring the issue presented by the case into clear definition. As the increasingly focused exchanges came to reveal, the case *did not* involve Cohen's right to express his views against the war, even in a courthouse. On this issue there could be no disagreement. Instead, the case involved his freedom to use a single word, "Fuck," in public. His claim was that the word, which by itself had negligible value, acquired value and First Amendment significance through its relation to the expression of an idea: that the war in Vietnam was unjust and the draft was likewise unjust. Was the constitutional stature of the word "Fuck" to be judged in isolation from "the Draft," or was it to be judged only as a *means* of expressing the antidraft message? What kind of relationship between a word and an idea does the First Amendment require? And what, exactly, was the nature of the word's contribution to that message?

On these questions, the burden fell to Michael T. Sauer, who was arguing the case on behalf of the State of California.

> *Question:* What would he [Cohen] be convicted of violating? A statute that says that, persons being then and there present, he . . . engaged in tumultuous and offensive conduct, is that correct?
>
> *Mr. Sauer:* I believe we conceded that it was not tumultuous.
>
> *Question:* That there was offensive conduct.
>
> *Mr. Sauer:* Conduct by displaying. . . .
>
> *Question:* And "conduct" is what?
>
> *Mr. Sauer:* Wearing the jacket and walking in the courtroom.
>
> *Question:* Well, wearing the jacket . . . the conduct was precisely what?
>
> *Mr. Sauer:* Displaying the sign on the jacket by the fact that he was walking with the sign displayed on his back.
>
> *Question:* The walking wasn't the offensive conduct—just the walking—was it?
>
> *Mr. Sauer:* Merely walking, no.
>
> *Question:* No. And so what was the conduct?
>
> *Mr. Sauer:* Displaying the sign.
>
> *Question (by Justice Marshall):* The words were . . . printed on or sewn on or whatever it was . . . his jacket?
>
> *Mr. Sauer:* They were painted on.
>
> *Justice Marshall:* How many people [were] in the hallway?
>
> *Mr. Sauer:* The record doesn't say.
>
> *Justice Marshall:* Well, what is there in the record, in testimony that shows that these words were [in fact] offensive to any person in the building at that time?
>
> *Mr. Sauer:* There is nothing in the record, Mr. Justice Marshall.
>
> *Justice Marshall:* Well, suppose he had on his jacket: "I dislike the draft"?
>
> *Mr. Sauer:* Then I doubt if we would be here, Mr. Justice Marshall.
>
> *Justice Marshall:* So, it's the word, isn't it?
>
> *Mr. Sauer:* Yes.
>
> *Justice Marshall:* Isn't that all you have?

Mr. Sauer: A word, yes. I think collectively throughout the case it's been referred to as three words.
Justice Marshall: I see what you mean.

The problem presented by Cohen's actions, in short, was not the message he chose to convey—"I dislike the draft"—or even the environment of the courthouse in which he chose to convey it, but the word with which he chose to convey it. As Justice Marshall put it in his question, it was not "I Dislike the Draft" but "Fuck the Draft." With the problem narrowed to the manner with which he spoke, the central issue for freedom of speech was the utility, or value, of a single word in relation to the antidraft message. This issue breaks down into two separate inquiries: (1) What *relationship* must a word have to a message? and (2) What *contribution* must it make to the message, to qualify as speech under the First Amendment?

The first inquiry concerns "intent": Did Cohen consciously intend, at that time and in that place, to express his views through the word "Fuck" or did he display the word inadvertently, as a by-product only of his response to the chill of the morning? The second concerns what we mean by speech: What does the word "Fuck" contribute to Cohen's message, and should that contribution, itself, count as speech for purposes of the First Amendment?

Nimmer argued on Cohen's behalf that the word "Fuck" added something of constitutional value to Cohen's message. He asserted that we need to see the word because it gives us as "self-governing people important data . . . [by which] to know that [Cohen] feels this deeply about this subject." The argument seems to ring a bit hollow—unsatisfying because incomplete, as if a corner had not been squarely turned—as it did, in the end, for the Supreme Court. Surely, it could be argued, the identity of a speaker and the depth of his or her feeling can be adequately conveyed without brutish expletive, at least for an audience of otherwise unsuspecting, disinterested men, women, and children.

If Nimmer's argument is instead a more poetic one—that the word conveys qualities of passion, feeling, and personality—its emphasis on "data," on information that supports rational self-governing choices, disguises the aesthetic and emotional dimension of the poetic reference. The solution to the First Amendment problem posed by Cohen's actions would require a more direct approach focusing explicitly upon, rather than sidestepping, the value, poetic or otherwise, of the expletive, itself, as speech.

The State of California, of course, took the view that the word "Fuck" could be isolated from its context. The question could then be asked whether "Fuck" contributed anything of significant social or political value to public discourse and the exchange of ideas in a self-governing, democratic society. As with obscenity, which, according to the Supreme Court, plays no significant constitutional role in the exchange of ideas and is therefore not protected speech for purposes of the First Amendment, removal of a single expletive—perhaps, in 1968, *the* expletive— from public discourse can be accomplished with little risk to the essentially rational ends of the free speech guarantee.

But the State of California's view has problems as well. First, expungement of the word from public conversation must be based not on the whim of government "taste" but on real evidence of harm or offense to those who hear it. If actual harm need *not* be proved, there would be no effective limit on government's power to parse and censor language. But in Cohen's case the state was forced to admit that there was "nothing in the record" to "show that [Cohen's] words were offensive to any person in the building at that time"—even to the three police officers who saw the message on the jacket.

Second, the state's argument notably ignores the view that free speech is a personal liberty of the individual, not just a mechanism of self-government; that speech says something about the person expressing it, not just (or even very much) about the message conveyed. The individual's liberty to speak is not, under this view, restricted to reasoned, rational or well-mannered speech. Emotion, feeling, faith, and depth of conviction color our speech, enliven it, personalize it. While the qualities of reason and good manners may be capable of definition and quantification, a speaker's emotion and feeling cannot. This asserted conflict between reason and emotion under the First Amendment may have been the underlying premise of the questions posed to Sauer by Justices Stewart and Marshall at the close of the oral argument.

> *Justice Stewart:* So it's not the—it narrows down to this one four-letter word, is that it?
>
> *Mr. Sauer:* That is correct, a word that we contend, and the Court of Appeals said, is not generally accepted for public display. . . .
>   The argument has been made that we should have a democratic

dialogue. I agree that conversation is important if the streets are to be used for public arguments. I don't believe this type of language has to be [imposed] upon an unwilling public. . . . *[T]hings that at the moment are not accepted by all the public* [emphasis added].

Justice Marshall: Is everybody in Los Angeles walking down the street who might use that word subject to be[ing] arrested?

Mr. Sauer: If they were displaying the word we would consider that to be . . .

Justice Marshall: Have you got jails big enough?

The City of Los Angeles apparently thought so.

But Paul Robert Cohen never went to jail.

Following oral argument, when the justices convened in their formal conference room, they debated Cohen's fate, voted on the result to be announced, and then placed the case in the hands of Justice Harlan, whose opinion transformed it from a simple little case into a larger-than-life symbol. Justice Harlan's opinion in *Cohen v. California* was to take its place among those very few opinions that shape the law and the culture, partly because of the broad sweep of the questions that emerged from the case. But, more important, this was because, true to his reputation as a justice of great analytical skill, intellectual integrity, and candor, Harlan met head-on the two most difficult, but fundamental, issues the case raised: What is the true meaning of "speech" protected by the First Amendment? Must the constitutionally protected act of "speaking" be a self-conscious, intentional one?

These questions are of practical legal importance because, if Cohen's actions were (like obscenity) not protected speech, the State of California would not have to show any special justification for regulating it. The will of a democratically elected majority, whether entirely sensible or not, would be sufficient justification for the law. Like a prohibition against jaywalking, which satisfies the Court's minimal requirement of rationality and thus can be applied to anyone who jaywalks, whether there is any traffic in the street or not, if Cohen had not been engaged in the protected act of "speaking" when he displayed his jacket in public, he could claim no special protection against the state's reasonable regulation of his language, whether or not his words offended anyone.

On the other hand, if Cohen's action amounted to protected "speaking" and the words he used were protected "speech," the state's ability to regulate it would be severely limited by the First Amendment. The state would have to prove what it couldn't prove at Cohen's trial: that Cohen specifically intended harmful consequences to flow from his actions, and that those consequences were highly likely to occur.

Justice Harlan did not begin his opinion with these issues, however. Instead, he began it in an almost self-deprecating way, in a voice that conveyed the apparent irony that Cohen's case would raise such fundamental questions about freedom of speech. "This case," he wrote, "may seem at first blush too inconsequential to find its way into our books, but the issue it presents is of no small constitutional significance." With this brief and evocative introduction, Harlan turned to defining the constitutional questions presented by Cohen's case. In order, as he put it, "to lay hands on the precise issue" in the case, he first disposed of the issues that the case *did not* involve.

The case was not about conduct but about speech—"the *words* Cohen used to convey his message to the public. The only 'conduct' which the State sought to punish is the fact of communication," he said. Moreover, the case did not involve the special need for restricting expression in courtrooms, for the law under which Cohen had been convicted applied to all public places.

Nor was the restriction of Cohen's speech justified by its effect on other persons present in the courthouse. No one could reasonably interpret the words on Cohen's jacket as a direct personal insult, and there was "no showing that anyone who saw Cohen was in fact violently aroused or that [Cohen] intended such a result."

Likewise, California's interest in protecting the legitimate sensitivities of the unwilling or unsuspecting viewers from having Cohen's distasteful mode of expression thrust upon them could not support Cohen's conviction. The words were displayed in a public place and, Justice Harlan observed, "we are often 'captives' outside the sanctuary of the home" and are obliged to "avert [our] eyes" where possible rather than "empower a majority to silence dissidents simply as a matter of personal predilections."

Finally, Cohen's message was not legally obscene. While obscene expression is not protected speech, it must be erotic, and in Harlan's view it was improbable that Cohen's "vulgar allusion to the Selective Service System would conjure up such psychic stimulation."

With the chaff thus separated from the wheat, Justice Harlan homed in on the true issue raised by Cohen's act. "Against this background," he said, "the issue flushed by this case stands out in stark relief. It is whether California can excise . . . one particular scurrilous epithet from the public discourse. . . ." Here Harlan draws us to the heart of the case: Does this one particular word, widely recognized as offensive, conveyed with seeming indifference to time and place, possess sufficient value to qualify as speech protected under the First Amendment? On this central question Harlan makes two arguments, one obligatory but ultimately insufficient, the other profound and pathbreaking.

The first, obligatory argument calls on the nation's commitment to individual freedom and the constitutional responsibility of each of us acting as free individuals, not as government, to make our own judgments about matters of taste as well as ideas. Harlan admonishes us that the "constitutional right of free expression is powerful medicine in a society as diverse and populous as ours." Its purpose is "to remove governmental restraints from the arena of public discussion, putting the decision as to what views shall be voiced largely in the hands of each of us." The consequences of this rule, he concedes, will "often appear to be only verbal tumult, discord, and even offensive utterance," but while the air "may at times seem filled with verbal cacophony," this fact is "not a sign of weakness but of strength." And if the authority to cleanse the air is lodged with the state, how "is one to distinguish this from any other offensive word?" Indeed, the Constitution leaves most matters of taste and style to the individual "largely because government officials cannot make principled distinctions in this area."

Describing Justice Harlan's first argument as obligatory but ultimately unavailing is not to dismiss it, for it expresses an important and historically warranted justification for freedom of speech in the United States. But as Harlan himself surely recognized, it cannot resolve Cohen's case unless we take the argument in absolute form — unless we agree with Justice Black that "no law" really means "*No* law" and, more basically, that Cohen's use of the word "Fuck" in reference to "the Draft," on his jacket, and in the courthouse corridor on the morning of April 26, 1968, was speech protected by the First Amendment.

Only if these assumptions are made would government be absolutely foreclosed from prohibiting speech based on standards of taste and decency — in Cohen's case and in all other imaginable circumstances. Only then could the Court avoid drawing *any* distinctions between speech and nonspeech — between "the fact of communication," as Justice Harlan put it, and First Amendment speech — and among types of speech that might be regulated and types of standards government might act upon in doing so. But this was a view that even Justice Black, the staunchest First Amendment absolutist on the Court, was unwilling to adopt in Cohen's case. He was of the view that Cohen's act was an "absurd and immature antic, . . . mainly conduct and little speech."

The absolutist position founders on the shoals of common experience. The same Supreme Court that decided Cohen's case also held the view that obscenity is not speech protected by the First Amendment. (Thus, "no law" does *not* mean "no law.") While Justice Harlan is technically correct that "Fuck the Draft" painted on the back of a jacket is not, legally, obscene, is this because, unlike obscenity, Cohen's words possess redeeming social value? Perhaps so, but we are entitled to know what, exactly, that value is and Harlan's first argument doesn't tell us. His argument that government should stay out of matters of taste and style seems self-evidently inadequate as an explanation: What else but taste and style is involved in government regulation of obscenity? Moreover, we are literally surrounded with other examples of government restrictions of speech, including laws requiring truth in advertising, laws prohibiting indecency in broadcasting, and restrictions on commercial fraud, libel, slander, and invasions of privacy.

Are these laws—and many, many other ones—unconstitutional government intrusions on what we say and do, unwarranted impositions of standards of taste and decency? Of course not. The examples of rules of order, truth in advertising, and fraud neither absolve nor convict Cohen, of course, but they do reveal the fact that while skepticism of government regulation of speech is a powerful principle animating the First Amendment, skepticism alone cannot provide the whole solution to particular cases such as Cohen's.

More basically, the absolutist position rests on the assumption that the message conveyed by Cohen's act was speech protected by the First Amendment. This is a conclusion that must be explained, not just declared. Harlan's first argument simply assumes it. The argument therefore provides, at best, a background—important, yet incomplete—for further analysis that focuses honestly and forthrightly on that basic question: Exactly what is it about Cohen's use of the word "Fuck" that makes it speech under the First Amendment?

Justice Harlan knew that the speech question could not be avoided. His second argument addresses it forthrightly, though he introduces it almost as an afterthought, a loose end that needs quickly to be tied.

Additionally, we cannot overlook the fact, because it is well illustrated by the episode involved here, that much linguistic expression serves a dual communicative function: it conveys not only ideas capable of relatively precise, detached explication, but otherwise inexpressible emotions as well. In fact, words are often chosen as much for their emotive as their cognitive force. We cannot sanction the view that the Constitution, while solicitous of the cognitive content of individual speech, has little or no regard for that emotive function which, practically speaking, may often be the more important element of the overall message sought to be communicated.

While we might have wished for greater elaboration of such a crucial argument—indeed, the only genuinely dispositive argument made in the opinion—its brevity does not detract from its importance. Protection for the emotional element of speech had been implicitly conferred in many prior decisions of the Court, but until June 7, 1971, the Court's opinions had always been predicated on a First Amendment devoted to reasoned, albeit often tumultuous, debate and rational public and private decision making. This was, in fact, the redeeming social value of free speech that, according to Justice Brennan, obscenity lacked.

The question posed by Cohen's action—the constitutional value of one word that cannot in all honesty be said to contribute to the *reasoned* understanding or articulation of an idea being expressed—had in the past been quietly ignored or avoided by the Court. It was simply assumed that a connection could always be made between spoken words and the reasoned expression of an idea. But for Justice Harlan such an approach would smack of intellectual dishonesty, or at least disingenuousness, for he saw that Cohen's use of the word "Fuck" did not contribute *reason* to his message; it could not realistically be defended as an articulation of an intellectual argument; it did not add information relevant to the message's rational explication. It simply added *force*.

In the hands and pen of a less able and intellectually forthright justice, the Court might simply have ignored the issue of the mere *force* contributed by Cohen's word, assuming by judicial fiat that all words are in some sense reasoned. But John Marshall Harlan was no ordinary justice. To argue that California's purpose in restricting Cohen's speech was to prohibit the idea he expressed (I dislike the draft) rather than the words he actually used to express it, simply couldn't be substantiated and wouldn't satisfy Justice Harlan's own exacting standards. Instead, Harlan said, communication involves reason *and* emotion, ideas *and* feelings. So also does speech protected by the First Amendment.

This was a statement extraordinary in its implications, unprecedented in its potential sweep. So before the celebration begins, we should analyze those implications and the underlying questions they raise about the meaning of speech and the place of emotion in the First Amendment. What does emotion contribute to speech? Do all emotions count? Is the value of emotion dependent on its connection to an idea? Does the speaker's motivation in communicating the emotion matter? Justice Harlan's opinion does not answer all of these questions. It only hints at the answers.

What Does Emotion Contribute to Speech?

Justice Harlan explains the emotional content of speech as that which expresses to others "otherwise inexpressible emotions"—qualities of anger, seriousness, fear, faith, and feelings that cannot be captured adequately in language. And he says that emotive force can, "practically speaking . . . often be the more important element of the overall message sought to be communicated."

Our own practical experiences with expressing disgust or anger illustrate his point. Buffy, the neighbor's dog, has just trampled down our prize St. Francis Hosta, reducing it to a bald stem. In addressing Buffy after the incident, we might yell toward the offending animal, "Buffy, you are a bad dog." But think how much more force would be added if we grabbed Buffy by the collar and said, "Bad pissant dogs like you should be euthanized!" "Pissant" and "euthanized" add emotional force to the "bad dog" message. The words, of course, are lost on poor Buffy, but the emotion with which we convey them isn't.

So what does the word "Fuck" add to "the Draft" in Cohen's case? In oral argument Justice Marshall had posited that "Fuck the Draft" is not the same thing as "I Dislike the Draft." What, then does "Fuck" add to the message? Justice Harlan concludes that the word adds an "otherwise inexpressible" emotion—not an idea or an argument or new information but an image, a degree of force, a personalization of feeling. The freedom of speech that Justice Harlan speaks of in his opinion, in other words, is not a function of social utility or political philosophy alone; it does not even depend, for its value, on the effects it has on hearers or viewers of the message.

The word "Fuck" need not prove its constitutional worth by its contribution to reasoned exchange of ideas. Instead, freedom of speech, according to Justice Harlan, is an individual liberty, an outlet for the expression of self, not just, or even necessarily, for the elucidation of others; and use of speech to add emotional force to a message is valuable as a manifestation of who the speaker is and what the speaker feels, not just what the speaker thinks.

What Emotions Count?

If emotions have value because of what they reveal about the speaker—not what they say but what they signify—does this mean that all emotions count equally as speech? Justice Harlan does not answer this question. He does say, however, that the emotions must be *those of the speaker*. This much was clear from the oral argument, where no one challenged the fact that Cohen was conveying his *own* emotions in relation to the draft. Assuming, as Justice Harlan did, that Cohen owned the jacket and knew what was on it as he walked through the courthouse, we must conclude that Cohen, himself, was strongly opposed to the draft; that the strength of feeling conveyed by the word "Fuck" was his own.

Had the jacket belonged to someone else, or had Cohen been ignorant of its lettering when he put it on that April morning, the case would be quite different. Then the emotion packed into the phrase "Fuck the Draft" would not have been his. Thus we might say that the strong-arm tactics of an unethical used-car salesman, for example, could be distinguished from Cohen's use of the word "Fuck" because in employing connivance, fraud, or threat, the salesman is not directly expressing himself. He may be acting out of fear, greed, or anger, but the manifestation of these emotions in his sales pitch is not intended to be, and is not, an expression of his own self but of his used-car salesman self.

Similar reasoning might serve to distinguish much obscenity, which is not protected speech, from Cohen's action, for while obscenity clearly expresses emotion—erotic feelings certainly qualify on that score—an author or producer of obscenity cannot always (or perhaps even often) claim with a straight face that the emotions so expressed are his or hers—that is, that the obscene portrayal is a means of expressing the author's or producer's own self (or, for a news organization, the institution's own editorial judgments), as distinguished from his or her commercial interests.

But a requirement that emotions be the speaker's own does not tell us which such emotions count for purposes of the First Amendment. Are *all* emotions — hate as well as love, anger as well as satisfaction, kind affection as well as violent lust — equal? Justice Harlan's opinion only hints at how this question might be answered. It suggests that the answer lies not in the emotion itself (love versus hate, for example) but in the purpose behind its expression. If the value of emotion under the First Amendment is as an expression of the self, then the expression of emotions that do not serve that function would not qualify for speech protection. Under this reasoning, emotional outbursts, whatever the emotion, such as yelling profanities while kicking a door in frustration, swearing in anger, or indeed most forms of spontaneous emotional rage, would qualify as speech if — but only if — they were intended to communicate those emotions to others.

But this may be too simplistic, even too easy, an answer. Are there no grounds for distinguishing among emotions? Where on the spectrum between painting "Fuck the Draft" on one's jacket and screaming obscenities alone in the woods, for example, does the racial epithet fit — the case of a white college student in a public university yelling "Nigger Go Home!" out the dorm window at passing African-American students? Harlan's view suggests that a racial epithet reflecting the speaker's own feelings that he or she intends to express to another would qualify as speech protected by the First Amendment, and thus would be protected from discipline or other forms of government restriction — at least absent an ensuing riot or an unavoidable act of physical violence. Are we willing to accept that conclusion? Is the emotion of racial hatred directed at members of a racial group distinguishable from Cohen's emotion of hatred directed at the draft and the Vietnam War?

Emotion and Ideas

Must emotion, to qualify as speech, be connected to an idea that is being expressed? And if so, what is the nature of that connection? On this question what Harlan did *not* say is as important as what he said. Imagine that emblazoned on Cohen's jacket was one word, "Fuck." It cannot be deduced from Harlan's argument that the word "Fuck" in isolation is protected speech. Nor does the outcome in Cohen's case hinge on the use of that one word, as the State of California argued.

Harlan says, instead, that the word "Fuck" adds emotional emphasis—force and feeling, not intellectual argument—to Cohen's antidraft message. The word's protection as speech, therefore, seems to *depend* on its connection to an idea but at the same time to be paradoxically independent of the message itself, going instead only to the *force* contributed by its expression to others.

The paradox is not explained by reference to the "others," the audience who felt the force of Cohen's word, for Justice Harlan did not say that speech that produces emotion in others has any free speech standing on that ground alone. Much speech produces emotion: a good movie, a daredevil act, a dirty film. But the audience is given no First Amendment right to emote by the *Cohen* case. What is involved, instead, is communication, and the Constitution's protection, Harlan says, is focused on the freedom of the person doing the communicating—in this case the expressing of Cohen's *own* feelings of anger and revulsion in relation to his *own* idea of opposition to the draft and the Vietnam War.

The emotion contained in the word "Fuck," in other words, is dependent on its relation to a message, but its First Amendment value lies not in its contribution to the content of the message but in the force of its expression by Cohen. As Marshall McLuhan asserted long ago, the medium *is* the message. Emotion, for Justice Harlan, is medium.

Speech and Conduct, Reason and Emotion

A final question concerns intent. Must the expression of emotion be a knowing and purposeful act by the speaker? Justice Harlan did not explicitly address this question. It was clear enough for him that by wearing the jacket as he walked through the corridors of the courthouse, Cohen intended to communicate the "Fuck the Draft" message—emotions and all—to those who saw the lettering on his back.

But this view of the case was not so clear to Justice Blackmun, then in his first year on the Court; or to Chief Justice Burger; or, most significantly, to Justice Black, the First Amendment absolutist ("No law means *No* law!"), who also joined Blackmun's dissenting opinion. They saw the facts differently from the other justices; they did not believe that Cohen seriously intended to engage in free speech while walking in the courthouse corridors on that chilly April morning in 1968. More basically, they were skeptical about Justice Harlan's emotive speech theory, for it swept too broadly and could not be effectively limited by proof of motive in a trial. Cohen's actions, Blackmun wrote, were no more than an "absurd and immature antic, . . . mainly conduct and little speech."

From the perspective of thirty years, Blackmun's view about use of the word "Fuck" may seem quaint, indeed almost naive, in our present environment of "uncivil" civil discourse. But perhaps we should not be too quick to judge, for much the same sentiment would be widely expressed in academic circles and in the public at large about the student thrusting the racial epithet from the dormitory window. Are there no ways in which we can insist on some moderation and restraint even in the expression of emotion?

The distinction between reason and emotion has deep and fundamental roots, reflecting among other things the contested separation of mind from body with its foundation in Western religious thought and in the Enlightenment. The *Cohen* case represents but a small fragment of this much larger mosaic.

It cannot be said, for example, that prior to Justice Harlan's decision in 1971 the First Amendment was the sole property of the Enlightenment—that the "speech" of which the amendment speaks consisted of reason and logic only, and that ideas and expression based in faith or feeling or passion had been evicted from the speech guarantee and left to inhabit smaller corners of the Constitution, like the religion clauses.

But the *Cohen* case did reflect the Court's discomfort with the place of emotion in free expression. This discomfort continues to this day, and is born of two main concerns. The first is the perceived correspondence between emotional expression and resulting action, or conduct, based on that expression. Emotion, in other words, fires passion and incites to action. It is dangerous.

The second concern reflects the nagging perseverance of Enlightenment thought, and in particular the deeply imbedded conviction that reason is most conducive to peaceful resolution of differences, even to the essential ingredients of civilization. In a free society, anarchy is domesticated by reason, not force.

As to the first concern, that the connecting glue between expression and conduct is emotion, two things may be said about the significance of *Cohen v. California*. By rejecting any necessary relationship between emotion and conduct, Justice Harlan did not erase the First Amendment distinction between speech and conduct. He did not, in other words, make it unnecessary to consider whether Cohen's action was conduct

The Jacket | 31

and not speech. Instead, he required that the distinction be formulated in altogether different ways that turn not on whether the expression at issue, such as Cohen's use of the word "Fuck," is "emotion" (which is every bit as much speech as is reason) or rests on "conduct" (which, the Court held, could be speech for purposes of the First Amendment if it expressed a message, whether reasoned or emotive) but, instead, on whether the communicative activity qualifies as "speaking." The distinction between speech and conduct, in short, remains a relevant one, but it does not rest on the presence or absence of emotion or on the faulty premise that speech and conduct are mutually exclusive of each other.

In bringing emotion under the protective mantle of the First Amendment, however, the Court did *not* say that all expression of emotion qualifies as speech, any more than the Court would say that any expression of reason is thereby, by definition, speech. Some expressed emotion, like some expressed reason, is not speech for purposes of the First Amendment because it does not qualify as "speech" under the First Amendment; it does not possess the attributes of human origin, intention, communicative purpose, and audience perception that "speaking" requires, according to Justice Harlan.

We might conclude that such disqualified expression, not being "speech," is therefore "conduct." But this would be mistaken, for it would not reflect the full implications of Justice Harlan's insight. As we shall see later, there may remain an independent and important role for the distinction between speech and conduct, though it will be a new role based on Harlan's view that the universe of communicative actions relevant to First Amendment analysis consists of *three*, not two, parts: (1) speech (some of which may be conduct); (2) conduct (some of which may be speech); and (3) nonspeech (which consists of events or actions that communicate but that are not the product of *someone's* communicative intention).

As to the second point — the Enlightenment idea that reason is conducive to peaceful resolution of differences and to the social order, itself — the *Cohen* case contains the seeds of a much more fundamental shift in First Amendment thought. But they are seeds only, for even after *Cohen* the Supreme Court has held tightly to the conviction that reason plays a particularly important and socially useful (if not necessary) role in judging the meaning and constitutional value of free speech.

From its beginning First Amendment thought has rested heavily on the Enlightenment idea that the best protection against dangerous ideas is the opportunity for competing ideas to he heard. Free speech has been conceived as a speech marketplace that serves as an outlet for our violent predispositions; a place in which competing views, not competing fists, do battle; an arena in which truth is sought and in which, therefore, the important thing is not that everyone be heard but that *everything worth saying be said*. So viewed, freedom of speech is an Aristotelian world of expression domesticated by reason.

By casting off the First Amendment's mooring in reason, the *Cohen* case opens up an entirely new world of expression, one in which expression is not simply "uninhibited, robust, and wide open," as the Court put it in its famous public-libel decision in *New York Times v. Sullivan*, but one in which expression is also calculatedly false, mean-spirited, and purposelessly harmful. It is a world that embraces, as it should, not only the purely emotional and aesthetic in art and literature but the purposefully degrading, violent, and destructive. It is a world that recognizes the emotional *force* of speech as speech itself, whether it is a force for good or bad.

John Marshall Harlan may not, of course, have intended to unleash these larger forces by his opinion in Cohen's case, a case that, he said, "may at first blush seem too inconsequential to find its way into our books." The implications of his embrace of the "emotive value" in speech, however, are inescapably broader and more profound. The fact that the Supreme Court has since fallen far short of embracing those broader implications does not disguise their more subtle manifestations, which can be found in the First Amendment claims lately made for the protection of hate speech; in the protections now accorded virtually all forms of commercial expression; and in the fact that the speech "marketplace" is now becoming as populated with PACs and special interest advocacy as is the political marketplace.

To observe these present conditions as facts is not to suggest that despair or celebration is the proper response. But what we should bear in mind as we contemplate these larger consequences is that Justice Harlan's lesson in *Cohen* had not one but *two* parts. Emotion should not, he told us, be evicted from the domain of speech. But saying that emotion *can* be speech does not mean that it always *must* be. Such a view would sweep away all distinctions between speech and conduct, for conduct is but emotion incarnate.

For Justice Harlan, therefore, a second question must also be asked: Is the emotion that claims protection as speech a product of a human, intentional, and purposefully communicative act that qualifies it as speech for purposes of the First Amendment? This question reflects the line Harlan draws between speech and nonspeech. It rests not on emotion versus reason or speech versus conduct but, instead, on "speaking," the necessary human predicate of those messages whose freedom from government restraint is captured in the word "speech."

Speaking as a Purposeful Human Act

The disagreement that surfaced in Paul Cohen's case between Justice Harlan, on the one hand, and Justices Blackmun, Burger, and Black, on the other, was not, in reality, about whether Cohen's actions were speech or conduct. Instead, it was about whether his actions were "speech." And this question boils down to a very basic and fundamentally important constitutional question: What does it mean to speak for purposes of the freedom of speech? Harlan's argument that the First Amendment protects the emotive force of speech is clearly premised on the presence of a speaker, someone who, like Cohen, intends by his or her voluntary exercise of free will to convey feelings through the emotional dimensions of language, intonation, and emphasis. But the reasons for this conclusion, and the definition of "speaker" that it implies, were not explicitly addressed in Harlan's opinion, for he assumed without discussion that Cohen knew he had the jacket on, knew of the lettering on it, and knew that people in the courthouse would see and react to it.

But while the subject does not find its way into Harlan's opinion, it lurks between the lines and in the ambiguities of the factual record of Cohen's case, where the justices in oral argument probed such questions as Cohen's motive for wearing the jacket (was it the chill of the morning or the message on the jacket or both?) and for removing it and carefully folding it when he entered the courtroom (how strongly did he *really* feel about the draft?). So we might ask, hypothetically at least, what would have happened had it turned out that Cohen picked up the jacket inadvertently as he left that morning for the courthouse, becoming aware of what he wore only as he entered the courtroom. Or what the result would have been had the jacket belonged not to Cohen but to a friend, and because it was a chilly morning Cohen simply swooped it up in a rush to get to court on time, having no intention to associate himself with its message, simply forgetting to remove it as he entered the courthouse.

If Cohen's act of wearing the jacket were inadvertent, and if the claim for protection of the emotive force of the word "Fuck" must be personal to Cohen, then the conclusion seems inescapable that under the First Amendment Cohen would not be exercising his "freedom" as a speaker, and the word he used would not be "speech." Likewise, if Cohen knew of the lettering on the jacket when he wore it in the courthouse, but the jacket were not his and did not reflect his own beliefs or emotions, his action could not be characterized as his speaking and any speech that occurred would not be his for purposes of the First Amendment. And so also we might conclude that the college student thrusting the racial epithet out the window on a dare, or in a drunken stupor, or in a fit of plain rage, or as a sick joke, unpossessed of a communicative will of his or her own, should not be given shelter under the First Amendment.

If the opposite result were reached — if Cohen's inadvertent act of wearing the jacket would not dispossess his act of First Amendment protection — then the speech would be lodged in the jacket itself and in the word it displayed, a disembodied sign whose communicative meaning arose strictly from those who saw it. This would open a vast landscape of potential First Amendment questions. Are all things to which people give meaning thereby protected speech? Is every possible meaning, no matter how idiosyncratic, protected by the First Amendment? Once loosed, such a definition of speech would rapidly consume all of human conduct and most animate and inanimate phenomenon as well. Trees, after all, are symbols with meaning.

Harlan was able to avoid this result by confining speech to the purposeful communicative act of a human being, at least in Cohen's case. The narrow ground for his decision, however, does not mean that no communication took place as Cohen walked down the corridor of the Los Angeles County Courthouse, nor even that no First Amendment speech took place irrespective of Cohen's intent. Assuming that someone saw the jacket, communication clearly did occur. But First Amendment speech, on the one hand, and "communication," on the other, are not necessarily the same thing. Harlan left the relationship between the two ambiguous, a judgment to be deferred until another day and another case.

Is speech that has no author, no *one* expressing his or her *own* ideas or emotions — is the artifact of language itself, freed of intention, authenticity, origin, and so on — constitutionally protected by the First Amendment? If so, why? The *Cohen* case helps us to define this question more narrowly, it helps us see what speaking and speech are all about as an exercise of liberty, but it does not solve the riddle of the constitutional status of disembodied speech—communication that has no author.

If the First Amendment protects the speech—the words, the message—and not the speaker's liberty to express them, it would be much easier to argue, as California did in Cohen's case, that the word "Fuck" contributes little if anything to the message of disdain for the draft and the war. It would be easier, in short, to dismiss the word as an antic only, a loose and aimless emotion with no human origin or identity, mostly conduct and little speech, whose expungement from the public dialogue would cost little. This, of course, is precisely what the Supreme Court had done when it concluded that obscenity "lacked redeeming social value" and therefore was not speech.

Justice Harlan's approach, in contrast, made such an escape impossible. Cohen's case, he said, involved much more than the speech that was uttered—the word, *its* content, *its* value. Indeed, the word "Fuck" was incidental to the First Amendment issue presented by Cohen's actions. The case involved, instead, Cohen's claim of liberty, for which the word was simply an instrument rather than an end in itself. Liberty, or speaking, is something less easily dismissed even when the way in which it is manifested seems unimportant, even juvenile.

The First Amendment's protection of speech, as opposed to speaking, is an issue to which we shall return in later chapters. Justice Harlan could ignore it by focusing strictly on the liberty to speak in Cohen's case. But the issue lay immediately beneath the smooth surface of his remarkable opinion. The issue goes to the very heart of what we mean by freedom of speech under the First Amendment. The fact that there is no clear answer to it discloses how little we understand about our most precious freedom, and how, ironically, the closer we look the less we know.

ADDITIONAL READING

Alexander M. Bickel, *The Morality of Consent* (1975).

Lee Bollinger, *The Tolerant Society: Freedom of Speech and Extremist Speech in America* (1986).

Thomas I. Emerson, "Toward a General Theory of the First Amendment," 72 *Yale Law Journal* 877 (1963).

Daniel A. Farber, "Free Speech Without Romance: Public Choice and the First Amendment," 105 *Harvard Law Review* 554 (1990).

Steven G. Gey, "The Apologetics of Suppression: The Regulation of Pornography as Act and Idea," 86 *Michigan Law Review* 1564 (1988).

Alexander Meiklejohn, *Free Speech and Its Relation to Self-Government* (1948).

Robert Post, "The Constitutional Concept of Public Discourse," 103 *Harvard Law Review* 601 (1990).

Story Two

The Author

(McIntyre v. Ohio Elections Commission,
514 U.S. 334 (1995))

What matter who's speaking, someone said, what matter who's
speaking?   —Samuel Beckett

This is a story about anonymity, about speech with no named author. While it is possible, as we shall see, for speech to have *no* author at all, in our story an author does exist. She simply fails to identify herself. Her story forces us to think about the role authors play in the First Amendment. Is speech somehow incomplete, a lesser order of "speech," without a known author? And what, precisely, *is* an author for purposes of the *freedom* of speech? Does speech lack significance without an author, just as a tool lacks function without a hand that wields it? Or is the author a sometimes useful but ultimately expendable appendage? Do we as listeners or readers sometimes supply the author, just as our imagination brings characters in a novel to life?

The view that affixes speech to its author rests the First Amendment's protection firmly on the freedom of a "speaker," requiring that we explore the meaning of *freedom* and whether its enjoyment is available only to individuals who "speak"—to First Amendment authors. Who is our anonymous author, and was her act of speaking, even under the cover of anonymity, an exercise of her *freedom?*

In contrast, the view that detaches speech from its author rests the First Amendment's protection on the speech and *its* freedom, requiring that we define what, exactly, we mean by "speech." Are the words confronted by the audience in our story entitled to the label "speech" and thus to be free from government restraint?

Paradoxically, both views can be found in the Supreme Court's jurisprudence. But in our story they become intermingled, even confused. So part of our task will be to pull them apart, where possible, and attempt to straighten them out.

The incident occurred in 1988. It was a mistake, really — one of those things that just happen but then, once loosed, seem to take on a life of their own, as if fated. Margaret McIntyre was forty-seven. She lived in Westerville, Ohio, a suburb of Columbus, with her husband, Joe, and her three children: Kevin, a senior in high school; Shawn, a junior; and Kimberly, a seventh-grader. She was actively involved in her children's education, but unlike most of us she did not restrict her focus to her own children and the local PTA. She didn't like what she saw in the public schools in Westerville, and she decided to do something about it.

She had been active in the Westerville City School District for many years. By 1988, when our story begins, she had run for the School Board three times, each attempt unsuccessful. But that did not stop Margaret McIntyre. Her daughter, Kimberly, described her mother as "just a regular person who didn't like what was going on." Husband Joe described her, with an air of affectionate indulgence, as more outspoken than he. But the descriptions are incomplete, if not also understated. Margaret McIntyre, it seems, was passionate, and she was not one to mince words.

This is evident from the text of the leaflet she wrote, the one that caused all of the problems. She passed out her leaflet on April 27, 1988, at a well-attended public meeting in the gymnasium of the Blendon Middle School. The meeting had been called by the school superintendent to discuss an upcoming referendum on a proposed school tax levy. In the audience were parents and other interested taxpayers and citizens, not all of whom were supporting the tax increase. The text of the leaflet tells us about the tax levy, but it tells us much more about Margaret McIntyre.

ISSUE 19 SCHOOL TAX LEVY

Last election Westerville schools, asked us to vote yes for new buildings and expansion programs. We gave them what they asked. We knew there was crowded conditions and new growth in the district. Now we find out there is a 4 million dollar deficit—WHY? We are told the three middle schools must be split because of overcrowding, and yet we are being told three schools are being closed—WHY? A magnet school is not a full operating school, but a specials school. Residents were asked to work on a twenty member commission to help formulate the new boundaries. For four weeks they worked long and hard and came up with a very workable plan. Their plan was totally disregarded—WHY? WASTE of taxpayers dollars must be stopped. Our children's education and welfare must come first. WASTE CAN NO LONGER BE TOLERATED.

PLEASE VOTE NO
ISSUE 19

THANK YOU. CONCERNED PARENTS AND TAXPAYERS

Margaret McIntyre wrote the leaflet on her home computer in advance of the meeting. She made copies at a local copy store and, with Shawn, Kimberly, and one of Shawn's friends in tow, proceeded to the meeting to hand them out.

The first mistake was McIntyre's. She didn't put her name and address on all of the leaflets. But it was genuinely a mistake, it seems. She was aware of the Ohio law requiring that election materials bear the name and address of the author or sponsor, but a local election official had told her not to worry about it because her leaflet was written and paid for by an individual, not by a group or political campaign organization. Nonetheless, she added that information to most of her leaflets, perhaps out of respect for the law's purpose or perhaps because of lingering uncertainties about the advice she had received.

But some of the anonymous versions slipped through the cracks. Inadvertence was apparently the culprit. We can easily imagine the scene: it is the day of the public meeting; Margaret McIntyre is sitting at her computer writing the leaflet, passion and excitement flowing through the keys; eagerly she prints the leaflet out, takes it to the local copy store to make some copies, then experiences nagging doubts about the advice she has received, orally and perhaps offhandedly, about omitting her name and address; she decides to add them though time is running out; she returns to the copy store for more copies, brings them home and places them on her cluttered desk, fails to keep the various copies straight; hurriedly fixes a meal for Joe and the children; she then gets everyone ready to leave, quickly gathers up the leaflets from her desk, stacking them together, and finally rushes off with the children to the public meeting, glad to have made the change but not really too worried about whether some of the anonymous versions were intermingled with the newer ones. Predictably, some of the anonymous leaflets were among those handed out to the gathered parents and citizens at the Blendon Middle School on April 27, and again the next night at another public meeting on the referendum.

The second mistake was not Margaret McIntyre's. Instead, it belonged to the school officials at the public meeting who decided, in what appears in retrospect, at least, to be a fit of small-minded legalism and bureaucratic literalism, to put a stop to McIntyre's leafleting. As people were entering the gym and moving to their seats in advance of the meeting, an assistant superintendent noticed that McIntyre and the children were distributing leaflets. Further investigation revealed that some were signed "Concerned Parents and Taxpayers." Armed with this fact, the assistant superintendent approached McIntyre, attempted to take the leaflets from her and, rebuffed, then informed her that she was breaking the law because the leaflets did not contain her name and address.

"I just thought he was being rude," her son Shawn said of the school official who tried to take the leaflets.

With all the fuss, interest in the leaflets was more likely heightened than dampened. We do not know whether Margaret McIntyre and the children continued to hand out the leaflets that evening, but we do know that the events of that first night did not deter her. A second public meeting on the tax levy was scheduled at a different school on the following evening. Margaret McIntyre was once again there with her leaflets, including (now advertently and, we may assume, defiantly) the anonymous ones. She was once again told that in distributing the leaflets she was violating Ohio law. She was once again undeterred.

The election was held later that spring. The tax levy proposal failed to receive enough votes and went down to defeat. But like McIntyre, the school officials, too, were persistent. They regrouped, decided to make another try, and scheduled a second election. The referendum failed again, this time apparently without the assistance of McIntyre's leaflets. The school officials, however, would not take no for an answer, either in their quest for the new tax levy or, it turns out, in their pursuit of Margaret McIntyre. On the third attempt seven months later, in November of 1988, the referendum passed and the tax levy took effect.

The sweet taste of victory following the election was apparently not enough for the school officials in Westerville, Ohio. They wanted not only to win but to get even, too. Margaret McIntyre had been a thorn in their side, it seems, and the wound had not healed. Five months after the levy had passed, and just over a year after she had passed out her leaflets at the public meeting in the Blendon Middle School, the assistant school superintendent who had first tried to stop her filed a complaint with the Ohio Elections Commission. He charged Margaret McIntyre with illegal distribution of unsigned leaflets.

This, it turned out, was the third mistake. And it was a big one. It did not appear so at first. The Elections Commission held a hearing, found McIntyre guilty, and fined her $100. While the record in the case does not disclose it, one would hope that at least some members of the commission rolled their eyes and wondered, if only to themselves, why their time was being wasted by this relatively trifling matter, which had all the markings of a personal spat.

The $100 fine was four times the amount McIntyre had spent to have her leaflets duplicated. But it wasn't much. Most people would have stopped there. Not Margaret McIntyre. She was a woman of passionate conviction, and now she had a new passion. For her it was not a matter of money but of principle — of her rights. "I'm standing up for mine," she said, "and I'm not letting them take them from me."

"One day," she told her husband, Joe, "it's going to get before the Supreme Court." And it did.

But before she got there, the case of the mistaken, anonymous little leaflet would assume much larger proportions. At a practical level it would become a battle fought over the right of a person to speak freely and anonymously, with the enforceability of election laws in forty-nine states and the District of Columbia hanging in the balance. At a theoretical level, courts would be forced to confront issues about the relationship between speech and its author that, surprisingly, had never before arisen.

The stakes first became evident in the Franklin County Common Pleas Court, the local district court to which McIntyre appealed the fine. The court sided with her. The Ohio law that applied to her leaflet, the court said, could not be constitutionally enforced against McIntyre's exercise of her First Amendment right freely and anonymously to speak her mind.

Following the Common Pleas Court decision, the State of Ohio weighed in, enlivened by the doubt now surrounding the enforceability of its election law. The state appealed the case to the Tenth District Court of Appeals, which reinstated the fine and declared the election law valid. Undeterred, though now having spent considerably more than the $25 the leaflets cost or the $100 fine she refused to pay, Margaret McIntyre appealed to the Ohio Supreme Court. The national implications of her claim were by now evident. The law was again upheld, but over the dissent of one justice.

By now five years had passed since the public meeting at the Blendon Middle School in April of 1988. Margaret McIntyre had predicted that "one day, it's going to get before the Supreme Court." She now had her chance, and armed with that chance, she requested that the Court accept her case for review. As the Court's decision to accept her case was pending, election officials from across the country—who would enter her case by filing their own briefs in the case if her request were granted—watched with bated breath. On February 22, 1994, the Court agreed to hear her case, nearly six years after it all began.

But this was not to be the last event in the unfolding drama of Margaret McIntyre's quest. She was genuinely elated at the Court's decision, looking forward optimistically to traveling to Washington, D.C., with Joe and her three children to hear *her* case argued in the coming fall. But Margaret McIntyre also had cancer, and she had been fighting it for some time. On May 6, 1994, almost a year before the Court would issue its opinion and six months before oral argument of her case, Margaret McIntyre died.

Joe had witnessed—indeed had lived with—his wife's persistence, her iron will in pursuit of her rights against all odds. "I'm standing up for mine," she had said, "and I'm not letting them take them away from me." So Joe took up his wife's battle, substituting himself for her as the named party in order to allow the case to proceed. Oral argument before the Court was held on October 12, 1994. The case was finally ended when the Court issued its opinion on April 19, 1995, reversing the Ohio Supreme Court's decision, declaring that the First Amendment protected Margaret McIntyre's right to distribute her anonymous leaflets, declaring Ohio's prohibition of anonymous campaign speech unconstitutional, and effectively voiding similar prohibitions in the laws of forty-nine states and the District of Columbia in the process.

The Problem of Anonymity

The Supreme Court does not explain its reasons for agreeing to hear a case, so we cannot know exactly why Margaret McIntyre's case was accepted for review. But a pretty good picture emerges from a question posed by Justice Sandra Day O'Connor to the lawyer for the State of Ohio at oral argument. "I would have thought that if the First Amendment stood for anything at all it stood for my right to put out a flyer on a street corner on an issue I felt strongly about without identifying myself. What does the First Amendment protect if not that kind of core political speech?"

Margaret McIntyre would have liked that question. But while Justice O'Connor's question is appealing, it is also rhetorical. It demands an absolute and unyielding conclusion, knowing no exceptions, while at the same time subtly limiting its scope to "my right to put out a flyer on a street corner on an issue I felt strongly about."

We know that the issue raised by McIntyre's case is broader than that, and we also know that there is no simple, pat answer. One need not look far to find instances in which anonymous publication is legally prohibited. Federal postal laws currently require that newspapers and other periodicals contain the name and address of the publisher. Political advertisements in print and broadcast media must identify their sponsoring organization. As individuals, we may not make a contribution to a political candidate or take out a television or radio ad supporting a candidate without identifying ourselves. Indeed, our gifts to charity cannot qualify for tax deduction if they are anonymous because the IRS demands that the charity issue a receipt. So much for anonymity, which is legally prohibited in all of these instances. And the Supreme Court made it perfectly clear (though logically obscure, if not inscrutable) that its decision in McIntyre's case would not disturb any of them.

It is therefore clear that while Justice O'Connor's question reveals an intuition, an instinctive sense of the case, it neither offers nor invites a workable principle of decision. The First Amendment issues raised by McIntyre's anonymous leaflet are too difficult to submit to such a question. They require instead that we ask when, if ever, and why anonymous expression should be protected by the First Amendment, and how, if at all, McIntyre's leaflet can be distinguished from the many other circumstances in which anonymous speech is now restricted — particularly in the political campaign setting. These questions, in turn, require that we grapple with the very concept of authorship and the constitutional significance of an author's relationship to a work.

Authorship and the Meaning of Texts

What, precisely, do we mean by the term "author"? Does "authorship" imply only possession of a legal claim to a work — a property interest residing in the person who produced it—or does it also have to do with the creativity, originality, and meaning of a work, and thus reside partly in the work itself, springing from the work rather than attaching to it? The Oxford English Dictionary defines "author" as "the beginning of anything." Does a work "begin" only with its production, or does it also "begin" when it takes on meaning in the hands of the reader? What is the relationship between a work's author and its authority? Does a work's *authority*—its true meaning, perhaps, or its force or significance—flow from the person who produced it, or does authority flow out of the work itself—from *its* meaning, or from the meaning *it* inspires? If a work's authority resides only in its production, can an anonymous work *ever* have authority?

These questions are not unfamiliar to the United States Supreme Court, for they lie at the heart of the Court's most important task: interpreting the meaning of the Constitution. The First Amendment serves as a good example. It reads, "Congress shall make no law . . . abridging the freedom of speech." In applying this injunction to anonymous campaign speech by individuals, how is the First Amendment's meaning to be found? The answer cannot be found in the text itself, for "abridge," "freedom," and "speech," to name but three words, are not self-defining. Is the First Amendment's meaning and authority, then, to be discovered in the mind and intention of its author, the person who produced it? But what if we do not know who *the* author of the First Amendment is; what if there was more than one author who participated in formulating the language, and even more "authors" who ultimately agreed to it by ratifying it, and who did so for their own reasons or with their own interpretations in mind? Must we, then, also look to the First Amendment's text in a different way, discovering meaning by its significance to *us* as readers, bringing a sense of history, of cultural and political experience, and even of personal conviction to the task of giving the words meaning? And if we do so, are we not acknowledging that the "beginning" to which the term "author" relates occurs partly with the reader, flowing from the text itself, and not with the author who first produced the text?

The Supreme Court's task in interpreting the Constitution, of course, is a specialized one dealing not with anonymity, as such, but with the need to give concrete meaning to an ambiguous text with a known, if somewhat shrouded, origin and history. The problem of authorship and its relation to meaning is analogous to that posed by McIntyre's case, but the specific issue of anonymity—the issue raised

by *complete* lack of information about an author, with meaning residing only in the text and its readers — does not further compound the
Court's task of interpreting the Constitution. The answers to the distinct questions posed by McIntyre's complete anonymity, therefore,
must be found in other illustrations.

Fortunately, history provides many examples upon which we can
draw in the fields of literature, politics, and even journalism. Perhaps the
most widely known example of anonymous speech is the writing of
William Shakespeare, whose identity remains unknown and hotly
debated to this day. Why did he choose to remain anonymous? Was
Shakespeare's decision the product of a deep sense of privacy, or did he
prefer to avoid the retribution that might flow from his frequent depiction of royalty in lightly derisive and humorous — or in deeply and
darkly tragic — ways? Was it fear of retaliation, aversion to fame, apprehension of derision, or simply whim that motivated him? We can ask the
same question about Samuel Clemens, who wrote under the pseudonym
Mark Twain, or about such writers as Georges Sand (a female French
novelist) and P. D. James (a female mystery writer).

Were these authors driven to pseudonym out of fear, because of a felt
need to preserve a separate life of their own, in order to attract a wider
and more accepting audience, or for reasons of whim and caprice? In
most cases we can't know, and therefore, perhaps, we shouldn't need to
know because their motive doesn't matter. This much, at least, we are
compelled to say in the face of actual experience.

But maybe we can say even more than this. Perhaps we can say also,
at least with these authors, that their true identity has little to do with
the value and meaning of their work. Their works are works of literature — often great literature — and all are works of fiction. The true
identity of Shakespeare is a source of curiosity — the human appetite for
intrigue seems ever insatiable — but his work speaks for itself, perhaps
the better so unhindered by the trappings of authorship. Would the force
and universality of the phrase "much sound and fury signifying nothing," which inspired William Faulkner, be improved upon, or even
altered in any significant way, by knowing the identity of its author?
Does it matter that the man who created Huckleberry Finn was Samuel
Clemens, not Mark Twain? In these works, as in all works of fiction,
whether good or bad or middling, the true author disappears behind the
veil of the characters and the drama of the events. The characters are the
principal actors; the truth, if any, is in their depiction. And they, in turn,

are products of our imagination as readers, drawn along by the author's narrative but brought to life in our own minds.

Can it not be said, at least with fiction, that we, the readers, are the authors, each of us unique in what we make of the tale and in the way we imagine the characters to be? Isn't the meaning and authority of a work of fiction in the reader's mind's eye? This appears to be a point of near-universal acknowledgment — and more than occasional despair — by those who write fiction. The idea of anonymous speech and the quest for understanding its value for purposes of the First Amendment, therefore, may possess an oxymoronic quality when applied to fiction. As Samuel Beckett observed, "What matter who's speaking, someone said, what matter who's speaking?" Authorship, we might say, resides in the work itself.

But Margaret McIntyre's leaflet was not a work of fiction; it was a work of nonfiction. As such it raises a different set of concerns about anonymity and about authorship and meaning in works that purport to be true. To put the point a bit differently, but perhaps more helpfully, we must inquire into the meaning and role of the "author" for works of nonfiction, a genre of writing that embraces statements of fact, whose truth is declared, and statements of opinion, of whose truth we must be persuaded.

McIntyre's case involved both fact and opinion. The Supreme Court approached the issues raised by her leaflet by asking two questions, both focused on the justifications for her choice of anonymity. Did she have sufficient reason — based perhaps on fear of retribution — for withholding her identity? Were Ohio's reasons for forcing disclosure of her authorship sufficiently compelling? The answers the Court gave were both unclear and confusing, even muddled and inscrutable. The reason for this lies not in the answers the Court tried to supply but in the fact that the Court began by asking the wrong questions. In focusing on McIntyre's motivation (which, the Court ultimately concluded, did not matter) and on the purposes underlying Ohio's law (which, the Court said, did not justify the indiscriminately broad prohibition exacted by the law), the Court simply assumed without discussion that the anonymity of works of fact and opinion should be treated equally for purposes of the First Amendment.

But is all nonfiction to be treated the same? Is the relationship between the work and its author different in some kinds of nonfiction than in others? These questions must be addressed by asking a different question than the Court did: What role does the author perform in works that purport to be true? To address this question, let us return to the distinction between works of fact and works of opinion, recognizing that the distinction is an artificial one—works of nonfiction generally comprise fact and opinion. Margaret McIntyre's leaflet, of course, was a bit of both.

Fact and Authority

Works of fact purport to declare truth. They do not persuade but assert. They do not interpret but observe. Or so some would have us believe.

"Facts," of course, are not so simple as this. While many people today bemoan the era of "new journalism"—a journalism of fact filtered through the writer's eye and the writer's values, thus "interpreted"; a journalism premised on the absence of "true" fact and on the inextricability of ideology and reality—it remains the case that journalism continues to be the dominant form of nonfiction based largely on, and explicitly devoted to, representing fact. The other dominant genre is found in advertising, both commercial and, most relevant for present purposes, political advertising. Much, if not most, advertising purports to be factual, and its textual content is heavily factual. To be sure, it is cleverly geared by use of image and inference to shaping an opinion, but news is hardly to be distinguished from advertising on this ground. Margaret McIntyre's leaflet, too, was largely factual, focusing on the purpose of an earlier bond referendum that supplied funds for new schools; the subsequent (and implicitly inconsistent) decision to close three existing schools; and the rejection of the school-boundary plan formulated by residents who served on an appointed commission.

What is the relationship between an author and a statement of fact? We might conclude that if all works that purport to be factual were in fact so, the identity of the author of the statements would be unimportant. That journalism holds to this conceit even today is manifested in the continuing practice of anonymous news articles. "Just the facts, ma'am"—"what matter who's speaking?" But we know this as a conceit only. Statements of fact are not always true, or accurate, or even fairly selected and put. And we need not adopt the entire deconstructionist philosophy (that all reality, including what we think of as fact, is a product of culture, politics, and ultimately power) to recognize the rightness of the insight embodied in the "new journalism": the meaning of fact is a product of our ideology and individual perception, and its representation is a function of a process of discovery, selection, and presentation. This is the stuff of the inadvertent falsehood and the unfair depiction.

Because we know this, we might conclude that we need further information upon which to judge whether and how something purporting to be factual is, in fact, so. We usually trusted Walter Cronkite when he reported a fact because we believed, based on our experience with his reporting, that the fact was likely to be true and, more important, likely to have been placed in a fair context that permitted us, as viewers, to make our own judgment about its significance to our own beliefs. But Sam Donaldson is a different matter. This is not because we disbelieve those things Donaldson reports as fact but because we understand that there is something more—something unsaid—lurking behind the facts he chooses to give us. And so while we watch him, and even admire him for his audacity and perseverance, we filter his facts through a different lens, suspending disbelief a little bit less for him than for Cronkite, recognizing that he is bringing his own prejudices and values, which we know because we know him, to the journalistic table.

Surely Margaret McIntyre, too, brought her own "angle" to the depiction, selection, and representation of the facts included in her leaflet. But what was it? Her story is consistent with two very different possibilities. On the one hand, in this time of tax protests and public discontent with the workings of government, a time in which the inclination to speak is stronger than the inclination to listen, McIntyre's leaflet has a familiar ring. Was she a foot soldier in that larger battle of political ideologies and moral absolutisms, bringing its preconceptions and prejudices to the factual representations in her leaflet? Or was she, on the other hand, "just a regular person who didn't like what was going on," as her daughter, Kimberly, described her—a plainspoken person honestly trying, grammatical warts and all, to alert us to the facts? Without her identity as author of the leaflet, we just don't know, and lacking that knowledge, we may dismiss her leaflet as the work of an extremist when, in fact, it isn't.

Margaret McIntyre's leaflet, of course, did not purport to be journalism—the presentation of "objective" fact in a straightforward manner. It had an avowed purpose, announced to the reader by its admonishment "PLEASE VOTE NO" and by its "author," "Concerned Parents and Taxpayers." Unlike journalism, there was no conceit of dispassion. Moreover, in requiring that the leaflet contain her name and address, and no more, the Ohio law arguably required disclosure of the least useful information to the reader. Except for those persons who knew Margaret McIntyre (and would presumably be adequately informed by seeing her passing out the leaflets in the gym), her name and address would contribute little in the way of reader discernment. But this is quibbling with the means Ohio employed to achieve its end, not with the end itself—the need, with statements of fact, to supply readers with adequate information about authorship to make judgments about intention, presentation, and authority. The fact that Margaret McIntyre's leaflet disclosed its avowed purpose, and that her name and address, alone, may have given the reader less information than might ideally be desired, does not refute the point that disclosure of her authorship would have provided information useful in judging the writing, itself.

When facts have no author we are missing a critical piece in the significance of the work. Nonfiction, and particularly factual nonfiction, is a representation not of the author or of the reader but of the objective world. Inherent in its very definition as nonfiction and fact are such qualities as representation (*re*presentation), intention, authenticity, authority. Representations of fact, in short, are reinterpretations inextricably and necessarily bound to their author, whose identity itself is part and parcel of its narrative. Because it cannot stand alone, fact-based nonfiction must have an author. Otherwise we can make nothing of it, for it lacks representation, intention, and authority, just as a plain sign on the roadside announcing "God is Dead" lacks significance, lacks the elemental qualities of nonfiction. Without more, the sign, if anything, is fiction.

So we may conclude that without an author, representations that purport to be true because they are fact lack a quality that we deem central and necessary to the genre. This does not necessarily mean, of course, that anonymous statements of fact are not "speech" for purposes of the First Amendment, for that is a different question to which we shall turn in due course. But it might mean that even if they are protected speech, the protection accorded them should be different and more limited than that given factual statements with an author. We might, for example, conclude that with respect to the factual assertions in Margaret McIntyre's anonymous leaflet, its incompleteness for its declared purpose—presentation of historical fact relevant to its persuasive purpose—makes it a lesser order of "speech" and therefore less generously protected under the First Amendment.

Or we might conclude that while an author is required, authorship need not always mean "name" but, instead, should be taken to require, as with Margaret McIntyre's leaflet, disclosure of sufficient information *about* the author (motives, "angle," standards of selection and presentation of facts) for the reader to make the necessary interpretive judgments about the meaning and credibility of stated fact. Under this view, Margaret McIntyre's leaflet was *not* anonymous.

Argument and Authority

The Supreme Court's forceful defense of Margaret McIntyre's First Amendment right to speak anonymously might, of course, be understood instead to mean that statements of fact need not have an author — a rejection of the argument that with factual representations the relationship between text and author is often sufficiently necessary, even definitional, to be required. But this would not be the correct reading of the Court's decision. In the settings of libel and misrepresentation, for example, the Court has implied that facts are less protected under the First Amendment than opinions. False facts, according to the Court, are not "speech"; false ideas, however, are. There are ample grounds in the Court's own opinions, in short, for imposing special requirements on statements of fact, and for distinguishing such statements from "opinion" under the First Amendment.

More important, in Margaret McIntyre's case the Court did not base its judgment about the protection for her speech on any particularized or careful analysis of her leaflet. But such an analysis would be necessary to support a conclusion that the leaflet was constitutionally protected as fact because in *her* case the purpose of the leaflet was openly avowed and her name and address would, in any event, add little of value. Indeed, the Court's broad-ranging — and frankly indiscriminate — discussion of the role anonymity has played in the past belies any careful attention to McIntyre's case or to the special role that authorship might play in works of fact, as opposed to works of opinion and persuasion.

Instead, the Court's decision appears to have rested on the fact that McIntyre's leaflet was an expression of *opinion*, not just of fact, and that its quality as opinion subordinated any claims about authorship that might be based on its factual content, thus avoiding any need to discuss its factual elements.

The Court: What interest do you . . . rely on here to support the State's ban?

Mr. Sutter [who argued on behalf of Ohio]: We think that this statute serves [to provide] information important to the voter, information that enables the voter to place a candidate on the political spectrum.

The Court: How about Mrs. McIntyre's address? Wouldn't that have helped inform the electorate?

Mr. Sutter: Yes, Your Honor, and that's required by the law.

The Court: All right, and how about her partisan affiliation?

Mr. Sutter: Your Honor, we think there is a point at which too much information would cross the line.

The Court: The public gets confused by too much information.

Mr. Sutter: No, Your Honor . . .

(Laughter)

The Court: Earlier Justice O'Connor brought up the tradition of pamphleteering, going back to the Federalist Papers. . . . Isn't there [a] venerable tradition attached to the lone leafleter in this country?

Mr. Sutter: I think there is a tradition. I think the aspect of anonymity changes the perspective of the case. We're not saying, and didn't say to Margaret McIntyre, that she couldn't speak, that she couldn't hand out literature, that she couldn't say whatever she wanted in that literature.

All we're saying is . . . that the State may require her to provide the public with access to a limited amount of pertinent information to help them make better educated electoral choices. . . . All we're asking for here is a minimal amount of additional information so that the electorate can evaluate the campaign message.

The Court: You know, in this context, though, it almost seems — when the leaflet speaks to the merits of a particular issue, as this does — that the electorate can take into consideration the fact that there is no identification of the speaker attached to the message and can conclude, if it wishes, that therefore it should be discounted.

I'm not sure how strong the State's interest is in forcing the information on the electorate. I mean, as a voter, I can say, well, here's an anonymous flier, and if they don't care enough to put their name on it, I'm going to toss it in the waste basket. I don't see why the State's interest is so strong.

Mr. Sutter: Your Honor, I think that is a difficult question. . . .

The Court's description of the leaflet as a work of opinion—of persuasive writing about truth—is surely accurate. While laced with fact, the leaflet openly argued that the school board had been dishonest, or at least disingenuous, in seeking funds for school expansion while simultaneously proposing school closings. It argued that the school system was rife with wasteful spending and guilty of making poor decisions. It argued that the new tax levy was not necessary because adequate funds would be available were waste eliminated, and that at the very least new funds should not be supplied until the school system put its own house in order.

But the Court's description of the leaflet as an expression of opinion does not, of itself, explain why a work of opinion might lay a special claim to anonymity, or why that special claim should override arguments against anonymity based on the representations of fact contained within it. Is opinion different from fact in its relation to the author? Is an author *less* important for a statement of opinion than of fact? Our intuition tells us the opposite; an opinion, after all, is necessarily *someone's*. How can it exist without an author?

At one level the answer to this question is plain. By its very definition opinion cannot (setting such technological frontiers as artificial intelligence aside for the moment) exist without an author. The construction of an argument leading persuasively to a conclusion seems necessarily to be a human act, a manifestation of consciousness.

But if we ask not about the existence of an author but, rather, about the author's identity, the answer is less clear. Margaret McIntyre's authorship of the leaflet signed "Concerned Parents and Taxpayers" was never in doubt; the issue presented in her case, instead, was the requirement that she disclose it. The free speech issue posed by her case, therefore, was whether statements of opinion, not fact, are necessarily and inextricably dependent on disclosure of the *identity* of the author. On this question our intuition may prove to have let us down.

The Court: Well, isn't there [a] potential for confusion when I walk up to the polling place and I'm handed six or eight or ten or twelve leaflets saying, vote for this, that, or the other person or issue on my way up to vote?

Mr. Goldberger [who argued on behalf of Margaret McIntyre]: Your Honor, I believe that the voters are capable of deciding for themselves. They operate in a political climate . . .

The Court: You just did not see my puzzlement last September when I was on my way into the primary!

(Laughter)

The Court: So that we do have an interest in knowing who is the speaker?

Mr. Goldberger: Well, I don't believe so, Your Honor, because the leaflets are — they speak for themselves.

Works of opinion are, in their essence, works of argument and persuasion. They disclose the thought processes of an author, whether those thought processes are logical or emotional, good or bad, complete or incomplete. The thought processes thus disclosed are neither true nor false. Instead, they are either persuasive or unpersuasive. Because fact *asserts* truth, we must know how to judge it; factual statements are not designed to persuade us of their truth but, rather, to declare it. Opinion, on the other hand, attempts to prove its truth explicitly; it lays no claim to hidden underlying truth or to secret undisclosed validation but, instead, lays its justifications and proofs out in the open before the reader. To the extent it fails to do so, it fails in persuasiveness and therefore in fulfilling its function. Yet it is still a statement of opinion — badly conceived, no doubt — and the identity of the author would affect neither its character nor its quality.

Because statements of opinion by definition contain within them the very grounds for their validity, perhaps the reader needs no known author. The reader is able to judge the tendered opinion on his or her own. If the work's logic is complete, it can be accepted or rejected on that ground alone. If its logic is incomplete, it can be dismissed as unpersuasive or the logical or emotional gaps can be filled in by the reader (who for this purpose then becomes part-author) and then judged for its persuasiveness. Do we really have to know Margaret McIntyre's identity to form our own conclusion about her argument (as opposed to the truth of her facts)? If we knew her name and address, would we be in any better position to judge the persuasiveness of her argument? While her identity might be *useful*, at least to those who know of Margaret McIntyre, as we do, is it a necessary ingredient without which her work lacks the quality of persuasive assertion of truth through opinion? Indeed, isn't there even some risk that knowledge of her identity might hinder rather than help our critical judgment about the arguments she makes?

Some of the greatest examples of anonymous writing have been non-fiction works of argument and opinion. The Supreme Court emphasized this in its opinion in McIntyre's case by focusing at some length on the examples of James Madison, Alexander Hamilton, and John Jay. These three framers of the Constitution were also the authors of the Federalist Papers, anonymously written articles, signed "Publius," that presented the arguments favoring ratification of the Constitution. The Federalist Papers were examples of pure and full reasoning in support of an opinion, and thus were perhaps the classic form of opinion-based nonfiction. Like McIntyre, Madison, Hamilton, and Jay each believed that their authorship should not be disclosed. Indeed, they likely felt that their identity would serve only to distract readers from their work and *its* function, introducing prejudice and the counterproductive element of personality into the process of reason and rationality celebrated as the eighteenth-century Enlightenment ideal. One might go further and say that the authors of the great works of persuasive nonfiction, even when we know their names, are incidental to the work itself. Would we think less of Plato or Socrates if we knew them well?

Margaret McIntyre's leaflet hardly stands up to the Federalist Papers or Plato's Dialogues, but the underlying question of the need for her identity as an author is the same. Her arguments—expressed stridently, laced with innuendo, and handicapped by poor grammar—are neither more nor less persuasive depending on whether or not her name is placed upon them. We know enough about the author from the argument itself, enough to dismiss it, accept it, empathize with it, capture its emotional fervor, measure its incompleteness.

This is what the Supreme Court decided. It did not matter, the Court concluded, whether Margaret McIntyre chose anonymity as a shelter from repression, or out of inadvertence, or as a small and idiosyncratic deceit. The Court's opinion would surely have been improved had it explained why it did not matter, but even without an explanation, it follows that if Margaret McIntyre's reasons for anonymity do not matter under the First Amendment, then the constitutional protection accorded her leaflet must have something to do with the inherent nature of her expression: that as an expression of opinion—*her* opinion—it possessed all of the qualities needed for full protection as "speech" for purposes of the First Amendment.

Speaking and Speech

The conclusion that Margaret McIntyre's anonymity was protected because she was expressing her opinion, her fundamental right of dissent and persuasion, may be satisfying, but it does not finally solve the puzzle of authorship that underlies Margaret McIntyre's case. Recall Samuel Beckett's haunting query, which circles upon itself, revealing its paradox. "What matter who's speaking, someone said, what matter who's speaking?" *Someone said.* Even when the author is unknown, must there be *someone* who is speaking? Does the First Amendment require that there always be an author, and must that author be *someone* (as opposed to some*thing*) in order fully to enjoy the freedom guaranteed by the Constitution?

If authorship can be said to reside in the text as well as in its creation, might it be said that the questions of anonymity and of authorship often collapse together, becoming one and the same—and becoming tautological, too, for what text does not, in this sense, have an author? Indeed, the song of the wind blowing through the aspen, the dog's bark, the random combinations of Scrabble tiles, all have an author when meaning springs from them. Or does the First Amendment require that anonymity and authorship be kept distinct, thus limiting *the Constitution's* protection to persons, not things; to speaking, not speech?

Without realizing it, the Supreme Court worried deeply about these questions as it addressed Margaret McIntyre's case. Her case, of course, did not raise them directly, for her leaflet had an author. The leaflet was produced by her intentional act and reflected her beliefs and ideas. It was a product of McIntyre's freedom and a reflection of her intellectual free will. But like a lingering second thought that just won't let go, Beckett's question haunted the McIntyre case.

And rightly so. The Supreme Court did not have the freedom to decide McIntyre's case in isolation. It was engaged in *making* law, not applying it, and in making law the Court is obliged to rest its decisions on reasoning that transcends the facts of the case immediately before it. The Court was thus duty bound to ask and answer a larger question than that posed by McIntyre's leaflet. How can the anonymity of the leaflet be protected without at the same time invalidating a wide range of other laws prohibiting anonymous political advertisements and anonymous campaign contributions, including, most significantly, major elements of the Federal Election Campaign Act, which the Court had already upheld in a case decided in 1976? If the First Amendment gives full protection to anonymous speech, how can we justify treating some speech differently from other speech?

A possible answer lies in Beckett's query. To be fully protected in its anonymity, and indeed to be protected as an act of freedom under the First Amendment's guarantee of "freedom of speech," perhaps speech must have some*one* who is an author. This conclusion had already been implicitly reached nearly twenty-five years earlier by Justice John Marshall Harlan in his opinion in the *Cohen* case, discussed in "Story One." There Harlan rested Paul Cohen's right to display the epithet "Fuck the Draft" on the back of his jacket on the fact that the sentiment so expressed was *his,* and thus represented an exercise of Cohen's liberty as an individual to speak. McIntyre's leaflet, too, expressed *her* individual views, in her case an opinion rather than, as with Cohen, an emotion. While we do not know McIntyre's name and address when we read her anonymous leaflet, the fact is that there *is* an author—a human, free-willed agent whose own views are being expressed and whose *freedom* to speak is therefore being exercised.

Much advertising, in contrast, reflects the expression of an organization alone, speaking only for the organization, not for the individuals it comprises. Likewise, much political advertising reflects the views of a campaign organization as an organization, not of the individuals, as individuals, who belong to it; not, even, of the candidate for whom it speaks. Indeed, the most striking characteristic of speech produced by a political campaign is that it quite explicitly does not speak for itself, even as an organization, but for another (the candidate), who in turn does not vouch for the speech as his or her own. This is an endless circle of anonymity. The political campaign contribution possesses a similar quality, for the contribution itself is not the contributor's speech; it is instead a payment to support speech by someone else, who in turn speaks as an agent of the contributor, not for herself or himself.

The Court carefully distinguished McIntyre's case from these, "not deciding," it said, "whether the First Amendment's protection of corporate speech is coextensive with the protection it affords to individuals," and observing that "even though money may 'talk,' its speech is less . . . personal" than McIntyre's. Behind these judicious qualifications Beckett's haunting query can be vaguely discerned: Is *someone* speaking?

Can we say, drawing on Justice Harlan's principle of individual liberty to speak, that the corporate ad, the political campaign message, and the campaign contributions are not, really, cases of anonymous speech — cases, in other words, where *someone* is speaking though her or his identity is unknown? Are they instead cases in which there is *no author at all*? And if there is no author — no individual human being expressing his or her *own* free will — can the "speech" be described in any meaningful sense as the product of freedom?

In Margaret McIntyre's case the Court's answer is, at best, implicit: to be fully protected in its freedom, the Court implies, speech must have a speaker, an author. But the precise meaning of this principle and its concrete implications could be left unaddressed in McIntyre's case. Margaret McIntyre was not, after all, a political action committee but a real person. The hard work of charting new boundaries under the First Amendment would occur in other cases, to which we will turn later.

For now, however, we will have to abide the ambiguous distinctions upon which the Court rested its decision in Margaret McIntyre's case. Hers was an exercise in *freedom* of speech, her right to express her *opinion* about truth without identifying herself. Left for another day were cases involving claims of anonymity in works of fiction and works of fact. Left also for another day was a fuller explanation of the distinction between authorship and identity; between Margaret McIntyre's anonymous leaflet, which possesses an author but no identity, and anonymous political advertisements and campaign contributions, which possess an identity but, perhaps, no author.

Left for another day, in short, were fundamental questions about what we mean by the term "author" and its relationship to the freedom of speech protected by the First Amendment. In addressing them, the Court will have to confront the paradox at the heart of Beckett's query: "What matter who's speaking, someone said, what matter who's speaking?"

Margaret McIntyre did not live to experience her victory. But in the gritty determination that marked her life, she left a legacy. In fact, she left two legacies. The first is the affirmation of her right — and thus our right — to speak our minds freely and, if we choose, anonymously. The second legacy is the beginning of a deeper understanding of what is meant by "the freedom of speech" protected under the First Amendment.

Margaret McIntyre would be pleased.

ADDITIONAL READING

C. Edwin Baker, *Human Liberty and Freedom of Speech* (1989).

Anne Wells Branscomb, "Anonymity, Autonomy, and Accountability: Challenges to the First Amendment in Cyberspace," 104 *Yale Law Journal* 1639 (1995).

Joseph Raz, "Free Expression and Personal Identification," 11 *Oxford Journal of Legal Studies* 303 (1991).

Steven H. Shiffrin, *The First Amendment, Democracy, and Romance* (1990).

Story Three

The Corporation and
the Candidate
*(Austin v. Michigan State Chamber of
Commerce, 494 U.S. 652 (1990))*

In America the speech marketplace is populated as much by corporations as by individuals. Procter & Gamble speaks to us about detergents; Mobil speaks to us about energy policy and the environment; and through campaign contributions and PACs, corporations ranging from IBM to the ACLU speak to us with increasing frequency about the political candidates for whom we should cast our ballots. This, it seems, is the American way—just as, in the old days before Honda, Nissan, and others, it was often said, "What's good for General Motors is good for America."

But when General Motors speaks, who is really speaking? Is speech by General Motors different from speech by other corporations and organizations, such as the ACLU, the NAACP, or the UAW? And why should General Motors' speech be less valuable than Donald Trump's speech, even when they are saying the very same thing? These questions, interestingly enough, were at the center of the Supreme Court's oral argument in a case involving Richard Bandstra, a candidate for the Michigan House of Representatives, and the Michigan State Chamber of Commerce, which wanted to endorse him. The story behind the case concerns speech that has no speaker. It is not a story about speech that has no identified speaker—speech that claims no speaker but has one hiding behind a veil of anonymity, as with Margaret McIntyre's anonymous leaflet. It is instead a story about speech that claims a speaker but in fact may have none—no point of origin in a person who qualifies under the First Amendment as a speaker. It is a story, in short, about speech by corporations.

The story presses the question left ambiguous in Margaret McIntyre's case, the question posed by Samuel Beckett's haunting query: "What matter who's speaking, someone said, what matter who's speaking?" Must speech have an "author," and must that author, as Beckett implies, be *"someone"*—an individual freely expressing his or her own views? If so, when, if ever, can corporations be authors, or First Amendment speakers, when they speak?

Before turning to our story, some preliminary groundwork must be briefly laid. Specifically, four terms that will be central to the story must be distinguished: "communication," "speech," "speaking," and "First Amendment speech." For purposes of the First Amendment's freedom of speech, "speech" and "communication" are not the same thing. Communication may be defined as "an act or instance of transmitting" information, ideas, feelings, images, and so on. The term describes a process, a phenomenon, only a subset of which consists of what we call "speech." A bird's song communicates, but it is not speech. This is not because the bird's song, which is "communication," is inherently different from, say, a Bach suite, its human counterpart. The difference instead resides in the bird, not in the song, for speech resides only in people, at least for purposes of the First Amendment.

But all human acts of speech are not protected by the First Amendment. Speech, in other words, excludes not only what the bird sings but also what some people say. The Supreme Court, for example, tells us that obscenity is not "speech" for purposes of the First Amendment because it lacks "redeeming social value," appealing only to "prurient interests." This can hardly be said about the bird's song. Obscenity, therefore, is "speech" but not *First Amendment speech*—a further subset of speech falling within the protected ambit of the Constitution.

If speech is but a subset of communication, and if First Amendment speech is but a further subset of speech, what are the qualities that distinguish "First Amendment speech" from "speech"—from other forms of human communication? This is the question with which the Supreme Court was confronted in our story. Answering it required the Court to think about a final distinction between "speech" and "speaking." Is "First Amendment speech" necessarily tied, indeed limited, to the act of "speaking," a distinctly *human* act by which free will and individual belief is made manifest? If so, what about the message communicated by a corporation—the Pepsi ad, for example, that cannot be traced to the personal views of *any* person? What about speech that can be described only as an endless circle of anonymity, such as the message purchased by a political campaign, spoken not for the campaign organization itself but for the candidate, who of course disavows (where convenient) the campaign organization's speech as not being his or her own but the campaign organization's? While the campaign message is admittedly communication, and it is clearly "speech" in the sense that it is of human origin, does it also fit within the narrower category of First Amendment speech?

These questions arose in a peculiar setting. Our story does not involve anything so romantic as the bird's song, so delicate as a Bach suite, or so politically charged as obscenity or pornography. It concerns instead a decision by the Michigan State Chamber of Commerce to purchase an advertisement supporting a candidate, and to pay for it from the chamber's own funds. But mundane as the setting of our story is, the importance of the story and the Supreme Court's attention to it can hardly be underestimated.

In telling the story we will rely heavily on the transcript of oral argument before the Supreme Court, for the drama and intrigue lie not in the facts of the story but in the quite remarkable exchanges that took place in the Supreme Court's chamber. One cannot understand the Supreme Court's surprising decision in the case, or the profound impact it may have, without participating in the proceedings that began at exactly 1:00 P.M. on October 31, 1989. It was Halloween, a fitting day, perhaps, for the Court to explore Beckett's haunting query: "What matter who speaks, *someone said*, what matter who speaks?"

As Chief Justice Rehnquist brought the courtroom to order and announced the case, Number 88-1569, *Richard H. Austin v. The Michigan State Chamber of Commerce,* the first lawyer to the podium was Louis J. Caruso, the solicitor general of the State of Michigan. Mr. Caruso's burden was to defend the constitutionality of the Michigan Campaign Finance Act, first passed in 1976 as part of a wave of state campaign-reform legislation that swept the country in the wake of the Federal Elections Campaign Act of 1971.

Michigan's law contained a relatively unique provision that prohibited corporations from spending corporate funds to express public endorsement or support for candidates for public office. The provision was at once sweeping and limited. It applied to all corporations, large and small, profit and nonprofit, private and public. It did not, however, apply to any other forms of organization, such as partnerships, associations, political action committees, or the more loosely organized groups that often spring to temporary life to pursue an ideology or political agenda. Nor did the act's prohibition apply to the use of corporate funds in connection with referenda or other types of elections that did not involve candidates for public office. And the act left corporations free to lobby, to make campaign contributions, and to engage in a wide variety of other political activities; they were even free to organize efforts to endorse candidates in elections for public office as long as the funds used were separately raised from the corporation's membership for that purpose, were kept separate from the corporation's general treasury funds, and were controlled by the shareholders, if any, and the officers and management of the corporation. Corporate endorsement of candidates with corporate funds was the sole target of the Michigan law.

While the act had been in effect since its enactment in 1976, it was not until the summer of 1985 that it was challenged. The challenge was brought by the Michigan State Chamber of Commerce. The chamber is a nonprofit corporation and the parent organization for the various local chambers of commerce in cities throughout Michigan. Its membership numbers about 8,000, roughly 2,000 of which are individuals or unincorporated entities; the remaining 6,000 are corporations. As an organization the chamber's purposes are broad, ranging from economic development, education, and the encouragement of ethical business practices, to lobbying, disseminating its views to government officials at state and local levels, and actively engaging in the political process in support of its agenda.

In June of 1985 a special election was scheduled to fill a vacant seat in the Michigan House of Representatives. The Michigan State Chamber of Commerce had not made a practice of sponsoring its own advertisements in support of legislative candidates, but this was a special case. The chamber favored the Republican candidate, Richard Bandstra, whose views were consistent with those of the chamber. Perhaps as important, the special election gave the chamber an appealing opportunity in the political off-season to launch a challenge to the Michigan Campaign Finance Act. Complying with the act through creation of special funds or political action committees required substantial solicitation efforts that might, in a general election, have to be duplicated many times in various districts as contributions were sought from members to support their candidates. The special fund arrangement also meant that the chamber's advertisements endorsing candidates could not carry the name of the chamber but would, instead, have to be sponsored by a political action committee, and thus the chamber, itself, could not speak as an organization.

As the June 1985 midterm election approached, therefore, the chamber set upon its course of challenging the Michigan act. The chamber arranged to place a paid advertisement supporting Bandstra in the *Grand Rapids Press*. The ad's headline read "Michigan Needs Richard Bandstra To Help Us Be Job Competitive Again." Its contents focused on the need to reduce workers' compensation costs and to roll back the personal income tax rate. Bandstra would work for both goals. The ad bore the insignia and name of the Michigan State Chamber of Commerce. It was scheduled for publication on June 9, the day before the election. It never ran.

The Michigan act made the chamber's advertisement a felony punishable by a fine of up to $5,000 or imprisonment for up to three years, or both. The chamber had no interest in becoming a defendant in a criminal trial, of course, so as soon as the chamber purchased the ad, but before it was scheduled to run, the chamber also filed a lawsuit in federal court claiming that the act's prohibition violated the First Amendment and requesting that the judge enjoin enforcement of the act against the chamber. The chamber's strategy was scuttled, however, when the judge refused to enjoin the act's enforcement, and the chamber (after canceling the ad) was compelled to commence the long process of appeal that finally brought it, on Halloween of 1989, to oral argument before the United States Supreme Court.

As the beginning of oral argument approached, both of the lawyers who would address the Court were ready, having worked out their respective strategies for presenting their side of the case. "Naming" the chamber— giving it an identity, almost as a character in a novel is given identity— served as the metaphor for each side's strategy. The lawyer for the State of Michigan would try to de-anthropomorphize the chamber, describing it as "a nonprofit membership corporation" sapped of human qualities, emphasizing its abstract corporate status, with all the baggage of accumulated wealth and power that accompany it, and focusing on the diversity, political and otherwise, of its largely corporate membership and interests. The chamber's lawyer would take the opposite tack. He would give the chamber human qualities by describing it as a gathering together of like-minded people working for a common cause, an ideological organization formed "for the specific purpose of promoting economic development and the preservation and enhancement of the American enterprise system. Both the purposes and activities of the State Chamber of Commerce," he would declare, "are ideological"—and political.

As we will see, this dispute over naming the chamber was but one level on which contending ideas of speech and speakers were fought out. For the state, the chamber was to be seen as a corporation, a mere entity, an abstract creature of state law possessed of no mind or will of its own. The chamber saw itself, in contrast, as an organization of people joined together for ideological ends, gaining strength from their numbers. "Organizations" don't have ideologies; people do.

And so the struggle for naming the chamber—corporation or people—would serve as a surrogate for the deeper debate about whether the chamber was a "speaker" for purposes of the First Amendment—whether it was more like Bach or more like the bird.

As Caruso approached the podium and faced the nine justices, he knew that he would have but a few minutes to state the essence of his argument before the justices' questions began. His burden was to articulate clearly the reason Michigan prohibited corporations from publicly endorsing candidates for office—to define the "evil" that the law was designed to prevent, as the Court often puts it—and to explain why the breadth of the Michigan law was not excessive but was, instead, limited closely and narrowly to those instances in which the "evil" was likely to occur. The issue of the act's breadth was critical because the First Amendment had long been interpreted to require that laws restricting expression be narrowly confined in their reach only to problems with which the legislature is justifiably concerned. To prevent speech that causes a riot at street corners, for example, a state cannot constitutionally prohibit *all* speech on street corners. A law that sweeps too broadly catches within its grasp other speech that cannot be restricted, thus limiting the freedom of other speakers, who may adopt a safer course and remain silent in the face of a law that makes no sense in their case but that literally applies to them.

The purpose of the Michigan law, Caruso announced as he began his argument, was "the prevention of corruption and the appearance of corruption in the electoral process, by a legislative scheme aimed in part at corporations [that] reflects a legislative judgment that the special characteristics of a corporation require particularly careful regulation," a judgment, he added, that is entitled to "deference by the Court."

With this, the questions from the Court began.

Justice Sandra Day O'Connor: Why are labor unions excluded from the scheme, Mr. Caruso? Do they not pose some of the same dangers that corporate expenditures do?

Mr. Caruso: Justice O'Connor, labor unions are not excluded as such. If a labor union is incorporated, it is included. As a matter of fact, I believe there are 22 major labor unions in the State of Michigan incorporated, including the [Michigan Education Association], and they are included.

[It would become clear later in the argument, however, that perhaps the biggest unions, such as the United Auto Workers, and the unions whose views competed most directly with the chamber's, were not incorporated and were therefore not subject to the law.]

Mr. Caruso continued: And with respect to not including them expressly, . . . this Court has said many times we defer to legislative judgment as to those entities that require regulation. There may be some entities that pose the same problem and the same potential threat to the electoral process as do corporations, but we defer to the legislative judgment in this area, and . . . perhaps at some particular time the legislature may see fit to include labor unions — labor unions [that are] not incorporated — but they have not done so at this time.

The argument Caruso was making requires some further explanation. A law that restricts some but not all speech that presents a serious risk to the electoral process is ordinarily treated with suspicion because its exemptions may disguise a legislative preference for some ideas — the views of labor in this case — over others — the views of business. To prevent speech that causes a riot at street corners, for example, a state cannot enact a law that prohibits only riot-provoking speech that endorses communism. If it did, we would question whether the state's concern was really communism, not riots.

The issue raised by the labor union exemption, therefore, was not that the law applied too broadly but, instead, the opposite. The law failed to reach all of the activities that presented the danger of corruption and undue influence to which the law was directed. It thus raised the question of whether Michigan was more concerned about the ideas corporations would express than the corrupting influence that large and wealthy organizations might have on the political process.

But questions about the underinclusiveness of the Michigan law were suspended for the moment as Justice Antonin Scalia, the Court's toughest and most aggressive questioner, turned the Court's attention back to the law's overbreadth with his question to Solicitor General Caruso:

> *Justice Scalia:* General Caruso, why is there a greater risk to the political process for an independent expenditure by a family corporation, a closely held corporation [with] eight family members [who] want to spend the corporation's money for a particular candidate whom they think will favor their business? That . . . that is prohibited by this [law]. But if Donald Trump wants to come in and spend as much money as he likes, that is perfectly all right. Why wouldn't it make much more sense, if you are worried about the problem, to establish an amount of money as the criterion?
>
> *Mr. Caruso:* Well, the Court has [said] that corporations are given by state authorities certain benefits by virtue of the corporate form. They are given certain benefits in respect of liability, certain benefits in respect of taxes, certain benefits in respect of perpetual life. And what the Court has seen in the past, . . . the legislature has seen . . . and has provided against their taking advantage of that— [of] those particular advantages given to corporations and turning them into an advantage in the electoral process and in the political arena. Now, this Court has said that the legislature's judgment in this area is one that we will defer to.

The weaknesses in Caruso's foundations were beginning to show. In his response to Scalia's question about Donald Trump, Caruso had shifted subtly from defending a law designed to root out corruption to defending the law as a quid pro quo, the price to be paid by corporations for their preferred status in other areas. This was a dangerous line of argument, as will become evident, for by such logic a person who receives Medicare funds from the government could be required to give up some of her or his freedom of speech in exchange for receiving government benefits.

Perhaps detecting the weakness of his argument, Caruso attempted to disguise the argument in a second argument: that the Court, a nonelected branch of government, should defer to the judgment of the elected branch. But of course this argument, too, was dangerous (even though instinctively appealing to an increasingly conservative Court), for if taken too far it would read the First Amendment right out of the Constitution. The point of the First Amendment, after all, is to restrict what government can do, including the democratically elected legislative branch.

But Caruso was saved the embarrassment of Justice Scalia's rejoinder by Justice Anthony Kennedy, who interjected and once again shifted the topic to an entirely different area. Caruso, we might imagine, was beginning to get dizzy from the rapidly shifting lines of questions.

Justice Kennedy: Well . . . let me ask this. Everyone concedes, I take it, that an expenditure in an election — a direct expenditure — is speech. It *is* speech we are talking about, an expenditure . . . ?

Mr. Caruso: Yes, that is correct, Justice Kennedy.

Justice Kennedy: And I take it that the State must establish a compelling interest to restrict that speech?

[In referring to a "compelling interest," Kennedy is referring to the requirement that, with state regulation of speech, as opposed to conduct, the First Amendment requires more than the ordinary level of justification. There must be a *compelling*, as distinguished from a simply legitimate, or everyday kind of interest being served by a restriction on speech.]

Mr. Caruso: That is correct.

Justice Kennedy: And the means [referring to the law's prohibitions] are to be narrowly tailored [and not overbroad or underinclusive].

[To this Caruso nods his assent, though perhaps in trepidation.]

Justice Kennedy: All right. Then . . . it seems to me that Justice Scalia's question indicates that you have to give a specific reason why a [family] corporation . . . presents more of a danger than Donald Trump, and I didn't really hear an answer to that question.

Mr. Caruso [returning now to very dangerous ground]: The compelling interest is the fact that [corporations] have been given certain advantages by the state legislature for other purposes.

Question: Well, that's not an interest.

Mr. Caruso: Well, it's the fact, the fact . . .

Question: That's not an interest, that is just a rationale . . . that's just a rationale for the legislative exercise of power. That is not an interest. An interest is an evil that has to be corrected.

Mr. Caruso: The evil is . . . that by virtue of the fact that they are incorporated, corporations . . . gain an advantage, and they are able to amass great wealth in the economic sphere . . .

Question: But you have just been put . . . a hypothetical where that is not the case!

Mr. Caruso: Not in the family corporation case, that is true. But in the traditional corporations it is true. This Court has said [in earlier cases] that the big corporations as well as those less fortunate are nevertheless—may come within the prohibition because we refer—defer to the legislative judgment.

[The Court's questions now begin to evince increasing frustration from the bench.]

Question: But, but. . . . That does not sound to me—that does not sound to me like a compelling interest, and it does not sound to me like [the law is being subjected to any significant] scrutiny. That is just legislative deference.

Caruso now attempts to shift away from the quid pro quo rationale to the potential of corruption and unfair influence corporate expenditures pose for elections. But in doing so he pays a terrible price, exchanging haunting doubts raised by the family corporation for devastation to be wreaked by the ACLU (the American Civil Liberties Union, of which certain politicians must from time to time swear *not* to be a card-carrying member, and which was treated just like the Chamber of Commerce under the Michigan law). In his faltering presentation Mr. Caruso shows signs of impending crisis.

Mr. Caruso: That is . . . the fact is that the evil is a potential of corruption, of injecting monies that have been generated through the corporate process in the economic sphere to effect an equal—to *unequal* a playing field in the political arena. And that is what the . . . what is aimed at. Now, historically, corporations [have] been regulated. . . .

[Caruso was trying to shift the focus and place Michigan's law in the larger historical context of Michigan's regulation of corporate activities. But the Court would have none of it, and it bore in—*hard.*]

Question: As I understand . . . this statute, if a candidate Smith has been a member of the Ku Klux Klan, the ACLU cannot take out an advertisement explaining that fact and asking people to vote for Jones. Or am I incorrect? Can the ACLU do that, the ACLU being a nonprofit corporation?

Mr. Caruso: The ACLU? I don't know whether they are . . .

Question: It is a nonprofit corporation.

Mr. Caruso: . . . nonprofit corporation. If they do not come within the exception that has been cast by this Court [in an earlier case involving a right to life organization that could not, the Court said, be restricted in its campaign activities], I would say that that prohibition . . . yes . . . unless they did it through a segregated fund [a separate PAC]. Now, the fact is that there are . . .

Question: I find it very hard to see that the fact that they can make this expenditure through a fund in any way really mitigates the evil, but it certainly does diminish the message. I am not interested in what a PAC says. I am interested in what the ACLU says.

Mr. Caruso: The thing of it is, the segregated fund, they can do this, simply because the money contributed to a separate fund is money given for political purposes. Now, if we are permitting these corporations to use funds that have been generated for another purpose into the political arena, we are causing what the . . . this Court has . . . what the legislature believes to be a potential threat to the economic market . . . or [rather] to the political marketplace — and causing an unfair advantage to corporations over private parties. I would respect. . . .

[Justice O'Connor, who began the questions by asking about the labor union exception, now breaks in and inquires about another exception.]

Justice O'Connor: Mr. Caruso, there is some kind of a media exception in the statute. Can a corporation publish something that would include some candidate endorsement and sell it as a magazine or distribute it, and fall under the media exception?

Mr. Caruso: There is a media exception, but that media exception, Justice O'Connor, has to do specifically with news stories, commentaries, editorials, and the regular course of publication and broadcasting. . . . I think [ordinary corporations not in the media business] would be precluded by this statute. . . . [But] if they are incorporated *and* it is a news media [corporation], . . . they may be able to do that.

Justice O'Connor: Why doesn't that distort the electoral process?

Mr. Caruso [fairly twisting in the wind of the Court's rapid-fire and constantly shifting questions, responds simply, and perhaps with a certain disbelief]: Pardon?

Justice O'Connor: Why doesn't that distort the electoral process? I find it difficult to see what the evil being driven at here is. When it is a contribution to the candidate you can say, well, some candidates just have too much money at their disposal.

Mr. Caruso: Well, the fact is that . . .

Justice O'Connor: But here the only evil, as I understand it, is that there will be too much speech on one side of the issue, funded by vast amounts of money. Is that right? We distrust *too much* speech?

Mr. Caruso: Well, I wouldn't put it that quite way. We [don't?] mistrust too much speech, but the thing of it is they get . . .

Justice O'Connor: Well . . . how else would you put it?

[Caruso is now in very deep trouble, sliding downward and grasping wildly for a handhold. He gropes for an answer.]

Mr. Caruso: They get speech, they are able to get a great deal of speech, and perhaps very effective speech, by virtue of the fact that the state has given them an advantage . . . and put — and direct this thing toward the . . . in the electoral process, which . . . which the legislature has seen for many years to prohibit . . . even though they recognize . . . there are other entities that perhaps pose as much a danger or a greater danger than corporations do. But nevertheless, the fact is that the . . .

Question: Danger of what? [H]ere we are talking about whether a corporation, just like a private individual, can go out and express to the public that corporation's view, with, I assume, indication that this is the view of General Motors.

Mr. Caruso: That is right.

Question: So, you think that is a threat to the democratic process, that the state is going to be swept away by ads signed by General Motors, or whatever?

Mr. Caruso: Well, the thing of it is . . . here again . . . insofar as making contributions [to a candidate's campaign] is concerned and independent expenditures [for an advertisement supporting the candidate] is concerned, in today's society I don't see the effect being any different. In other words, this Court has prohibited in the past contributions by corporations, but [it has] not reached and answered the question on independent expenditures.

Justice O'Connor: Quite so.

Mr. Caruso: Pardon?

Caruso seemed, once again, a bit taken aback by the justice's too-ready agreement with his argument. It was in fact true that the Court had upheld restrictions on campaign contributions in the past—by individuals as well as corporations, it should be said. But that did not, as Caruso was implying, mean that restrictions on corporations purchasing ads supporting candidates were *therefore* constitutional. Indeed, the Court had earlier concluded that such independent advertisements purchased by individuals could *not* be constitutionally restricted. Caruso's analogy did not work and more importantly failed to supply an affirmative justification for the Michigan law. The colloquy continued.

> *Mr. Caruso:* Independent expenditures, I believe, today, with the political consultants—they abound in the states—and with the sophisticated news media we have today, electronic systems that we have, I think that money, independent expenditures, can be very skillfully manipulated in such a way that it would be just as much a benefit to that candidate . . . as contributions [are].
>
> *[The response (probably Justice Scalia's) was surprisingly acerbic]:* Right. People are getting too much information. That's the problem.
>
> *Mr. Caruso:* Pardon?
>
> *Question:* The people get too much—they get talked at too much. That is an evil.
>
> *Mr. Caruso:* The evil is that they get talked at too much by—because money has been made available.
>
> *Question:* Well, I don't care why. What is the evil in being talked at too much? I mean, I understand the evil of giving money directly to a candidate. It is close, you know, it could be very close to a bribe. But this is not giving money to a candidate, it is just talking. And you are saying that that is an evil?
>
> *Mr. Caruso:* It's more than just a bribe. Heretofore . . . contributions were prohibited on the basis that there is a quid pro quo . . . which doesn't exist in independent expenditures. [But] I think that it does. Nevertheless, the fact is that the corporations have an unfair advantage in the marketplace because they are in a position of generating monies. . . .
>
> *Justice Scalia:* [Can Michigan prohibit corporations] from giving contributions to religious charities, to religions?

Mr. Caruso: Why, I suppose it can. I don't think that the Michigan Campaign Finance Act prohibits that. As a matter of fact, the Act permits corporations to make direct expenditures and contributions without limit to ballot questions.

Justice Kennedy: Can it prohibit corporations from contributing to one party but not to another?

Mr. Caruso [again put off balance by the direction the questions were taking]: To one party and not to another? I wouldn't think so. I don't think they should be permitted to contribute to *any* party.

Justice Kennedy: I suppose you would think that the legislature could prohibit the nonprofit corporation from publishing a journal then—[like] the American Medical Association Journal?

Mr. Caruso: To do—to say what?

Justice Kennedy: Well, if corporations can be regulated, if there is too much speech, if that is an evil, why can't the state prohibit the American Medical Association from publishing its monthly journal?

Mr. Caruso: I don't believe they can prohibit that. That is not the issue here. The issue here, Justice Kennedy . . .

Justice Kennedy: Well, you're saying . . . that corporations have too much power, that there is too much speech, that this is an evil, the corporations gather a great deal of money, that they are created by the state. Therefore we [the Courts] give legislative deference. All of those arguments can be made to support the proposition that the AMA journal—that the ACLU newsletter—ought to be regulated by the state.

The ACLU had come up again, and it was not a happy hypothetical for Caruso. Notwithstanding the Michigan act's broad language, the law was clearly directed at the traditional form of business corporation, and the State of Michigan—as well as Caruso—seemed to have little interest in wrestling with public interest groups like the ACLU. This must have seemed a delicious dilemma to a conservative Court, and Justices Kennedy, O'Connor, and Scalia jumped at the chance to rub it in. Caruso attempted to wiggle out.

Mr. Caruso: But not in . . . in candidate elections is what we are talking about. Not anything other than candidate elections.

[But the justices would not let him escape.]

Justice Kennedy: We are talking about a matter of principle! And we are asking you to tell us what the evil is in the speech the nonprofit corporations present in election campaigns. And all of the comments you have made so far would equally support the proposition that you can prohibit the publication of [the ACLU's] monthly newspaper, or prohibit [corporations] from giving to churches, as Justice Scalia asked, or that you can require them to give money to one party and not to the other.

Mr. Caruso: I don't know of anything like that being in the Campaign Finance Act. . . .

Question: And the ACLU?

Mr. Caruso: The ACLU, that is . . . The ACLU may come within the exception . . . if it is a political action group . . . .

Question: Have you read the amicus briefs in this case? [Amicus briefs are written arguments filed with the Court by persons and organizations that are not parties to a case but will be directly affected by its outcome.]

Mr. Caruso: Pardon?

Question: The ACLU has filed an amicus brief in this case. Have you read it?

Mr. Caruso: Yes.

Question: Don't they indicate . . . that they take corporate contributions, and therefore they do not qualify under [our earlier decision in the right to life case for an exemption]?

Mr. Caruso: If that is the case, if that is correct, then I suggest . . .

Question: Well, do you have any reason to doubt that what they've said is correct?

Mr. Caruso: No, I have no . . . no . . .

Question: All right, then the ACLU doesn't qualify under that case.
    [Mr. Caruso proceeds to dig himself a deeper hole.]

Mr. Caruso: Then I would say that—I would say that the ACLU, if they take corporate contributions, if they get involved in the electoral process, they are a conduit for those corporations to put money into the electoral process.
    [And then the Court lets him slide to its bottom.]

Question: Isn't it true that the ACLU is a membership, nonprofit corporation?

Mr. Caruso: Yes.

Question: That is a little different from General Motors, isn't it?

Mr. Caruso: It's totally different [from] General Motors.

Question: How does it compare with the Michigan Chamber of Commerce?

Mr. Caruso: Pardon?

Question: I mean, we're talking about a nonprofit membership corporation on the one hand, versus a profit-making corporation like General Motors, on the other. How about the Michigan Chamber of Commerce, which is the corporation involved here?

Mr. Caruso: The Michigan Chamber of Commerce, I would say, looking at it on a spectrum . . . comes someplace in between, and we suggest closer to General Motors. . . . [T]hey have been established by business corporations, they have an 8,000 membership, 75 percent of those members are business corporations. . . . They have . . . a very sound financial resource to draw on. . . . The Chamber is in a situation where they can have a serious impact on the political process.

Justice Scalia: By which you mean a lot of speech?

Mr. Caruso: Well, if that is the way you want to cast it, Justice Scalia — a lot of speech — I suppose that is true. But it is . . .

Justice Scalia: But no other thing that you are directing this narrowly at except that they'll have too much speech?

[No response. Justice Scalia repeats the question — for which there is, of course, but one answer: submission.]

Justice Scalia: I mean, there is no other element of a corporation that accounts for the legislature's restriction here, except for the fact that they will have a lot of — of political speech?

Mr. Caruso: They have a very . . . their presence — a corporation's presence in the political marketplace is very formidable. Just the very presence is formidable.

Mr. Caruso's career with the case is now all but finished. He has been placed in a box from which there is no escape. If the Court insists that the State of Michigan have a clear, articulable, and compelling — even substantial — justification for its law prohibiting endorsements of candidates by corporations, and that the law catch in its grasp no more speech than fits the justification, but all of the speech that does, the case is lost. Even accepting the state's mushy theory about corporate wealth and too much corporate speech — a justification far removed from the themes of corruption and undue influence with which Caruso began — the examples of the labor unions, the family businesses, the AMA, and, worst, the ACLU make a shambles of the law's rationality. The state's argument has been utterly devastated. It is so full of holes that it is no longer identifiable.

It was at this point, when even to Caruso it may have seemed that all was lost, that a softball—an easy, leading question, a hand extended as a means of escape—was tendered. And it came from a surprising source: Chief Justice Rehnquist. But a little digging would reveal that the source was not all that surprising, for the chief justice was no proponent of corporate free speech. Beginning with a lone dissent in a little-known but fascinating case decided in 1986, involving a public utility company's claim that its free speech was violated by a requirement that it include a public interest group's message about energy conservation in its monthly billings, Rehnquist had begun to stake out his own position that corporations are not First Amendment speakers. The extension of the First Amendment's protection to speech by corporations based on "individual freedom of conscience," he said, "strains the rationale . . . beyond the breaking point. To ascribe to such artificial entities an 'intellect' or 'mind' . . . is to confuse metaphor with reality."

The escape Chief Justice Rehnquist offered to Caruso led in a direction different from that which Caruso had taken thus far. It shifted the focus from the state's justifications for restricting protected speech to the dramatically different question of whether the chamber's advertisement *was* speech at all. If it was not speech protected by the First Amendment, all of the fussing about hypothetical cases by Justices O'Connor, Scalia, and Kennedy would be irrelevant, for when the state regulates non-speech activity, it needs little by way of justification or narrow tailoring to satisfy the demands of the Constitution; it can, in short, enact sloppy and messy laws.

The chief justice's question seems gentle, almost understated, pointing the way out of the dilemma but letting Caruso discover the answer.

> *Chief Justice Rehnquist:* Isn't one of the reasons you are urging why corporations like this were treated differently—or *could* be treated differently from individuals—that the stockholders of the member corporations could find their funds put to uses that they had not intended?
>
> *Mr. Caruso:* That is exactly right. As I have mentioned earlier, Justice—Mr. Chief Justice—that these monies that are put in by the stockholders by way of investments [are] for economic benefit and

economic gain, to earn profits. And they certainly do not anticipate those monies being used in the—to—in the electoral process to urge the election of a particular candidate. And they [the stockholders] have free speech rights. Their free speech rights might be violated by the fact that the corporation is going out and spending monies [that have] been put in for other purposes.

The clear implication of the chief justice's question had been that corporations don't speak; their stockholders, as individuals, do. But for the stockholders to speak through the corporation, they must know what is being said on their behalf, and agree with it. Unfortunately, by this point Caruso was apparently too far disoriented by the flurry of earlier questions to really grasp the question. He may have been aware that his time was—thankfully—short, perhaps even anxiously awaiting the red light that would signal the imminent end of his argument, his ordeal. His answer started out fine but quickly took a wrong turn, veering toward the free speech rights of the stockholders rather than the inability of corporations, as entities distinct from—and not reflecting the individual views of—their members or stockholders, to engage in First Amendment speech.

The chief justice thanked Caruso for his argument, which is customary for the Court, and invited him to be seated. Caruso no doubt left the podium with relief, and certainly with gratitude that the relentless questioning was finally concluded. Did Caruso, who had been so badly pummeled, yet realize the favor the chief justice had extended him, the helping hand offered—too late, perhaps, just as the time allotted for his argument came to an end?

If Caruso had a hard time of it before the Court, the same cannot be said of his opponent, Richard D. McLellan, of Lansing, Michigan, who argued on behalf of the Michigan State Chamber of Commerce. His burden was to anthropomorphize the chamber, to give it an identity, even a personality and system of beliefs, to make it a First Amendment speaker rather than an abstract, impersonal, artificial entity created by the state and treated as a legal "person" only because of a legal fiction. Mr. McLellan's argument was smooth, self-confident, rarely visibly perturbed by unanticipated questions; a model of oral argument.

In Caruso's defense, it should be said that defending a statute's constitutionality is always much more difficult than challenging it, just as the affirmative side of an argument is more difficult than the negative. Caruso was saddled with the act the Michigan legislature had passed in 1976. It was not a pretty act, but he was not free to change it, and he had to defend it in all of its applications, warts and all. McLellan, on the other hand, could shape his argument around a coherent theory of his *own* design, and if fault lines appeared, he could shift nimbly to other grounds for doubting the law's validity. McLellan knew that such flexibility was his greatest asset, and that its absence was Caruso's greatest liability.

But McLellan also knew something else: while his argument would be the easier to make, his case would be the harder to win. From cases the Court had recently decided, he knew that he could count on the votes of only three justices: Kennedy, O'Connor, and Scalia. Even their votes were far from certain, but their combined and almost coordinated attack on Caruso no doubt gave McLellan a greater measure of confidence. McLellan's burden, then, was to gather the votes of two of the remaining justices, each of whom in one way or another had expressed views at odds with the chamber's claim.

Chief Justice Rehnquist, of course, had expressed his disdain for freedom of speech by corporations in the earlier public utility case. Justices Brennan and Marshall, the two remaining justices from the Warren Court of the 1960s, had supported federal and state laws restricting campaign speech but had drawn the line on government's power to limit such speech in a very recent case involving Massachusetts Citizens for Life, a nonprofit group whose ideological mission was deemed sufficiently clear and pervasive that the corporation's speech could be traced to the views of its members as individuals, and therefore could not be restricted. Justice Blackmun, too, had joined that opinion. He was now third in seniority among the justices and was widely seen as fitting within the diminishing liberal block of the Court, at least in cases involving individual civil liberties.

Justices Stevens and White were the "wild cards" for McLellan. Their earlier votes fit no neat ideological or philosophical pattern. Stevens tended to see cases in his own, and often idiosyncratic, way. White was the consummate pragmatist, less concerned about elegant theory than about the cold, hard facts and realities of cases. So it was likely that McLellan had shaped his theory of the case around the views of Stevens and White—a theory resting firmly on the premise that the chamber was an organizational vehicle by which its members expressed their ideological views. This theory required that McLellan quickly and decisively—before the questions began—give the chamber a different identity as a speaker, a different name, from the "corporation" label urged by Caruso.

McLellan was surely aware of the difficulties he faced as he approached the podium and began his argument:

> *Mr. McLellan:* Mr. Chief Justice, and may it please the Court.
>
> The Michigan State Chamber of Commerce is a nonprofit Michigan membership corporation. It was organized in 1959 for the specific purpose of promoting economic development and the preservation and enhancement of the American enterprise system. Both the purpose and the activities of the state Chamber of Commerce are ideological. The state Chamber lobbies in the state capital on legislation. It is actively involved in ballot question campaigns and referenda in the State. It educates its members and the public with respect to public policy issues. It maintains a separate segregated fund for the purpose of making political contributions to candidates. And it rates candidates on a job provider index.
>
> But the state Chamber of Commerce does not communicate its views to the general public with respect to candidates because Section 54 of the Michigan Campaign Finance Act makes it a felony . . . for the Chamber to engage in such communications.
>
> *Question:* Can it communicate the ratings?
>
> *Answer:* It cannot. Not if those are in any way in support of or opposition to the election of a candidate. [And with the Chamber], their purpose in speaking is ideological and it is designed to influence the election or defeat of a candidate.

The ground had been set. With the elegance of simplicity, McLellan had cast the chamber as an ideological organization—a speaker with a viewpoint—that acted directly in the political process to promote that ideology on behalf of its members, and that made no excuses for its expressed desire to influence the course of public affairs, including the election of public officials. Influence over elections was what the chamber *sought*. It would not rest its claim on its lack of influence but on its First Amendment right to seek *more* influence through speech.

McLellan was then asked about the law's exemption for unincorporated labor unions. He used the question to emphasize further that the case involved a struggle of ideologies, not of entities or money.

> *Mr. McLellan:* In Michigan the political marketplace is largely characterized by the contest between the forces of organized labor and business. And the Michigan law, because it treats the Michigan Chamber of Commerce differently than its primary adversaries, which were identified in trial as the United Auto Workers and the AFL-CIO, this disparate treatment creates . . . a disadvantage to the Michigan State Chamber of Commerce in carrying out its purposes, which [are] to be a political and ideological organization within the State of Michigan. . . . Mr. Caruso and the State have argued that the amassing of wealth is the important state interest. And unions, particularly the major labor organizations in the State of Michigan, are able, because of their size and their broad membership base and the special advantages they have under the law, to amass substantial wealth.
>
> *Question:* Do they do that through their own funds, or do they set up separate funds for doing that?
>
> *Mr. McLellan:* In Michigan . . . they use their general union treasury funds. . . .

In emphasizing the resources of unincorporated unions and their relative advantage over the chamber, McLellan was treading on thin ice, for he was coming close to accepting the argument, by making it himself, that correcting imbalances in the speech marketplace caused by access to resources with which to speak might justify government regulation. This, of course, was simply one form of the state's argument. The Court did not, however, pursue the point, but one justice questioned the degree of advantage the unions enjoyed.

> *Question:* You suggest that there are no limitations, legal limitations, on how much [and] how unions can use their funds for political purposes?
>
> *Mr. McLellan:* There is not in the Michigan Campaign Finance Act, Your Honor.
>
> *Question:* But members certainly have remedies, don't they? . . .

Mr. McLellan: They — members do have the rights . . .

Question: . . . under the federal labor laws.

Mr. McLellan: This Court has recognized that, in that there are other laws that protect union members. [Such laws include the right of union members to withhold a portion of their dues that would be used to support political positions, or candidates, with which they disagree.]

Question: So unions really aren't all that free to just use their amassed wealth to — for political purposes, are they?

Mr. McLellan: No, they are not. There are federal restrictions on them.

Question: Well, there are also constitutional restrictions, aren't there — which would apply to the use of funds in state elections?

Mr. McLellan: Yes. It would. A member of a union would be able to assert his or her constitutional interest.

Question: And unions nowadays usually have a mechanism for that, don't they?

Mr. McLellan: Yes.

Question: And your organization, so long as it doesn't endorse a particular candidate . . . could still campaign with respect to issues as much as you like, is that correct? You could publicize an issue statement to the electorate, not just lobby in the legislature . . . so long as you don't identify it with a candidate . . . right?

Mr. McLellan: That is correct.

Question: And you can make all the arguments you want to your membership in connection with soliciting funds for your political action fund . . . which is then free to spend the money . . .

Mr. McLellan: Correct.

Question: Why is that? I am a little interested in the difference between — why is it so important that you are not, that you be free to operate without going through the fund that the statute provides for, the separate fund?

Mr. McLellan: The primary operational reason is that PACs [political action committees authorized by federal law to raise funds from groups of donors to support candidates] have a significant, negative image in the public. And the State Chamber of Commerce . . . has a very strong reputation. . . . And to be able to speak with your own voice, with your own name on the bottom of the advertisement — this is the view of the State Chamber of Commerce . . .

With this line of questions McLellan had been led—willingly—to the heart of the case. The case was not about the unions' disproportionate power or about the administrative complexities of setting up many separate funds and undertaking many solicitation efforts. It was instead about the chamber's desire to "speak with [its] own voice." It was about the chamber's status as a speaker under the First Amendment; about the chamber's claim that its speech was "First Amendment speech." On this question the closeness of the chamber to the views of its individual members was to be the critical question, as it had been for Justices Brennan, Marshall, and Blackmun in the earlier Massachusetts right to life case. This was a more delicate and complex argument than at first appeared, as McLellan knew. The justices' questions now turned to the complexities.

> *Question:* But the problem is that when you speak with your own voice you purport to represent 8,000 members who all agree on your—[on] what you are saying. Whereas when you [use a separate] fund you are sure that everybody who contributed to the fund authorizes you to speak in that way. Isn't there that potential misunderstanding—[indeed, isn't that] why it is stronger speech when it purports to represent all 8,000 members, *even though* they haven't all contributed to the fund?

McLellan is surely aware that the questions are leading him in a dangerous direction, but he holds his ground. In this he has no real choice, for if *his* case must turn on whether all eight thousand members specifically agree with every candidate endorsement the chamber makes, he has lost. His only recourse is to stand firm and resist that conclusion, emphasizing the *chamber's* role and the *chamber's* ideology, making the *chamber* a "person"—a speaker protected by the First Amendment.

> *Mr. McLellan:* The Michigan State Chamber of Commerce, every member, corporate or individual, must subscribe to the objectives of the state Chamber.
> *Question:* I understand. But they don't all have to vote for the same candidates for office.
> *Mr. McLellan:* No, and they may not. In fact they—it is a diverse membership. There is a—it is a widely diverse membership, in size and function of business . . .

> *Question:* And of course you want to be able to use your accumulated funds from dues, you don't want to have to go back to anybody.
> *Mr. McLellan:* That is right. We don't want to have to . . .
> *Question:* And if you are going to set up a fund, you are going to have to go raise some money.
> *Mr. McLellan:* We don't want to go through the same . . .
> *Question:* And you may not be able to raise it from everybody, because they don't agree with you.
> *Mr. McLellan:* That is correct.
> *Question:* Which means that your speech is restricted [by having to solicit contributions for a special fund each time the Chamber wants to endorse a candidate].
> *Mr. McLellan:* Our speech is restricted. If we have to use that mechanism, there are substantial burdens. . . .
> *Question:* It is not only restricted, but if it weren't restricted it might be misleading, too.

McLellan had stood firm through this line of questioning, knowing, we must suppose, where it was leading but having no choice but to submit to it, standing firm, answering forthrightly, not wanting to appear evasive or to reveal the least insecurity in his client's case. But it must have been painful. And at the end of the line of questions, one of the justices had lowered the boom. "It is not only restricted," the justice asked, "but if it weren't restricted it might be misleading, too"—because it would imply greater support than the speech actually enjoyed among the chamber's membership. It was not a question but a statement, and little good could come of an attempt to argue the point. It was best left alone, and that is exactly what McLellan did. He said nothing.

After a momentary silence that might, to McLellan, have seemed like hours, the questioning resumed, but now on another tack:

> *Question:* What difference does it make in your argument that you speak for a nonprofit corporation? Can't the same arguments you are making be made for corporations that are in the business for profit?

The tack was not a good one for McLellan, though surely he had anticipated it as he prepared for oral argument. His direct and immediate response proved that, but he may nevertheless have regretted the need to answer it. The question required that he take one of two critical forks in the road. The first fork would treat the chamber's nonprofit, membership status as a critical fact distinguishing the chamber from General Motors on the ground that it was differently ideological, that its members all shared that ideology even if they might not agree with the specifics of its application to particular candidates, and therefore that the chamber was speaking for its members.

The second fork rejected any distinction between the chamber and General Motors. Both were legal "persons" and were entitled by the First Amendment to speak freely. The fact that the members or stockholders didn't agree with the message spoken — indeed the fact that they were not aware that a particular message was being spoken — was irrelevant because the corporation, the entity itself, is the speaker for purposes of the First Amendment. This would be a hard and controversial argument to make, at least in such plain terms, for it imbues a corporation with too much independent stature and gives its owners none at all. Still, McLellan may have had no choice but to make the argument. His client's interests were not only those of the chamber but also of its members, six thousand of whom were profit-making corporations that also wanted freedom to speak.

Moreover, the fact that most of the chamber's members were corporations meant that there was no safe route of escape on the first fork of the road even had McLellan been free to take it. Any effort to separate the chamber from profit-making corporations would quickly collapse under the ensuing barrage of questions about the corporate members, followed by questions about exactly how *they*, as corporations, could hold an ideology — and if they couldn't, how the chamber could claim an ideology based on *their* agreement to it. McLellan, it turns out, had a tough balancing act of his own — indeed, in some respects it made Caruso's simple (but factually flawed) approach look easy.

And so McLellan took the second fork in the road. He really had no choice, but his bravery is to be applauded, even as we sympathize with his plight.

> Yes, the same argument can be made [for profit as well as nonprofit
> corporations]. And we would make it. In this case . . . there has
> been no showing of any state interest that would restrict independent
> dent expenditures generally. There [were] no legislative findings

dealing with independent expenditures. There was no evidence submitted at trial that would suggest that there is something inherently corrupting or potentially corrupting by corporate independent expenditures generally. So, in answer to your question, yes. We do not think that that is a significant distinction.

This is the first time this Court has considered the constitutionality of a state law that bans independent expenditures . . . with regard to a candidate, by an ideological corporation that has business corporation members. And we suggest that the analysis that this Court has made [in earlier cases, where limits on individuals were stricken,] with respect to independent expenditures generally is equally applicable in this case.

McLellan's argument, in short, was that corporations—*all* corporations—should be treated just like individuals for purposes of the First Amendment's freedom of speech. The Supreme Court had stricken limits on independent expenditures—advertisements supporting candidates, for example, by groups that are unaffiliated with the candidate's campaign organization—in a major 1976 case that had challenged the Federal Election Campaign Act of 1971. But the Court's decision applied only to individuals and groups of individuals acting in concert—the equivalent of political action committees—not to corporations.

McLellan had staked out his claim clearly and directly—perhaps a little more clearly and directly than he would have wished. But he had stuck firmly to it. After a brief round of questions on a different topic, McLellan was prepared to sum up, pull his arguments together for one last time and, with likely relief, step down. But as he was finishing with his brief summation, in which he again referred to the chamber's "ideology," he was interrupted by a justice:

May I just inquire, what do you mean by an "ideological group?" I understand it is a sort of a single issue group where there is just one issue, such as right to life or something like it, [where it is] very clear that [the members] all have the same approach to the problem. But one of the points you made earlier was [that] the Chamber of Commerce, by its very nature, is very diverse in the various interests it represents. And, sure, everybody is in favor of democracy and against crime or something like that, but do you call that—is that enough to make it an ideological group?

If the question seemed innocently framed, the innocence had a clever and ruthless quality. This was *not* a question McLellan wanted to pursue at any length. Nothing was to be gained for him by probing the particulars of the chamber's governance processes, the range of its activities, the political composition of its membership, or—worse yet—the nagging fact that most of the chamber's members were themselves corporations. He therefore tried to duck.

> *Mr. McLellan:* I believe an ideological group—it does—it is an ideological group.
> *Question:* Well, would General Motors be an ideological group, because all the shareholders want to make money and believe in free enterprise?
> *Mr. McLellan [cautiously]:* No, I do not think it, General Motors, is an ideological group.
> *Question:* Simply because they are a profit-making corporation?
> *Mr. McLellan [now regaining his footing]* No, simply because they are organized for a different purpose. I think that you can identify those groups that have organized themselves to primarily advocate ideas, not all necessarily political ideas, but they are ideological in that sense.
> *Question:* Would there be any nonprofit or membership corporation . . . that would not be an ideological group within your concept?
> *Mr. McLellan:* Yes. Some health care groups . . . may not be ideological. Certainly, I think that they would be supporting [health care needs, but] their purpose would not be ideological.
> *Question:* What about a trade association—the Automobile Manufacturers Association or something like that—who seek to promote the welfare of the automobile industry?
> *Mr. McLellan:* In general, trade associations, I think, are organized for largely public policy and ideological purposes. . . . Civic action organizations, like the ACLU, NAACP, are the more common examples of ideological groups. But the State Chamber of Commerce, trade associations, environmental groups, are equally ideological in that sense. The fact, from our perspective, that . . . the Chamber represents business interests does not make it any less ideological.

It is hard to imagine a better set of responses to an uninvited and frankly unwanted line of questions. McLellan had simultaneously set the chamber apart from its members, yet distinguished the chamber from General Motors by defining *its* (the chamber's, *not* its members') "ideology" as different in kind from the nonideological purposes of General Motors. The responses didn't make McLellan's case — the six thousand corporate members of the "ideological group" (hardly the equivalent of a group of individuals banding together in common cause) were still a big problem, as was the unfortunate but necessary argument that the chamber's claim to be a speaker applied as much to General Motors as to the local ACLU chapter — but he had gotten by unscathed.

Having done so, and hearing no further questions, McLellan promptly said, "If there are no further questions, that concludes my argument. Thank you." To which the chief justice replied, "Thank you Mr. McLellan," and McLellan took his seat at the counsel table.

There followed a brief but uneventful, indeed unconstructive, rebuttal by Caruso, which added little and generated no questions. At its conclusion, the chief justice announced: "The case is submitted."

It would be hard to predict from oral argument which side had the better chance to prevail. McLellan had the better argument by far. His theory was tight, clear, and even elegant. But it was built on shaky foundations and the engineering was too subtle and overly complex: there *is* a difference, after all, between General Motors and the chamber or the ACLU, and a corporation's "ideology" is, intuition tells us, a different matter from an individual's personal system of beliefs. Caruso, on the other hand, was dealt serious blows in oral argument, and he seemed at times befuddled by the questions, bedraggled toward the end, and uncertain of his moorings. Yet his argument, though inelegantly put, was the more straightforward one — corporations *are* different from individuals, as a general matter — and his foundations were broad and clear. But his foundations were also mushy and the structure of the Michigan law built upon them was riddled with defects.

The argument brought all of this out, and more. But whether it changed any minds on the Court is a subject of some doubt. As the Court retired to its conference room on the Friday following Halloween to discuss and vote on the Michigan campaign case, it appears that the votes pretty well lined up as predicted. And when the decision in the case was announced just a few months later, on March 27, 1990, one did not have to read beyond the author of the opinion to know the result. The author was Justice Marshall, and with him were the chief justice (who had little patience for claims of corporate free speech), Justice Brennan, and Justice

Blackmun. Worse yet for the chamber, Justices White and Stevens also joined Justice Marshall's opinion. It was a veritable clean sweep for Michigan, whose law was upheld, and a total loss for the Michigan State Chamber of Commerce. Corporations, including the chamber, could be legally prohibited from endorsing political candidates.

Justice Marshall's opinion bore the markings of the oral argument. The Michigan State Chamber of Commerce, he wrote, was a large organization with a diverse membership and a broad set of purposes, "several of which are not inherently political." It thus lacked the "narrow political focus" that would be needed to "ensure that its political resources reflected political support" for its speech among the members. And the fact that the chamber's value to its members lay not only in its general political aims but also in the advantages membership conferred for the members' businesses meant that the members would have an "economic disincentive for disassociating with it if they disagree with its political activity." The chamber, in short, could make no claim that the views it expressed as an organization were the views of its members, as individuals. This was especially true, the Court noted, because of the "striking" fact that "more than three-quarters of the Chamber's members are business corporations."

These facts led the Court to the conclusion that the chamber — and its members —"are more similar to the shareholders of a business corporation than to the members of" an ideological group whose collective speech is but an instrument for the members' individual rights to speak. The chamber was more like General Motors than, say, the NAACP. General Motors does not "speak the mind" of its shareholders, and it has no "mind" of its own. It is the members, not the organization, who are qualified to speak for purposes of the First Amendment; their speech, and not the corporation's speech, is *First Amendment speech*.

Interestingly, the Court did not try to distinguish labor unions from the chamber. But the Court upheld the Michigan law that exempted them because federal law already limited their ability to expend general union funds on political activities over the active opposition of union members. Under federal law an objecting union member's dues cannot be used for political purposes to which he or she objects. Thus, the funds used for such purposes are *in effect* drawn from a separate fund consisting of those portions of nonobjecting members' dues that are directed to the support of political activity. By this reasoning the Court concluded that a union's political speech in fact reflected the specific views of its individual members, and thus would qualify under the First Amendment as speech by individuals, not speech by an artificial entity.

Because the chamber's speech did not qualify as fully protected speech under the First Amendment, the Court concluded that the purposes behind Michigan's law need not be particularly compelling. The mushy purposes of preventing the potential for abuse or corruption; of leveling the speech playing field by limiting corporate expenditures (which could be, but are not necessarily, large); and, most important, as it turned out, of assuring that speech by organized groups actually reflects the views of their members, were sufficient to support the ban on public candidate endorsements by corporations. The Court also concluded that the law's application need not be narrowly tailored to achieving its purposes. The fact that the law prohibited much speech that did not pose any of the problems the law was aimed at addressing—such as the speech by the family corporation, the ACLU, or the local public library foundation—and that it left unregulated much speech that presented those problems—such as Donald Trump, the unincorporated organization, even (notwithstanding federal law) the labor unions—did not matter.

The important point, instead, was that the law *was* tailored to distinguishing organizations that qualify as First Amendment speakers (like the Massachusetts Citizens for Life, labor unions, and, perhaps, the ACLU and the family corporation) from those that don't (General Motors and the chamber). Unless important First Amendment rights were at stake—which they weren't for organizations that do not qualify as First Amendment speakers—the Michigan legislature was free to exercise its own political judgment and legislate imperfectly. And it had. Michigan's law, which can be described only as mushy in its purposes and riddled with imperfections, was constitutional.

And the puzzle of the constitutional status of speech that has no speaker was, at least tentatively, unlocked. To Beckett's query, "What matter who's speaking, someone said, what matter who's speaking?" the Court could say that with the chamber there was no "someone speaking." The chamber's "speech" represented no *one's* views; it was not the product of the minds or will of its members, *as individuals*, and hence the chamber's speech was not "First Amendment speech."

Mr. McLellan must surely have been disappointed. His clients had lost—all of his clients, the chamber and its corporate members, too. The fault, of course, was not his; indeed, fault is not a relevant word when it comes to the Supreme Court's decision in a case. McLellan had acquitted himself and his clients stunningly well in oral argument. His theory was coherent, well presented, and sound. Lawyers don't really win or lose cases in the Supreme Court; the Court is too independent, too much responsible for its own choices, for a lawyer's argument—especially a fine one like McLellan's—to bear the burden of the outcome. While wishing that he had prevailed, McLellan might also, upon hearing of the decision, have taken some comfort in the fact that while his clients—corporations, business interests—were not entitled to the full protection of the First Amendment, they were not without the political power to protect themselves from excessive government intermeddling in their affairs.

But perhaps the Court's opinion caused McLellan also to reflect, even if for just a fleeting moment, on a simpler, earlier time, a time when people spoke for themselves, and when the influence of their ideas depended more on the strength or weakness of their reasoning than on the size of their media budget. Perhaps he even imagined that a bit of that romantic past could be recaptured in the present.

Mr. Caruso, on the other hand, was no doubt elated at the decision. He had been bloodied and beaten as he fought to defend Michigan's imperfect—indeed, flawed—law. But he had survived. The Michigan law had been upheld and the state's power to restrict speech produced and distributed by corporations had been confirmed. But did he fully appreciate the narrowness of the victory? Did he understand the challenges that lie ahead when the Michigan law is actually applied to the NAACP, or even to the ACLU with its corporate sponsorship? Was the victory *that* complete?

And might Caruso, perhaps late at night in the quiet of his study, have been moved also to reflect on what had transpired? And might he have wondered to himself whether, when all is said and done, the chamber's ad would have been all that harmful—indeed, whether the battle had not really been about corporations speaking but, instead, in a paradoxical twist of First Amendment fate, simply about "too much speech"?

If so, perhaps Mr. McLellan had the last word.

ADDITIONAL READING

Lillian BeVier, "Money and Politics: A Perspective on the First Amendment and Campaign Finance Reform," 73 *California Law Review* 1045 (1985).

Owen Fiss, "Free Speech and Social Structure," 71 *Iowa Law Review* 1405 (1986).

Robert Post, "Managing Deliberation: The Quandary of Democratic Dialogue," 103 *Ethics* 654 (1993).

Buckley v. Valeo, 424 U.S. 1 (1976).

PART 2

Speech and Conduct

In part 1 we explored the meaning of speech and, more specifically, the role of the speaker in the freedom of speech. We discovered that under the First Amendment the human act of speaking is more important than the resulting speech itself. Indeed, speech that lacks a speaker because it is not the product of speaking may be entitled to little if any protection under the First Amendment, perhaps because it makes no sense to speak of its inanimate "freedom." Focusing on speakers under the First Amendment has permitted the Supreme Court to escape the need to define "speech" itself; what is protected is the human activity of speaking, not just "speech." But the "speech" question cannot be so easily escaped.

In part 2 we will consider the meaning of "speech" from a different angle. If speech is the product of a human act, we might say that it is the product of the act of "speaking." All human acts, of course, do not constitute "speaking." What standard do we apply in distinguishing acts of speaking from all others?

The divide between acts of speaking and other acts has traditionally been defined by the distinction between speech (speaking) and conduct. This is the distinction to which our attention will be drawn in the stories that follow. Is human activity divisible into acts of speaking and acts of conduct? Or is some human activity *both* speaking and conduct?

Speaking is an intentional human act; speech is its product. But speech is also the product of other forces: what people do (conduct) as opposed to what they say; and what meaning is given to what people do and say. Speech, in other words, is not the product of an isolated act but of a participatory one involving words and deeds, intention and inadvertence, personal and social meaning.

These are the puzzles that we begin to explore in the first story, "The Burning Cross," which focuses on speech and conduct, and in the second story, "The Artist," which expands the focus to the larger yet deeply related question of meaning.

Story Four

The Burning Cross
(R.A.V. v. St. Paul, 505 U.S. 377 (1992))

The First Amendment's Holy Grail

The First Amendment says that government may not "abridg[e] the freedom of speech," which the Supreme Court has interpreted to mean that government can rarely and only for the most compelling of reasons invoke its power to regulate speech. Conduct, on the other hand, is not free. Government can regulate it broadly and for just about any reason, and in any way, that a democratically elected majority wishes. But can conduct sometimes be speech? Can speech sometimes be conduct? Aren't these but two sides of the same coin: an act is either speech or conduct, with a single boundary separating them? Logic might tell us so, but for purposes of the First Amendment, logic isn't everything. Some speech, it turns out, is conduct, and some conduct is speech.

The quest for a single and coherent boundary between speech and conduct has been ongoing since the Supreme Court first began to interpret freedom of speech. Like the search for the Holy Grail, the quest for the boundary separating speech from conduct is never-ending, and the prize remains elusive, clouded in myth, a constant source of adventure.

The quest is based on important philosophical underpinnings. A principal justification for free speech is that it domesticates conflict, replacing the urge to violence with the more civilized process of reasoned discussion and disagreement. As Justice Brandeis announced in dissent in *Whitney v. California*, an early free speech case decided in 1927, "[T]he fitting remedy for evil counsels is good ones." Those who wrote the First Amendment, he continued, "believ[ed] in the power of reason as applied through public discussion, they eschewed silence coerced by law." Justice Oliver Wendell Holmes, Jr., ever the skeptic, put it more agnostically in his 1919 dissent in *Abrams v. United States*. "[T]hat the best test of truth is the power of the thought to get itself accepted in the competition of the market," he wrote, "and that truth is the only ground upon which [the people's] wishes safely can be carried out. . . . That at any rate is the theory of our constitution." Talk, not conduct, is what free speech is all about. "No one pretends," John Stuart Mill declared in *On Liberty*, "that actions should be as free as opinions."

The distinction between speech and conduct, then, is a quest for a way to free speech and thought without unleashing anarchy—to keep speech in its proper place, so to speak, and to draw distinct and enforceable boundaries between our freedom to think and say what we think, on the one hand, and our impulse to act on our thoughts and words, on the other. Our thoughts can be isolated from others, made accountable to no one; acting on our thoughts, however, is a collective act, requiring consent or democratic authorization.

From the beginning of First Amendment jurisprudence the divide between speech and conduct has been thought to hold the key to the puzzling relationship between individual freedom and the demands of the social order. But the quest for a single key to a single, simple truth has proved elusive, if not misguided.

There is no single, simple truth. This is the first thing we must understand about the relationship between speech and conduct under the First Amendment. Oliver Wendell Holmes, Jr., observed in 1919 in *Schenck v. United States* that the "most stringent protection of free speech would not protect a man in falsely shouting fire in a theatre and causing a panic." Under the First Amendment, Holmes said, "the character of every act depends on the circumstances in which it is done." Like shouting fire in a crowded theatre, speech may in fact constitute conduct because the resulting bedlam is so inextricably bound to the literal words uttered that their quality as speech is simply incidental, effectively engulfed. And it is likewise true that conduct, such as the raised fist, may be speech because its quality as expression at a given time or in a given place transcends its nonexpressive dimension.

These examples do not exhaust the possibilities. Actions, it turns out, can be both speech *and* conduct. Something as simple as camping out in a tent, which is obviously conduct, may also be speech when, for example, it occurs on the Ellipse in Washington, D.C., as part of a mass protest movement. And admitted speech, such as solicitation for a charity, may be treated as if it were conduct alone if, for example, it is undertaken at an inappropriate time—perhaps during working hours—or in an improper way, as with fraud or misrepresentation. The danger in being too literal about "speech" and too absolute in its protection is twofold: some admitted conduct that is but a benign part of expression will go unprotected; and some admitted speech that plays little or no part in expression or that coerces dangerous conduct will be erroneously protected.

So the First Amendment presents a rather untidy set of rules and distinctions when it comes to separating speech from conduct. Traditional analysis approaches the question at two levels. The first level is definitional: if the activity is speech, it is protected; if it is conduct, it is not. But some conduct, if sufficiently expressive, is defined as speech, and vice versa. The boundaries at the definitional level are obscure.

The second level looks to the causal connection between speech and conduct. If an activity that satisfies the definition of speech, such as advocacy of violence, presents a clear and present danger that the speech will immediately produce the violence, it will be treated as if it were conduct even though in every literal sense the act consists of speech. This is the origin of what has come to be called "fighting words," a type of speech that will prove important in our story.

Fighting words, the Supreme Court has said, come in two varieties: words directed at other persons that provoke an immediate breach of the peace, and thus present a clear and present danger of producing acts of violence, such as assault; and words directed at other persons that, themselves, harm those persons without anyone's being provoked to violence. It is this second variety of fighting words, where the harm resides in the words themselves and in their emotional or psychological force, that will occupy us in our story. It is here that the controversy over regulating hate speech resides.

The rules for distinguishing speech from conduct appear logical and coherent, though elaborate. But the definitions they rely upon and the rules of causation that they employ disguise profound ambiguity, giving an appearance of clarity where, in truth, there is none. They are the mask through which fealty to speech as the preferred freedom, absolutely protected, is paid.

Justice Felix Frankfurter had little time for pat solutions and constitutional absolutisms. For him the idea of a "preferred position of freedom of speech," and the clear boundaries and absolute protection the phrase implied, did not comport with the complexities of human behavior. "I deem it a mischievous phrase," he said in 1949 in *Kovacs v. Cooper*, referring to the "preferred position" shorthand, for "it carries the thought

[that] any law touching communication is infected with presumptive invalidity. It radiates a constitutional doctrine without avowing it."

When it comes to speech and conduct, the First Amendment is not simple but complex; not absolute but qualified; not clear but inscrutable. Its central quality may not be logic but paradox. Our story invites us to probe the paradoxes of speech and conduct. It does so, moreover, in a particularly strange way, for it is a story that involves more than the distinction between speech and conduct. It involves the additional — and surprising — question of whether actions that are clearly conduct and *not* speech should nevertheless be protected under the free speech guarantee of the First Amendment.

The Burning Cross

The story begins on the evening of June 20, 1990, in a neighborhood on the east side of St. Paul, Minnesota, called Mounds Park. Mounds Park was not one of those old and tired urban neighborhoods with poorly maintained houses crowded together, voicing despair and frustration. It was a nice, working-class neighborhood whose homes were large and well kept and whose lawns were well trimmed, where neighbors knew one another, cared for the appearance of their street, and raised their children in the American way. It was, in short, the kind of neighborhood that one expects to find in the upper Midwest. Mounds Park was also predominantly white, but not exclusively so. Black families lived in nearby apartments and had purchased homes in the neighborhood as well.

East Ivy Avenue is one of the streets running through Mounds Park. On one side of the street was the home in which Arthur M. Miller III lived. Miller was eighteen years old at the time and living with his father. He had a number of young friends in the neighborhood who would often gather at his house. Friendship and good, wholesome fun, however, were not the only things that brought the boys together. The bond that tied them was recreational in a different way as well, for when they gathered on that Wednesday evening in June 1990, marijuana, LSD, and alcohol were also on their minds.

Miller's father wasn't home that evening, so Miller was there alone with his girlfriend. During the course of the evening he and his girlfriend got into an argument and in the midst of the ensuing fight he broke a window in the house. So when five or six of Miller's friends came to the door of the house, Miller was cleaning up the broken glass. The friends came by to sit and talk and bum around, as one does in one's youth on summer evenings; they came also, according to one of them, in the hope that Arthur would have some "weed." The friends drank, used drugs, and apparently just lounged around. As the evening turned to early morning, the need for a new outlet apparently emerged from the increasingly hazy mists beclouding their minds.

"I drank all night. If I was sober I wouldn't even have thought about going along." This is what Miller said in his statement to the police, made some days later, after his arrest. According to Miller, whose objectivity can well be doubted, one of the youths "came up with the idea about a cross-burning. Everybody agreed." He continued, "I heard them talking about one of them getting chased by a bunch of black people by their house because they had a skin head." No longer languid, the group's conversation now became active and focused, and the boys' thoughts, dimmed by the effects of alcohol and drugs, turned to action.

The group proceeded downstairs to Miller's basement. There they searched for material with which to make a cross. They found two wooden dowels that would form the cross, tape to bind the wood pieces together, rags to wrap around the dowels, and paint solvent to soak the rags for the coming conflagration. Then, armed with the cross, they turned their attention to an object for their ill-begotten enterprise. They found it immediately at hand: the home of Russ and Laura Jones, located just across the street.

Russ and Laura Jones had recently moved into the Mounds Hill neighborhood with their children, attracted by the well-kept homes and the prospects of raising a family in a safe and clean and wholesome area with good schools and lots of other children. Being African American, the Joneses no doubt moved to the largely white working-class neighborhood with some apprehension but also with hope and optimism. Since their move they had experienced a few small acts of vandalism, but in a neighborhood with many children playing outside — children to whom property lines were irrelevant and a front-yard fence just another obstacle to be overcome — the source of the vandalism was ambiguous. Russ Jones was inclined to presume the best, not the worst.

There was cause for concern, however, for St. Paul had experienced its share of racial incidents. Indeed, concern about race relations and incidents springing from racial bias had motivated the City Council in 1982 to enact a law entitled "St. Paul Bias-Motivated Crime Ordinance."

While other laws already in effect would provide ample grounds for prosecuting cases of vandalism, disturbing the peace, and assault growing out of racial tension, the politics of the late twentieth century required, in St. Paul as elsewhere around the nation, a more explicit and direct legislative response—an opportunity, perhaps, for those in elected political office to claim a hand in arresting racial hatred, or at least an excuse that they had done all that they could do about it. So under the ponderous heading of the ordinance, the City Council enacted the following law:

> Whoever places on public or private property a symbol, object, appellation, characterization, or graffiti, including but not limited to, a burning cross or Nazi Swastika, which one knows or has reasonable grounds to know arouses anger, alarm or resentment in others on the basis of race, color, creed, religion or gender commits disorderly conduct and shall be guilty of a misdemeanor.

In its reference to "a burning cross" the ordinance seems to have exhibited prescience, at least as one now looks upon the events of that June evening in 1990. But of course the St. Paul ordinance was just a law. It could not anticipate what was to happen. Indeed, it could not prevent it. It could only punish the act after the fact.

Sometime after midnight of June 20, 1990, in the wee hours of the morning, Miller and his young friends, most of whom were under eighteen and therefore juveniles in the eyes of the law, turned their attention—and their paint-solvent–soaked, handmade cross—toward the Jones house across the street. Accompanying Miller were five or six others, including Jason Olson, age eighteen, who had come to Miller's house with two of his friends, hoping to get some marijuana, and Robert Viktora, seventeen, who was charged with Miller as a leader in the incident and whose prosecution under the St. Paul ordinance would find its way to the Supreme Court of the United States. Because Viktora was a juvenile, his case, *R.A.V. v. City of St. Paul, Minnesota,* would not bear his name, only his initials.

The youths were in a state of inebriated recklessness; they had now been drinking, smoking marijuana, and using LSD since the previous evening. With inept stealth the motley and disorderly group crossed the street and entered the Jones yard. The house was dark, for the Jones family had gone to bed. As they placed the cross in the front yard, the boys were anything but silent, their ineffectual attempts at whispers piercing the dark night air. No one, of course, admitted placing the cross and setting it afire; as with most such incidents, the act itself simply emerged from thin air as if produced by the force of will alone. But the boys were all in it together, and it really doesn't matter whose hand struck the match, for that hand moved as if directed by the passion of each.

"Everybody went in the yard," Miller would later tell the police. "I don't remember who lit it." But a match was struck and placed on the soaked fabric of the erected cross, and the cross was engulfed in flames, its shape leaping forth from the darkness, the reckless and hungry fire bringing the cross to life. The boys watched the evil symbol emerge from the darkness, transfixed in their drunken excitement, and then fled the scene, returning to the darkness. "I went into my house alone," Miller said, "in a couple minutes everybody showed up again and waited for the police to leave." Jason Olson and his two friends wanted to leave Miller's house "because," he said, "they didn't have any weed, but we couldn't because there were cops outside."

Russ and Laura Jones were asleep in their bedroom. Sometime after midnight they were awakened by the sound of voices outside. As they listened, it became apparent that the voices were coming from their yard. They got out of bed and went to the window. There, in horror, they witnessed a black family's worst nightmare: a cross burning in front of their house. Shocked and frightened, for themselves and, especially, for their children, they called 911. Police were quickly dispatched to their home.

Miller and his friends watched the scene from his house. Still high on drugs and alcohol, they felt no remorse or guilt—they couldn't have, or they wouldn't have done what they did next. Their watching was instead accompanied by a frenzied excitement—the kind, perhaps, that accompanies a childhood prank. Only this was no childhood prank, and these were not children. The squad cars were in the street and police officers were examining the scene. Miller and his friends awaited the departure of the police.

When the police finally left, the youths did not break up and slither away, sobered by what they had done. They did not return to their homes in the emptiness that follows catharsis, as a mob sometimes does after a lynching. Their hunger was not sated. Instead, they awaited the departure of the squad cars as a vulture awaits a lion's departure from a carcass.

"Let's go burn some more and be crazy," one of the boys said as the police departed. And they did.

With their emotions now raised to an even higher fever pitch by a mixture of drugs, alcohol, and adrenaline, Miller and his friends returned to the basement to begin the next stage of their loathsome enterprise. They built two more crosses, this time out of broken-furniture legs. Again they taped the crosses together, wrapped them in cloth, and soaked them in paint solvent. With the police gone and the neighborhood returned to darkness, they left Miller's house and proceeded first to the corner. There they lit a second cross across the street from the Jones house. They then proceeded two blocks up the street to an apartment house where other African-American families lived, where they lit the third cross. Twice more they witnessed their crosses emerge from the night's darkness, engulfed by hungry flames.

Their deeds now done, the group returned to Miller's house. But even then their malevolent thirst was apparently not yet quenched. They wanted to do more, to continue their crazed enterprise. Their further plans were dashed, however, when, according to Olson, Miller kicked "us out of his house because his dad was coming home."

Russ Jones was quickly jolted out of his benign complacency by the events of the early morning of June 21, 1990. Whatever the source of the earlier incidents of vandalism, there could be no doubt about the motivation behind the cross-burning in his front yard and the second across the street. A powerful combination of emotions — fear, helplessness, danger, anger, shock, isolation — buffeted Russ and Laura Jones with an intensity that few white Americans could understand. The burning cross was the evil symbol of the Ku Klux Klan. It conveyed a message not of oppression but of stark, unmitigated fear.

Morning finally dawned, following what must have been a sleepless night of fear and apprehension, confusion and despair. One can imagine the Joneses looking out at the spot where the symbol of hatred and anarchy and bigotry had burned, perhaps guarding the truth from their children, who wouldn't understand and shouldn't have to know, finding little solace in the light of day. Their world — their optimism and hope — had been cruelly and crudely wrested from them.

But it turns out that they were not alone, nor were they unwelcome. With the morning came also an outpouring of sympathy and support from their neighbors and from city officials. The police investigation of the three incidents — as well as other incidents that were never linked to Miller and his friends — was swift, and within a few days Miller and his friends were tracked down. Miller and Viktora, alleged to have been the leaders in the incidents, were quickly charged with violating the St. Paul Bias-Motivated Crime Ordinance. It was the first time the ordinance had been used, even though it had been on the books since 1982. Miller was charged as an adult, pleaded guilty, and was sentenced to thirty days in jail. He, at least, admitted his guilt and accepted his punishment.

The same cannot be said of Viktora, who would come to be known in the annals of the law as R.A.V. He did not plead guilty but, instead, challenged the law's constitutionality under the First Amendment's guarantee of free speech. The juvenile court judge who first heard his case agreed with him and dismissed the charges. But the judge's decision was appealed by the City of St. Paul to the Minnesota Supreme Court, where the juvenile court decision was reversed and the case sent back for trial. The trial never took place, however, because Viktora appealed the Minnesota Supreme Court decision to the United States Supreme Court, which agreed to review the case.

On June 22, 1992, almost two years to the day from the Joneses' nightmare, the Supreme Court issued an opinion reversing the Minnesota Supreme Court's decision and invalidating the St. Paul Bias-Motivated Crime Ordinance as inconsistent with the First Amendment to the United States Constitution. The Court's opinion takes but two sentences to state the facts:

> In the predawn hours of June 21, 1990, petitioner [Robert Viktora] and several other teenagers allegedly assembled a crudely-made cross by taping together broken chair legs. They then allegedly burned the cross inside the fenced yard of a black family that lived across the street from the house where petitioner was staying.

With this brief, disembodied statement, the First Amendment descended with full force on the City of St. Paul, Minnesota.

The charges against Viktora under the St. Paul ordinance were subsequently dropped.

The Supreme Court Opinion

"Doctrine Radiated but Not Avowed"

Were the cross burnings by Robert Viktora and his drug-influenced and recklessly juvenile group of friends acts of speech protected by the First

Amendment or were they conduct not entitled to the First Amendment's protection? In the Supreme Court's First Amendment jurisprudence, this question breaks down into two parts. First, was the act of lighting the cross speech? Second, even if speech, was the act sufficiently brigaded with resulting conduct—with a resulting evil, or harm, that government can properly act to prevent—that its speech elements were transformed into conduct for purposes of the First Amendment?

On the first question—whether Viktora's participation in the cross burning was speech—the five justices who joined the Supreme Court's majority opinion were unanimous . . . unanimously silent. This surprising fact is hard to comprehend. Its explanation can be found only in the peculiar—some would say Byzantine—pathways of First Amendment reasoning employed by the Court. *Whether or not the act was speech or conduct*, the Court's majority opinion effectively stated, the ordinance was unconstitutional because it failed to sweep within its prohibition other cases involving undisputed speech acts that arouse, in the words of the ordinance, "anger, alarm, or resentment" on grounds *other than* "race, color, creed, religion, or gender." The ordinance was therefore too narrow in its scope, violating the First Amendment rule that government restrictions on speech must be neutral, not singling out particular ideas for punishment. This was a conclusion that went to the *general* terms of the ordinance, not to Viktora's particular case. And this was why the Court could treat the facts of Viktora's case almost cavalierly, for the facts really weren't relevant to the general issue the Court chose to address.

The Court's reasoning, it should be added, had a peculiar twist. Because the Court rested the ordinance's infirmity on the ground that it singled out only some, and not all, grounds upon which the speech or conduct subject to its provisions could be restricted—only anger and alarm grounded in race, religion, or gender were covered—the effect of the Court's decision was that the ordinance's constitutionality could be saved only by restricting *more*, not less, speech. This led Justice White, in bewilderment, to dissent bitterly from "the folly of the opinion," which he characterized as "an arid, doctrinaire interpretation, driven by the frequently irresistible impulse of judges to tinker with the First Amendment."

To which he might have added, quoting Holmes, "To rest upon a formula is a slumber that, prolonged, means death."

When Is Conduct Speech?

Can the question of whether Robert Viktora's act was speech be ignored as easily as the majority opinion would have us believe? Was the pure formalism of the Court's approach to the case too clever, as Justice White suggested? If, as White believed, Viktora's act was *not* speech—if it was instead simply conduct, "fighting words" falling completely outside the First Amendment, as the Court has long described such speech—was there any good justification for reversing *Viktora's* conviction, given that *his* action could legally be punished because it could claim *no* protection as speech under the First Amendment? Why should Viktora be absolved of responsibility for his *conduct* simply because some other person engaging in some other act of speaking (use of an offensive word or phrase in a college speech, for example) at some future time might be wrongly prosecuted under the ordinance—an ordinance, it should be remembered, that had *never* been used in the eight years of its existence before Viktora, Miller, and four or five other boys had chosen on that June evening of 1990 to drink, smoke pot, take LSD, and finally in the wee hours of the morning to burn a cross in the front yard of the black family that lived across the street?

Perhaps there is an adequate answer to these questions, but to discover what it is and then to judge it one must begin by exploring the issue the Court chose, expediently, to ignore: Was Viktora's act speech for purposes of the First Amendment? In the *Cohen v. California* case, Justice Blackmun, joined by Chief Justice Burger and Justice Hugo Black (the First Amendment absolutist), had described Paul Cohen's wearing of a jacket emblazoned with the words "Fuck the Draft" as an "absurd and immature antic, . . . mainly conduct and little speech." If the sentiment was wrongly applied to Cohen's act, would it nevertheless be a fit description for Viktora's?

Justice Harlan's opinion in *Cohen* treated Cohen's act of wearing the jacket emblazoned "Fuck the Draft" in the Los Angeles County Courthouse as speech because Cohen was intentionally trying to communicate his views to others through the jacket's message, and the four-letter expletive was a purposeful means of expressing his emotions, his strength of feeling on the issue of the draft and the war. Cohen's act, in short, was speaking; it was immature, crude, and insensitive, but it was nevertheless part of an effort by Cohen to communicate ideas to others.

The fact that the means he used to express his feelings were distasteful did not alter the basic speech quality of the act.

Whether Viktora's act of burning the cross (or, more accurately, allegedly participating in its burning) was, like Cohen's act, speech, thus turns on how we judge *his* conduct and *his* motives. The speech quality of Viktora's act is not determined by asking whether *an* act of burning a cross, in theory, *could* be an act of speaking, or whether the burning cross, itself, had expressive meaning as a symbol. Just as Justice Harlan insisted in *Cohen* that the First Amendment question revolved around *Cohen's* use of the phrase "Fuck the Draft" and not whether the phrase itself, out of its particular context, was in some abstract sense "speech," so also the question for Viktora is whether *his* actions in burning the cross were acts of *speaking*. As Holmes said, the "character of every act depends on the circumstances in which it is done."

Unfortunately, Viktora's case was seen as an abstraction from the very start, beginning with the juvenile court's decision to dismiss the charges because the ordinance was faulty even though its application to Viktora's case may not have been. As a consequence, no trial was held and no evidence adduced on the particulars of the boys' actions that June evening. So in addressing *Viktora's* conduct and *his* motives, we will have to proceed on a certain degree of surmise, based on the facts available to us from public—and unchallenged—accounts. But what those accounts tell us, if true, is that there is substantial reason to doubt that Viktora's acts constituted "speaking" for purposes of the First Amendment.

The act of speaking has three essential qualities. It must be purposeful, not inadvertent or unintended; it must be geared to communicating ideas or information to others; and the ideas and information must be those of the speaker. Ample room for doubt exists on all three scores in Viktora's case.

Following his arrest, Miller told the police, "I drank all night. If I was sober I wouldn't even have thought about going along." If we indulge the well-grounded assumption that Viktora, too, was by the wee hours of the morning well under the influence of alcohol, marijuana, or LSD, or some combination thereof, can we easily assume that he was capable of a "purposeful" act, especially one based on the specific intent to express a coherent idea to an identified audience?

In the criminal law, actions undertaken under the compulsion and judgment-distorting influence of drugs can be excused or mitigated (though grudgingly and infrequently, it should be added) on the theory that one cannot be held responsible or morally culpable for choices made under such circumstances. In short, the requisite *intent* required by the criminal law cannot be found. Is it not possible, by analogy, to say that for speaking to occur a similar clarity of mind, a coherence of purpose, must exist? Is the swaggering bellow of the lurching drunkard on the city street late at night something we should define as speaking for purposes of the Constitution?

Even if in some minimally adequate sense Viktora knew what he was doing, who was he speaking *to*? Speaking, at least for purposes of the First Amendment's protection, requires more than the coincidence or inadvertence of an audience; it requires an audience to whom the speaker *intends* to express himself. Who was Viktora's audience? It is improbable that Viktora's conduct can be seen as communication to the five or six other boys who participated with him in the cross burning, for theirs was a joint, collective act directed not to one another but to some other object. Was the object simply the venting of hate, the wild and crazy expression of inebriation, pointed nowhere and to no one in particular? Or can we say that in their drunken mob psychology, the boys had formulated a plan to burn the crosses as a means by which to express their racism to the neighbors, the city, the public at large? Perhaps so, but only perhaps, because the course of events, capped off by the decision, once the burning had begun, to "burn some more and be crazy," belies any such coherent communicative strategy, much less the individual capacity to form its intent.

There is, of course, another possibility. Did Viktora and his friends intend to communicate a message—*their* message—to the Jones family, a message bearing the symbolic imprint of the Ku Klux Klan? If in their inebriation they lacked the capacity to form any meaningful intent, much less this one, we can of course dismiss the possibility. And even if we assume that they *could* so intend, the message they set out to express to the Jones family must, to qualify as *their* speech, be their own. It must reflect *Viktora's* free-willed decision to express the ideas as *his*, or at least to express the ideas of his own conscious choice. But Miller's statement "If I was sober I wouldn't even have thought about going along" and Jason Olson's description of the decision to burn again as a decision to "be crazy" suggest something very different. It suggests that the Jones family was not the communicative object of a message but at best the communicative instrument; not the intended recipient of the message but instead part of the message itself. If this is so, Viktora would not be "speaking" to the Jones family for purposes of the First Amendment but speaking through them, and thus the act of speaking—of communicating to others—could not transpire in the absence of another intended audience, of which there is no evidence whatever in the facts we know. And if there was no speaking by Viktora, his action would amount not to speech but simply to conduct, for purposes of the Constitution.

Speech and Harm

Let us assume, even in the face of all of the information we have, that Viktora was capable of forming the necessary intention, and that he did in fact intend by his act to express his own feelings of racial hatred and violence to the Jones family by the act of burning a cross in their yard and another across the street from their home. Must we, based on all of these assumptions, unlikely as they appear, acknowledge that Viktora's act was speech protected by the First Amendment? Or might we even then ask, as Holmes did, whether the "character of the act . . . in the circumstances in which it [was] done" was so brigaded with conduct, so directly and immediately productive of resulting harm, that it should be treated, like shouting fire in a crowded theatre, as mere conduct and not speech? This view of the case would fit the classic mold of "fighting words"—words that in their immediacy are but part and parcel of resulting harm, and are therefore not protected as speech under the First Amendment; words that are directed specifically at another person, intended by their communication to that other person simply and solely to cause immediate harm to that person by the very idea expressed.

This is a case very different from that presented by Paul Cohen's walking through the Los Angeles County Courthouse with a jacket that said "Fuck the Draft." In the *Cohen* case Justice Harlan was quick to point out that there was no evidence that Cohen intended to cause anyone harm, much less that he intended to inflict harm by the words alone on any specific and known person who he knew, in fact, would be harmed. Cohen's case, instead, was about standards of taste and about the freedom to express the emotional strength of one's conviction in circumstances in which people might be shocked and offended but not harmed in any but an intellectual way.

When the case is of a different sort, as with Viktora's intending to hurt and, indeed, expel the Joneses from the neighborhood by the very

message he directed at them, would much of value to the First Amendment be lost by a decision to treat the act as conduct, not speech? Is the
kind of communicative act we have hypothesized for Viktora really different from acts of fraud, coercion, blackmail, or extortion, all of
which can occur through the medium of "speech" but none of which
we consider protected acts of speaking for purposes of the First
Amendment?

During the course of the oral argument in Viktora's case the justices
openly worried about this question. But they did so rather aimlessly and
without ultimate resolution.

> *Question [posed to Edward Cleary, Viktora's lawyer]:* With respect
> to words that injure, is it your position that the only words that
> injure that can constitutionally be punished are threats?
>
> *Mr. Cleary:* No, Your Honor.
>
> *Question:* Threats to immediate harm?
>
> *Mr. Cleary:* No, Your Honor. I'm not suggesting—
>
> *Question:* How do You—where do you draw the line?
>
> *Mr. Cleary:* I believe, Your Honor, that that—I'll be very honest. I
> think that's a very hard line to draw, and I think that's perhaps the
> crux of this case to a certain degree, is the offensiveness idea and
> how—
>
> *Question:* Mr. Cleary, . . . it depends case by case on the reaction of
> the person who hears the words, is that right?
>
> *Mr. Cleary:* That is as I understand it, Your Honor.
>
> *Question:* So you can use any language whatever in a Quaker com-
> munity, if you are in a solid Quaker community, you can be much
> more insulting than you can somewhere else. Does that make a lot
> of sense?
>
> *Mr. Cleary:* No, but it does rely on the audience reaction . . . the
> reflexive violence idea, and everyone is going to be different. . . .
>
> *Question:* Might it not be a reasonable man standard? I guess you
> would have to consider Quakers not reasonable men, at least inso-
> far as their strong aversion to violence is concerned, but might that
> not be the standard? I mean, if you happen to be in a pacifistic
> community, why should the law take that into account, why
> should the law subject these people to that kind of abuse which
> other people would be provoked to respond to with violence?
>
> *Mr. Cleary:* I agree—

The issue of the precise harm caused by the boys' act was also the subject of a colloquy with Thomas Foley, the attorney for Ramsey County, who argued that the St. Paul ordinance was constitutional.

> *Question:* Mr. Foley, would you address the concern expressed by [Mr. Cleary] that the ordinance is limited only to fighting words [words that produce immediate harm] that arouse anger, alarm, or resentment "on the basis of race, color, creed, religion, or gender" and not other fighting words that could cause the same reaction in people [for reasons other than race, etc.]? The argument is that the statute is underinclusive.
>
> *Mr. Foley:* Your Honor, it's our position that the statute is not underinclusive, that this is a fighting words case, that this is [therefore] unprotected conduct [and not speech], and that the City of St. Paul has the right to determine which harms it can proscribe within the limits of its jurisdiction.
>
> *Question:* So you're saying fighting words simply [are] not protected speech as such, and therefore we can select anything within the category of fighting words . . . is that what you're saying?
>
> *Mr. Foley:* Yes, Your Honor.
>
> *Question:* What if the burning were done in front of the Ramsey County Courthouse?
>
> *Mr. Foley:* Your Honor, we believe this ordinance would not be applicable if the burning cross was done in a public forum or in a political parade of some sort. It's only when the conduct in this case is done in a manner to inflict injury or cause an immediate breach of the peace that it violates [the] ordinance. . . . There is an element of intent with the ordinance saying [that the cross-burner must] "know or have reason to know that it would arouse—"
>
> *Question:* Mr. Foley, I'm having trouble with terminology and it may be my fault, but I have assumed that [this court's prior decisions] spoke to two different categories [of "fighting words" that could be punished], the "words that injure" category and the "fighting words" [that incite others to violence] category.
>
> Are you claiming that this is a fighting words case or a word or expression that injures case?
>
> *Mr. Foley:* We rely more heavily on the inflicts injury prong, [that the cross burning itself inflicted injury] to the family, the Jones family. The burning of the cross in the middle of the night outside of their

home is more than just outrageous conduct. It is direct harm to
these people, causing fear, intimidation, threats, and coercion. . . .

Question: Your theory is that because the category of words that
inflict injury [is] outside the First Amendment's protection, it is not
an objection in this case that the particular words . . . are identified
by content [i.e., race, religion, and so on]? Is that a fair statement
of your position?

Mr. Foley: We think they can be content-based under those circumstances.

These exchanges make clear the Court's interest in defining the precise
"harm" to which the ordinance was directed. Was it the harm the act did
to the feelings of the recipient—"anger, alarm, or resentment"—or did
the harm take more objective and physical form through the violent
reaction of others? The implication, of course, is that the First Amendment requires those on the receiving end of speech to brace themselves
against the offense, anger, and hurt that will befall them, even when they
have been singled out as targets by one whose motive is just that, and
nothing else.

But just how firmly must we brace ourselves before responsibility for
the harm can be shifted from the listener to the speaker, from its object
to its creator? Is it obvious that Russ and Laura Jones's feelings of stark
fear and brutal intimidation are a lesser form of harm than a physical
assault, perhaps because the harm is comprehended and internalized
rather than physically felt? Was the Klan's reign of terror and intimidation more benign than its acts of arson? Is destruction of the spirit less
condemnable than destruction of a building?

Where should we draw the line between shouting fire in a crowded
theater and causing a panic in which people might be trampled, on the
one hand, and wearing a jacket emblazoned "Fuck the Draft" in public,
knowing that children will be present and many hearers will be deeply
offended and emotionally upset, on the other?

Tucked beneath the smooth logical veneer of the Supreme Court's
opinion in Viktora's case, disguised by the formalism of the Court's
"underinclusiveness" rationale, lurks the inescapable line-drawing question. What harms caused by speech are sufficiently grave to justify treating the speech that causes them as conduct that can be made the subject
of regulation by a democratically elected majority? Harm to the hearer's
or reader's or viewer's sense of good taste, decency, and sound values is

not sufficient, according to Justice Harlan's opinion in the *Cohen* case. But the possibility—indeed likelihood—of being trampled in the theatre is sufficient, according to Justice Holmes.

Are the horror, the stark fear, the sense of helplessness, devaluation, and rejection that Russ and Paula Jones felt sufficient harm to justify treating Viktora's act as conduct and not speech? Or is such harm—for it surely *is* harm—too ephemeral, a product only of thought and belief? If "ephemerality" is the answer given, is the result it yields in Viktora's case a necessary (or at least acceptable) price that must be paid for freedom of belief and expression? Why, we might ask, must the Joneses' freedom to maintain *their* beliefs—beliefs of dignity and equality and opportunity and safety—be sacrificed in the name of preserving the cross-burners' beliefs, *especially* when the cross-burners' beliefs, such as they were, were only dimly if at all visible through a cloud of alcohol, marijuana, and LSD?

This is a question not of theory but of fact. Theories provide a structure for understanding facts, not for ignoring them. But this lesson was lost on the Supreme Court's majority, for neither facts nor answers to the difficult question of harm can be found in the majority's opinion in Viktora's case. The opinion simply refused to face up to it, escaping through a device of pure abstraction that condemned the ordinance's failure to sweep within its reach all possible kinds of action that might produce traumatic emotional harm—or even, for that matter, all possible kinds of action than might produce a bonfire in one's front yard. It was left to Justice White, joined by Justices Blackmun, O'Connor, and Stevens in frustrated and bitter dissent, to insist, without the legal force of a majority opinion, that Viktora's act was *not* speech, and to accuse the majority of "legitimat[ing] hate speech as a form of public discussion."

But if we are left without an answer from the Court's majority in Viktora's case, we are still left with the question, which is open because it was ignored. What kinds of harm are sufficient to justify restrictions on speech? In pondering this question, we remain, at least for the present, haunted by Justice Harlan's opinion in Paul Cohen's case, haunted by the questions his remarkable and factually rich opinion compels us to address:

- Is the plight and the hurt felt by Russ and Paula Jones when confronted with a burning cross in their yard in St. Paul, Minnesota, in 1990 different in articulatable ways from the shock and revulsion felt by a family and their children when confronted with "Fuck the Draft" on Paul Cohen's jacket in a courthouse corridor in 1968?

- Is the burning cross the cultural equivalent today, in a society now numbed by expletives and obscenity, of the word "Fuck" displayed on the back of a jacket in a public building in an earlier day, in a very different climate and social order?

- Can we distinguish the family's claimed right, in 1968 or even today, to a public culture that consists with rather than undermines the values of moderation, decency, and commitment to reason, from a black family's claimed right to a culture free of racial terror and the relics of racial violence?

When all is said and done, perhaps the only difference between Robert Viktora and Paul Cohen is the passage of two decades. We might, of course, hope that this is not so, for if it is, the First Amendment would have to be taken to mean, at its base, that the culture can insist on no public virtues whatever; that no requirements of intention, of communicative purpose, or of consciously formed thought can be placed on the act of speaking; and therefore that we can not even insist that the protected and sacred right of speaking freely be *at least* a self-conscious act that "eschews violence coerced by" force.

Perhaps the sentiment expressed in 1971 in Cohen's case by Justice Blackmun, then new to the Court, and shared also by Justice Black, then a veteran at the end of his career who was known, among all of the justices, as an absolutist on First Amendment issues, somehow seems less quaint and anachronistic when transplanted to the present in the form of a burning cross lit by a group of boys acting on whim and impulse, under the influence of alcohol, marijuana, and LSD. Was Viktora's act, too, an "absurd and immature antic . . . mainly conduct and little speech?"

If not—if Justice Harlan's reasoning in Cohen's case in 1971 would compel a similar result in Viktora's case in 1992—are we prepared to swallow the bitter pill thus tendered? Justice Holmes put it well, if unsatisfyingly, in his famous 1919 dissent in *Abrams v. United States*:

> But when men have realized that time has upset many fighting faiths, they may come to believe even more than they believe the very foundations of their own conduct that the ultimate good desired is better reached by free trade in ideas—that the best test of truth is the power of the thought to

get itself accepted in the competition of the market, and that truth is the only ground upon which their wishes safely can be carried out. *That at any rate is the theory of our Constitution. It is an experiment, as all life is an experiment.* (Italics added)

What if we could ask Holmes, were he alive today—the same Holmes who defined truth "as the system of my (intellectual) limitations"— whether the success of the American experiment really must depend on Robert Viktora's freedom to burn a cross in the Joneses' front yard?

We might be surprised at his answer.

Let us return, in closing, to the beginning. What does Viktora's case reveal about the distinction between speech and conduct under the First Amendment? It reveals a distinction that is theoretically imperfect but practically necessary; an approximation only of when an act has the necessary qualities of speaking. It reveals a line that can be neither clearly drawn nor wholly ignored, and whose enforcement calls upon the less tidy demands of judgment as well as the elegant abstractions of philosophy.

As Alexander Bickel, one of the greatest constitutional scholars of the twentieth century, expressed it in his wonderful book *The Morality of Consent*, freedom of speech rests fundamentally on the proposition that for speech to *remain* free, "violence must be the monopoly of the State." Speech must, at a minimum, be a product of individual freedom and will, not of inadvertence or caprice or simple brute force. Its quality as expression, not violence, must be judged, as it was not judged in Viktora's case, against Holmes's observation that "the character of every act depends on the circumstances in which it is done." For if Robert Viktora's undeniably "absurd and immature antic" was conduct, and not speech, the Supreme Court's decision to grant it shelter in the name of the First Amendment would not be folly but tragedy.

To borrow Justice Frankfurter's turn of phrase, it would "radiate a constitutional doctrine without avowing it."

ADDITIONAL READING

Richard Delgado, "Words That Wound: A Tort Action for Racial Insults, Epithets, and Name-Calling," 17 *Harvard Civil Rights/Civil Liberties Law Review* 133 (1982).

Richard Fallon, Jr., "Two Senses of Autonomy," 46 *Stanford Law Review* 875 (1994).

O. W. Holmes, "Natural Law," in *Collected Legal Papers* 310 (1920).

Frederick Schauer, "The Phenomenology of Speech and Harm," 103 *Ethics* 635 (1993).

Clark v. Community for Creative Non-Violence, 468 U.S. 288 (1984).

The Artist: *Carnal Knowledge* as Art, Pornography as Subordination, and the V-chip as Family Values

(Jenkins v. Georgia, 418 U.S. 153 (1974))

And now, I said, let me show in a figure how far our nature is enlightened or unenlightened:—Behold! Human beings living in an underground den, which has a mouth open toward the light and reaching all along the den; here they have been from their childhood, and have their legs and necks chained so that they cannot move, and can only see before them, being prevented by the chains from turning round their heads. Above and behind them a fire is blazing at a distance, and between the fire and the prisoners there is a raised way; and you will see, if you look, a low wall built along the way, like the screen which marionette players have in front of them, over which they show the puppets.

I see.

And do you see, I said, men passing along the wall carrying all sorts of vessels, and statues and figures of animals made of wood and stone and various materials, which appear over the wall?

You have shown me a strange image, and they are strange prisoners.

Like ourselves, I replied; and they [the prisoners] see only their own shadows or the shadows of one another, which the fire throws on the opposite wall of the cave?

True, he said; how could they see anything but the shadows if they were never allowed to move their heads?

And of the objects which are being carried in like manner they would only see the shadows?

Yes, he said.

And if they were able to converse with one another, would they not suppose that they were naming what was actually before them?

Very true.

To them, I said, the truth would be literally nothing but the shadows of the images.   —Plato, *The Myth of the Cave*

Plato's allegory is about meaning, about how the meaning of what we see is a function of what we know. Our story is also about meaning: the meaning of speech, and more specifically the meaning of movies about sex. Is sexual intercourse portrayed in a movie the true image, or is it instead a shadow of another image, such as liberty and freedom, hopelessness and despair, lust and immorality, love and intimacy, subordination and inequality?

If we draw on Plato's allegory, the question of a film's meaning is, at one level, a question of epistemology. The term "epistemology" is defined as the "theory of the nature and grounds of knowledge." It thus concerns how we know what we know, not how we select that which we might *choose* to know. When we hear a "chirp" we perceive a bird, not a car. We have not *chosen* to reject "car" in favor of "bird," for to do so we would have to perceive both ideas from the "chirp." Instead, all we know from the chirp is bird; epistemologically speaking, we do not "know" car.

What we know is a result of what we perceive, and perception, as Plato understood, is a subtle and complicated thing. Perception is the construction of *a* reality, not *the* reality. We do not perceive the visual image that lies before us. "The eye and brain," Ulric Neisser wrote in "The Processes of Vision," an important article published in 1968 in *Scientific American*, "do not act as a camera or a recording instrument. In perceiving, complex patterns are extracted from that input and fed into the constructive process of vision." What we perceive, in other words, is not the image before us but, rather, what our neurological filtering systems make of the fragments of color and texture as they are first deconstructed and then reconstructed in light of our experience, language, culture, and social relationships. "The perceptual object," as Christian Metz put it in a 1980 article entitled "Aural Objects," "is a constructed unity, *socially constructed*, and also (to some extent) a linguistic unity."

The meaning of an act of sexual intercourse depicted on film, then, is a product of the viewer's act of perception. If the viewer sees prurience but not despair—just as a listener hearing a chirp would see a bird and not a car—can we describe the perceptual act of ascribing that meaning as a *chosen* one, as a self-conscious social, even political, act in which the viewer perceives a range of possible meanings but elects only one based on personal preferences and values and prejudices?

Or might the act of giving meaning instead be an epistemological one, the product of an unconscious, deeply imbedded process reflecting learned patterns of culture, language, and experience, revealing to the viewer only the image that passes through the filtering lens of perception? Is meaning, as Plato suggested in *The Myth of the Cave*, a shadow only, the only thing we can see through a template that shapes the image we perceive?

Our story involves the distinction between epistemological ignorance, on the one hand, and political preference, on the other. Which of these, ignorance or politics, explains a southern town's failure to perceive racism in the early 1960s; which of these explains the same southern town's failure to perceive the "art" in sexual intercourse a decade later; and which of these explains a northern town's failure to perceive parody in sexual bestiality in 1995? In each instance messages imbedded in the images of racism, sexuality, and bestiality were ignored in the constructive process of ascribing meaning. Was each town's ignorance a conscious political choice, or was it instead a sign of epistemological ignorance: of simply not seeing?

Should a community whose ignorance is borne of epistemology—of failure to see because the lens through which the community "saw" prevented the other meaning from being perceived, much as a template placed upon an image changes it into something else—be able to preserve its ignorance, its template, much as the Amish struggle to protect their children from knowledge of the outside world? Can a community be conscious of its blindness (though unaware of what it cannot see) *and* wish to preserve it? Is such an act a political act, or a benign act of epistemological ignorance, the political act consisting instead in the acts of those who would force them to see that which they cannot see?

Catharine MacKinnon, a brilliant and controversial First Amendment scholar, claims that when a woman views an eroticized depiction of violent rape and sees not sex but subordination, hers is an epistemological act, not a political one. Subordination is the meaning she sees, not the meaning she *chooses* to see; indeed, MacKinnon claims, subordination is the meaning that most of us see, male and female, young and old alike. If she is right, then to describe what we see as a political act with First Amendment consequences, when it is an epistemological one, is to confuse the act of refusing the forbidden fruit with the act of forcing others, through pornography, to eat it. The political act, MacKinnon claims, is the pornographer's, not ours.

This issue lies at the center of another contemporary development: the V-chip. Recently embraced with the force of law and the fervor of moral imperative, the V-chip is a mechanism to be installed in all television sets that will allow each of us to shape what we and our children see, and thus, perhaps, also to shape what we know. By programming the mechanism to block out sex or violence in advance even of its production, much less its broadcast, the viewer can avoid choice, and thus avoid knowing. The V-chip is thus much more than a technological marvel, it is an epistemological miracle.

The debate over pornography and the V-chip thus have something in common. Both raise a fundamental question at the heart of the First Amendment: Must the First Amendment be read to require that everyone else pay the price for the pornographer's act by sacrificing the ignorance we wish to maintain?

Not always, as it turns out. But to find out when and why we must turn to the beginning of our story, to the Deep South in the civil rights era and to the mysteries of obscenity law.

Carnal Knowledge

In 1972 the movie *Carnal Knowledge* opened in Albany, Georgia.

The theater was the Broad Avenue Cinema, located in downtown Albany. It could have been the kind of theater that most Americans frequented in their youth, with Saturday matinees for the children, movies that families could attend, and of course popcorn, soft drinks, and candy. The theater manager was Billy Jenkins, a businessman who managed the Broad Avenue Cinema for Martin Theaters, an Atlanta chain. *Carnal Knowledge* was playing in Albany and on Main Street in theaters across the country, to an audience of nearly twenty million people.

Albany was a town that believed in law and order, with an emphasis on "order." Just a few years earlier Martin Luther King, Jr., had been jailed there four times, each without incident. The civil rights movement had come to Albany, beginning in the bus depot and spreading thereafter, through protest and resistance, to all quarters of the community. But the police chief's unyielding demand for law *and* order had left the civil rights movement stillborn in Albany, forced to move on to other venues. And in the court of public opinion Martin Luther King, Jr., was humbled and the chief was made a national hero.

The citizens of Albany were for the most part decent people. The community had values, and while its values can be criticized for the selectivity with which they were applied, once adopted they were fiercely embraced. Principal among Albany's values was the characteristically southern convention of courtesy and propriety in one's public demeanor. "Obscenity" was thus a dirty word, and it was given broad definition.

In 1972 Albany was a town possessed of its own history, its own culture, its own values. *Carnal Knowledge* was not welcome there.

Albany lies about one hundred miles south of Macon, well beyond the grasp of Atlanta's "New South" orbit. Tuscaloosa, Alabama, lies some two hundred miles west, over occasionally rolling but dominantly flat southern-pine country. This is the Deep South, hot and steamy in the summer but green and lush, too. Albany is just east of the low, rolling foothills of the Piedmont's southern extreme.

The name of the town seems discordant to a northerner, who associates it with the capital of New York. So as not to confuse Albany, Georgia, with its northern namesake, perhaps, the name is pronounced with the accent on the second *a*, which is mounted high and with a muted twang. The city's location in southern Georgia plants an image of a small, rural, steamy, racially divided southern town. But with a 1972 population of some sixty thousand, 40 percent of whom were African American, it did not fit the classic stereotype of the small, backwater southern town whose racial divisions were enforced by a brutal sheriff and a well-placed railroad track.

Not that Albany had no racial divide. It did, and like most towns in the Deep South the divide was deeply ingrained in the culture. In Albany's case, however, the railroad track was redundant, for the racial divide was enforced not by one but by two officers of the law: a brutal sheriff *and* a hard-nosed, astute, take-all-prisoners, law-and-order police chief. During the "time of racial unrest," to which we shall turn shortly, the brutality was provided by Sheriff Cull Campbell, an unreconstructed man given to using force to solve problems. The law and order was astutely provided by Police Chief Laurie Pritchett, described in a December 1961 *Newsweek* story as "a red-haired, red-faced former paratrooper" who, by comparison with Campbell, was fairness incarnate. As Howard Zinn put it in his book *You Can't Be Neutral on a Moving Train*, "Campbell would beat somebody bloody and Pritchett would call for an ambulance."

Albany has a notable, if not always commendable, history. President Jimmy Carter's childhood nanny, Annie Mae Rhodes, lives there today, as she did in the 1930s when she traveled twenty-one miles north on Route 19 and nine miles west on Route 280 to Plains, Georgia, where she worked in the Carter home. There, beginning at age sixteen, she supplied young Jimmy with sweet-potato pie and peanut bread, and a lifelong friendship. When, in 1994, her Albany home was destroyed in a flood, President Carter turned his attention from nuclear arms in North Korea and reinstalling President Aristide in Haiti, rolled up his sleeves, and helped "Mrs. Annie Mae" get back on her feet by working on her new house from Habitat for Humanity.

Albany is also the "Quail Capital of the World." Each year the town hosts the Celebrity Quail Hunt attended by famous sports, movie, TV, and entertainment VIPs, as well, recently, as General Norman Schwartzkopf and Chuck Yeager. The city also bore the less notable distinction, in 1994, as the city with the nation's highest percentage of single-parent households, just ahead of New York City.

But Albany's most notable claim to fame traces back to 1961 and 1962, in the early, grim days of the civil rights movement. It was in Albany that the fates of the Reverend Martin Luther King, Jr., Sheriff Cull Campbell, and Chief Laurie Pritchett would be drawn together with jarring and improbable results. It all began in late 1961 in the wake of the Montgomery, Alabama, bus boycott. Three young civil rights activists, Charles Sherrod, Cordell Reagan, and Charles Jones, of the Student Nonviolent Coordinating Committee (SNCC), who were later joined in what would be known as the Albany Movement by a coalition of groups including the NAACP, Congress of Racial Equality (CORE), Southern Christian Leadership Conference (SCLC), and the Baptist Ministers' Alliance, selected Albany as the first step in a coordinated effort to bring full-scale integration to cities throughout the South. Beginning with the then-segregated Albany bus depot and train station, SNCC organized sit-ins, marches, protests, and voter-registration drives to integrate Albany from top to bottom, from City Hall to department stores, restaurants to schools, bus transportation, theaters, and churches. It was nothing less than an attempt to transform the city's soul.

In the short run, at least, the city's soul resisted. But the city's reputation didn't. As the *New Republic* put it in March of 1962:

> This sprightly, but mannerly and basically well-meaning south Georgia city has lately attained an undesired and at least partially undeserved national reputation as the prototype of all the relics of the Middle Ages that are stubbornly refusing to surrender to the 20th Century. This is the result of the arrests of 700 Negroes, including the Rev. Martin Luther King, on the technical charge of parading without a license in a demonstration against segregated seating on the city bus lines. But the reputation is fantastically wrong. Albany is simply a community that has a wolf by the ears and cannot discover any safe way of letting go.

A conflict that cannot be escaped or resolved must at least be managed. Here Chief Pritchett shone through. Law and order was his theme, and he pursued it relentlessly, arresting and jailing 50 people here, 170 there, 15 people elsewhere, and so on, including on one occasion in 1962 a group consisting of the Reverend Martin Luther King, Jr., and 69 priests, ministers, and rabbis. Pritchett's distinction was not to be found in his skills of arrest and prosecution (which were possessed in equal measure by many police chiefs in the South) but, rather, in the evenhandedness with which he applied the medicine. His answer was simply to arrest everyone, young and old, black and white, northerner and southerner, saved and sinner.

Pritchett's medicine was generously doled out for every breach of the law, distributed in a matter-of-fact, nonjudgmental, and orderly way. And he did this with an eye to quelling any eruption of passion and violence, often removing the most notable of the arrestees to "living quarters" in other counties. Pritchett is reported to have arrested Martin Luther King, Jr., four times but in each instance to have released him from custody quickly enough to avoid his being made a martyr. *Everyone* who distributed handbills in violation of the Albany ordinances was arrested, whatever their message, a policy described by the *New Republic* in July of 1963 as a "mockery of the Bill of Rights [made] thus . . . very precise, being limited principally to ideas."

For this Pritchett achieved not ignomy but fame. He was invited to a symposium sponsored by the Ford Foundation, where he shared his skills and tactics with other police chiefs. He was widely praised in the media for maintaining law and order (and, not coincidentally, segregation) in Albany. He "earned this praise from the establishment press," according to Howard Zinn, "by simply putting into prison ('nonviolently,' as he boasted) every man, woman, and child in the city of Albany who tried to exercise their constitutional rights of free speech and assembly."

Racial segregation, it seems, was part of the warp and woof of Albany, deeply ingrained in the culture and outlook of all citizens, black and white, young and old. How else can we imagine an existence permeated from top to bottom, imbedded in every act and gesture, at every moment, by the horror of racial segregation?

Charles Sherrod, Cordell Reagan, Charles Jones, and all of the others came to transform Albany's soul by lifting its shadowed veil of ignorance—wresting it away, in fact. But Albany, for the moment at least, could not be made to see so easily. It resisted being led from the cave into the light.

One gets the distinct impression upon reading about Albany at the time of the civil rights protests and ten years later, when *Carnal Knowledge* played at the Broad Avenue Cinema, that not much had changed between 1962 and 1972. To be sure, the characters were new, as was the surface appearance of the town. But the soul was still intact—a soul that consisted not only of racial division but also of small-town southern values of mannerliness, religiosity, and (always) law and order. There was, it seems, a coherence of values, a belief in limits, an old-fashioned idea of propriety in one's public conduct and, importantly, in matters related to sex.

Or so it could have seemed in early 1971 as the sheriff, in concert with the district attorney, launched a program of investigation and seizure of allegedly obscene films that were playing in Albany's movie houses. The enterprise was a systematic and relentless one intended to purge Albany of obscenity. In July and August of 1971, for example, as many as forty-three films were investigated by the sheriff's deputies. Six months later, in January of 1972, *Carnal Knowledge* got caught in the trap.

On an afternoon in early January, Lynn Stout was among the patrons who walked up to the ticket booth at the Broad Avenue Cinema. He purchased a ticket and then proceeded inside to see the movie that was playing. The movie was *Carnal Knowledge*. Stout thus joined roughly twenty million other Americans who watched a critically acclaimed film depicting the experiences of two young men whose lives were centered unrepentantly and unfulfillingly on sex. The film dwelled on their sexual activities and on their conversations, which likewise were dominated, with increasing emptiness and despair, on sex. By today's standards the film was not explicit, at least in the graphic sense to which we have become accustomed; it could best be described, instead, as sexual and sensual, representational but not explicit.

After the film was over, Stout rose from his seat and walked out of the theater with all of the other patrons who had seen *Carnal Knowledge* that afternoon. The dinner hour was fast approaching, and most of the patrons probably headed for home. But home was not Stout's destination. He headed, instead, for the district attorney's office.

On January 13, 1972, Stout returned to the Broad Avenue Cinema, this time in his official capacity as chief investigator for the Dougherty County Sheriff's Office, and he was armed with a search warrant. With 150 or so people watching *Carnal Knowledge* at the time, Stout proceeded to serve the warrant on Billy Jenkins, the manager, and seize the film. As Stout later testified, Jenkins "is the man that I served the warrant on. He's the man that gave all the orders to rewind the film and to have the people leave the theater and etcetera."

Carnal Knowledge, as it turned out, achieved a special distinction in Albany. In the days following Stout's visits to the Broad Avenue Cinema, *Carnal Knowledge* was seized three more times in other Albany theaters. Albany, it seems, took sex seriously.

On March 6, 1972, a warrant was issued for Billy Jenkins's arrest on a charge of distributing obscene material, a violation of Georgia's Criminal Code. In a remarkable example of justice's swiftness, his trial was held just fourteen days later, on March 20–21.

The trial itself was unexceptional as obscenity trials go. Characteristically for Albany, it was orderly, efficient, and short. Apart from testimony about the time and circumstances of the seizure and arrest, the location and admission policy of the theater (the film was R rated), and testimony about other dirty films and magazines that had not (yet, one suspects) been seized in Albany by the sheriff's officers, the only direct evidence of the film's obscenity was the film itself, which the jury, after its lunch break, was taken to view in the same Broad Avenue Cinema from which it had originally been seized.

There was nothing untoward about this rather spare proceeding; the United States Supreme Court's decisions had said that a jury could decide on a film's obscenity based on the jury's viewing of the film, alone, without any testimony about its meaning or value. And for a lawyer defending an obscenity case in a small rural southern town, bringing fancy movie critics or academic types into the courtroom to lecture the jury about the "proper" standards of taste and aesthetic judgment could be risky business, indeed. After all, the citizens of Albany are capable of making their own aesthetic judgments. Or so the theory went.

More notable than the brevity of Jenkins's trial, is the fact that it occurred not once but twice. The first trial ended in a mistrial because one member of the twelve-person jury held out for acquittal and hung the jury. The trial judge thereupon dismissed the jury and set the matter for retrial the next day. After a second, similarly short trial, followed by a matinee showing at the movie house, the case was once again submitted to the jury on March 22.

The state prevailed the second time around, but not without difficulty. On the afternoon of March 22 the judge charged the second jury, and the jurors retired to the jury room for deliberations. The jury returned to the courtroom late that afternoon to report on its deliberations. The transcript reveals the following events:

The Court: Mr. Foreman, have you been able to reach a verdict yet?

The Foreman: No sir, we haven't.

The Court: Do not tell me how you stand for acquittal or conviction; tell me simply how you stand numerically.

The Foreman: Well, Judge, we have had one vote and I would say that it would be about five and ten and that would not be for sure because some said that they were not committing themselves.

The Court: Well, we have this problem. Under the law, you are required to stay together and experience has shown that if you go to a hotel to eat that it will take about an hour and a half or something like that.

I was just wondering . . . if you would like to deliberate until around 7:30 and then we will arrange for you to be set up over at the hotel and you can make your arrangements to spend the night and have your meal and resume your deliberations in the morning. Does that sound reasonable to you?

The Foreman: Well, it will take awhile for them to set up at the hotel and suppose we just wait in the Jury Room until they set up at the hotel and we can just use that time to deliberate.

The Court: All right, we will do that. If you haven't reached a verdict at that time, then we will just let you make arrangements to spend the night and to get your meal and to resume deliberations in the morning.

The Foreman: Can I ask you this? I think that a dictionary would be of some help if it were available to us.

The Court: Ordinarily not. There is no dictionary which has been introduced into evidence and you can resume your deliberations and we will let you know when arrangements are made.

[Later that afternoon, the jury returned to the courtroom.]

The Court: Mr. Foreman, are you still unable to make a verdict?

The Foreman: We haven't reached a verdict or close to it.

The Court: You are not close to it?

The Foreman: No, sir.

The Court: All right, arrangements have been made for whatever you want to have to eat at the hotel and arrangements have been made for rooms.

Now, if you will, be back in the morning after having your breakfast over there and be here in the Courtroom in this box over here at 9:00 o'clock in the morning. . . .

The Court [following a discussion with counsel off the record]: If any of you should want to pick up a magazine, is there a magazine counter over there? Is there any objection to them getting a newspaper from out of town? Does anybody have any objection to that?

[There being no objection, the hearing was then recessed and the jury went to the hotel. The next morning, March 23, 1972, the jury returned to the courtroom.]

The Court: All right, Gentlemen, if you will, go to your Jury Box and resume your deliberations.

[After a period of deliberations in the Jury Room, the jury returned to the courtroom.]

The Court: Mr. Foreman, do you have any communications that you would like to make?

The Foreman: Well, I think we have just finally reached it, Judge. I don't know if we stayed there 'til the 4th of July that we would get much further.

The Court: Has there been any change?

The Foreman: Yes, sir, it's 11 to 1.

The Court: Well, some jury is going to have to pass on this case.

The Foreman: We have tried very diligently to reach a decision and it just looks like that it is impossible. We will be glad to do whatever you wish us to do.

The Court: Well, try it a while longer and if you then find that you can't do it, we will have to re-evaluate it. At this time, I—would like to reiterate that I am not trying to force a verdict, but unless somebody has some deep abiding conviction that he cannot give up through reason and thinking, a verdict should be made because both the State and the Defendant wants this Jury to pass on this question.

The Foreman: I can't say that it would help any, but if it could be done, if you could—could you read the charge? It might help some; I don't know.

The Court: Is there any particular part that you are interested in?

The Foreman: I don't believe that it would be any particular part. We have tried to ascertain the particular question and haven't been able to get one.

The Court: I will be glad to do that if you think it would be helpful.

The Foreman: I don't know whether that would be in order or not. I thought that I would ask it.

The Court: Do you have copies of the code Section that you have requested?

The Foreman: That's correct, sir.

The Court: I can give you the whole charge again, but I don't know that that will help because—why don't you go back to your Jury Room and discuss any specific questions that you want to ask about the charge or whatever the law may be and then write out your request and I will tell if we can answer it.

The Foreman: All right.

[Following further deliberations, the jury returned to the courtroom.]

The Court: Mr. Foreman, have you been able to reach a verdict?

The Foreman: We have, Your Honor.

The Court: All right, Mrs. Gable, receive the verdict and publish it, please.

The Clerk: State versus Billy Jenkins. We, the Jury, find the Defendant guilty, this 23rd day of March, William M. Dorsey, Foreman.

Following the reading of the verdict, the judge promptly dismissed the jury. With little further ado, the judge then sentenced Billy Jenkins to twelve months probation and fined him $750.

A dinner and a good night's sleep at the local hotel, combined with a gentle, last minute nudge from the judge, appears to have done wonders.

Billy Jenkins appealed his conviction to the Georgia Supreme Court, claiming that the jury's determination that *Carnal Knowledge* was obscene was unsupported by the evidence, and that the Georgia obscenity law violated the First Amendment. In an opinion issued on July 2, 1973, the Georgia Supreme Court, over the dissent of three of its members, held that the evidence supported the verdict of guilty, that the Georgia obscenity law was constitutional, and that Jenkins's conviction would stand.

Jenkins then sought to have his conviction reviewed by the United States Supreme Court. In the fall of 1973 the Supreme Court agreed to hear Jenkins's appeal and set his case down for oral argument on April 15, 1974. The case, formally entitled *Billy Jenkins v. Georgia*, would soon become known as the *Carnal Knowledge* case.

It is hard to imagine a less enlightening Supreme Court oral argument than that which occurred in the *Carnal Knowledge* case. Louis Nizer, a famous and extraordinarily skilled lawyer from New York City, argued on behalf of Billy Jenkins. There is no evidence that he took his client's case for granted, though surely he was optimistic. *Carnal Knowledge* had been seen by millions of people and had met with great critical acclaim. But no lawyer who is experienced at oral argument before the Court, as Nizer surely was, would expect, much less be prepared for, near—indeed virtually dumb—silence from the bench. That is what he got.

Over the course of his presentation, Nizer was asked few questions, none of which really challenged his position that *Carnal Knowledge* was protected speech and not obscene, and most of which seemed more grudgingly obligatory than serious, asked as if in obeisance to an obligation to *appear* interested and engaged than genuinely to be so. Between the questions, which were bunched together at three points, Nizer was left to fill seemingly vast stretches of time with a monologue—a monologue that became increasingly difficult to sustain without repetition, and that strikes one upon reading it now as disturbingly directed at no one, as if the justices were not really listening but just biding time, tapping their fingers impatiently with one eye on the clock. As he sat down at the completion of his argument, Nizer must have felt disoriented, wondering why he had been left with a formalistic duty only, a duty, in effect, to spend half an hour talking to himself.

The lawyer who argued for the State of Georgia, Tony Hight, was the executive director of the District Attorneys Association of Georgia in Atlanta. His experience was similarly strange. His oral argument was marked by long periods of silence, perhaps even indifference, from the justices, only occasionally punctuated by questions focusing almost exclusively on technical, even arcane, procedural aspects of the Georgia jury and appellate procedure. Such matters, while largely incomprehensible, were not irrelevant to the case, but they hardly justified the Court's exclusive focus on them, a focus so dominant that virtually nothing was asked about the *constitutional* issues presented by the jury's finding that the film was obscene. On the constitutional issues Hight, like Nizer, was left to a monologue which, for him too, seems to have had no audience.

How can we account for the Court's utter, and apparently conscious, disinterest in the First Amendment speech issues raised by the Albany jury's decision? There can be only one answer to this question: the result in the case was obvious to the justices from the beginning; oral argument was a hollow ritual only, a duty imposed by tradition and carried out in form but not in substance. This would become clear later when the Court announced its decision in the case, a decision that would unanimously reverse Jenkins's conviction and declare that *Carnal Knowledge* was not obscene. The opinion would be written by Justice Rehnquist, the justice most likely, some would say, to sympathize with the State of Georgia.

But if the outcome was foreordained by the time of oral argument, why did it take until June 24, 1974, more than two months after oral argument and at the very end of the Court's term, for Justice Rehnquist to announce the opinion? Could it be that explaining the decision was more difficult than arriving at it? If so—and there is reason to think so based on reported accounts of Rehnquist's struggle to formulate his opinion—the explanation may lie in two knotty First Amendment matters that lay just beneath the surface of the case: (1) whether a work's *quality* can play a legitimate role in measuring the degree of its First Amendment protection, and (2) whether a work's *meaning* can be left to a jury as the interpretive voice of a community's social and cultural values.

Does the First Amendment Foreclose Judgments about Quality?

The explanation for the Court's apparent conviction from the very beginning that a tragic error had taken place in the Albany courtroom seems clear enough. *Carnal Knowledge* was not, after all, just *any* dirty movie. It was not *Sex Kittens*, one of those anonymous (and fictitious) stag films that inhabit seedy and decrepit theaters located on the wrong side of town. *Carnal Knowledge* played in five thousand theaters on Main Streets of virtually every American town, to a huge national audience. It received national attention and critical acclaim: reviewed by Vincent Canby in the *New York Times;* written about by Studs Terkel in the *Chicago Daily News* and George F. Will in the *Washington Post;* and nominated for an Academy Award. Its actors were not the nameless and invisible denizens of the pornography trade. They were instead Jack Nicholson, Candice Bergen, Art Garfunkel, Ann-Margret—famous actors and, more to the point, serious and accomplished artists.

Carnal Knowledge may not have been the full film equivalent of *Ulysses*, but it surely wasn't the equivalent of *Sex Kittens*. It was not a movie *of* sex, but one *about* sex: about the emptiness and ultimate destitution and self-destructiveness of sex *as sex;* about moral despair and decay.

We can safely assume that the justices knew much of this even as they gathered to vote on accepting the case for review, and we can be certain of it when, following oral argument, they gathered in their private conference room to discuss the case and cast their votes on Jenkins's fate. They had been repeatedly—indeed relentlessly—reminded of the film's stature in the briefs presented to them in the case. The Author's League of America, which was only one of the organizations that filed briefs *amicus curiae* (briefs submitted by interested groups that would be affected by the decision, as "friends of the Court"), quoted from a review of *Carnal Knowledge* that appeared on July 3, 1971, in the *Saturday Review:* "Not only is the film, overall, the best acted in years; it is also the most mature of all those American films that have attempted to deal with the subject of sex in these ultra-liberated cinematic times." "[A]ll of the reviewers" of the film, the brief stated, "considered, and evaluated, 'Carnal Knowledge' as a film of serious literary and artistic value." Another *amicus* brief was more direct, declaring it "inconceivable that a movie such as this—which many critics found to be one of the ten best of the year; which had a star (Ann-Margret) nominated for an Academy Award; and which scores of reviewers analyzed on a sophisticated level, debating the ideas and values which it contained — could be found to be without serious literary, artistic or political value." Yet another brief simply announced: "Twelve jurors bring no greater aesthetic expertise to 'Carnal Knowledge' than they would to 'Ulysses,' 'Waiting for Godot,' or 'Les Demoiselles D'Avignon.'"

Nizer, however, left no room for misunderstanding about the film's stature and quality, even at the late date of oral argument. And he didn't mince words in doing so.

> *Mr. Nizer:* Indeed, your honors, . . . it is unthinkable that this picture should be confused with hardcore pornography.
>
> The film depicts two college students over a span of about 30 years. They grow older but they don't grow up. They are preoccupied with sex. But the picture is not. It does not involve the senses with erotica, driving out all other ideas, which is the typical characteristic of hardcore pornography.
>
> On the contrary, it depicts the failure of the boys' lives, though they are successful in their professional careers, because they cannot establish meaningful relationships and they are ultimately crushed by boredom, loneliness and impotency.
>
> The film deals with the human predicament resulting from the enthronement of impersonal detachment, the inability to love and the sequelli of cruelty and psychic illness. And this artistic treatment of this problem which besets this decade has evoked many social and philosophical studies, has been the subject of plays from Strindberg to Tennessee Williams, and . . . is why the *New York Times* reviewer called it "profound" . . . and the *Catholic Film Newsletter*, despite some reservations, called it "a perceptive and brilliant put-down of a certain lifestyle." [T]he many critics throughout the country who have heaped similar praise upon this picture certainly could not have been fantasizing.
>
> The story in "Carnal Knowledge" predominates over any visual presentation. The greatest care was lavished on sets, lighting, camera effects, musical score, brilliant ensemble acting, all under the direction of [Mike] Nichols, acclaimed among the most gifted of cinemagraphic artists who synthesized the ancient arts of painting, writing, composing, acting in a new universal medium and the resulting dominant effect of the picture as a whole is a sincere and

earnest effort to create a literary and artistic work. *And to confuse that result with pornographic imbecility is cultural illiteracy."*

To confuse *Carnal Knowledge* with obscenity, *as the jury had,* "is cultural illiteracy." These are strong words, indeed. And they are no doubt true, too, depending, of course, on one's perspective.

But to confuse such baldly political sentiments with the makings of a Supreme Court opinion justifying the First Amendment's protection for *Carnal Knowledge* but the absence of such protection for *Sex Kittens*, is an altogether different matter; for *Sex Kittens* could likewise be characterized as a reflection on the moral destitution of sex "for its own sake," or the centrality of sexuality to life, even in a post-Victorian but still repressive social order. To be sure, *Sex Kittens* did not play on Main Street; it was not seen by twenty million people; its actors were not famous; its director was not acclaimed; its budget was not over $3 million; and it was certainly not seriously reviewed in all of the right places.

But can the size of the audience, or the fame of the actors, or the views of critics be employed as the indicia of "quality" for purposes of First Amendment? Can we afford to let them be so? *Sex Kittens* might have had a huge (though demographically different) audience, too. Its stars may be household names to millions of people. It, too, may have met with critical acclaim in its own critical quarters.

To rest judgments of quality on such factors is to choose not among films but among cultures. This is the dilemma in which the law of obscenity finds itself, even today.

The question can be put bluntly: Is it conceivable that the First Amendment's protection can be made to turn on the *quality* of expression rather than on the fact of its communication? To even entertain the idea that qualitative distinctions can be made, that good films deserve more protection than bad ones, would in some quarters be heresy. To expressly adopt it would be deeply inconsistent with many of the strongest currents of First Amendment jurisprudence. As Justice Harlan had declared in *Cohen v. California* just three years before the *Carnal Knowledge* case, "[T]he constitutional right of free expression" is designed "to remove governmental restraints from the arena of public discussion, putting the decision as to what views shall be voiced largely in the hands of each of us." Matters of taste and style, he continued, are left to the individual "largely because government officials cannot make principled distinctions in this area." Just as surely, placing matters of taste and style under the First Amendment in the hands of movie reviewers would be equally pernicious. What is important under the First Amendment, he said, is the "fact of communication."

In view of this, it may seem odd that the arguments made on behalf of Billy Jenkins and, through him, of *Carnal Knowledge*, were so explicitly couched in terms of quality, which in turn was made a matter of "cultural literacy." This was an unfortunate choice of words, but the rules the Court had created in the obscenity field may have left Nizer little alternative.

After years of huddling together in a small viewing room deep in the recesses of the Supreme Court Building, watching allegedly obscene movies whose legal fate had been left to the final, unreviewable aesthetic and cultural standards of "nine old men," the United States Supreme Court had at last managed, just a year before the *Carnal Knowledge* case, to delegate questions of "value" and community standards of taste in obscenity cases to the lowest reaches of the polity — to put the definition of culture squarely in the hands of the citizens who inhabit particular cities, towns, and communities.

The delegation was accomplished in a 1973 Supreme Court decision in *Miller v. California*. The *Miller* case involved the unsolicited mass mailing, by Miller, of advertising brochures containing pictures of men and women engaged in group sexual activities. Miller was convicted under California's obscenity law and appealed his conviction to the Supreme Court, claiming that the pictorial advertising brochures constituted speech protected by the First Amendment.

The Supreme Court's prior obscenity decisions had said that materials falling within the legal definition of "obscenity" did not qualify as speech and were therefore not protected by the First Amendment. But those earlier decisions had also left the Court, not the jury, with the ultimate responsibility in each case to determine whether the materials were, in fact, obscene. It was this ultimate responsibility that had obliged the justices in their darkened basement room to watch the dirty movies, read the dirty books, view the dirty magazines and, in Miller's case, to review the dirty, unsolicited, advertising brochures. By so doing, each justice was exercising his solemn constitutional duty to supervise the quality of aesthetic and political judgments rendered by juries throughout the United States.

As it turned out, the facts of the *Miller* case were not terribly important to the Court's decision in the case. This was because the Court had something very specific in mind when it decided to accept the *Miller* case for review. The Court's interest lay not in Miller's sleazy brochures but, instead, in announcing new rules for distinguishing obscenity from expression protected under the First Amendment, rules that would limit—indeed eliminate—the Court's obligation to supervise the jury's *qualitative* judgment by delegating virtually complete authority to the jury.

To this end, the Court's opinion in *Miller* announced a new definition of obscenity. Juries were thenceforth instructed by the Supreme Court to base their decisions on three questions:

1. whether, to "the average person, applying *contemporary community standards,* . . . the work taken as a whole appeals to the prurient interest";
2. "whether the work depicts or describes, *in a patently offensive way*, sexual conduct specifically defined by the applicable state law"; and
3. "whether the work, taken as a whole, lacks *serious* literary, artistic, political or scientific value" (emphasis added).

The jury would be required to answer each of these questions. And it could do so, as it did in Billy Jenkins's case, on the basis of no more evidence than the film itself. Thus, for the Albany jury the question was whether "to the average person applying contemporary community standards" of Albany, *Carnal Knowledge* appealed to the prurient interest; whether, to those citizens of Albany who were serving on the jury, it depicted sexual conduct in a patently offensive way; and whether, taken as a whole, the jurors in Albany judged it to lack *serious* literary, artistic, political, or scientific value. If the Albany jurors satisfied their constitutional obligation to answer these questions and rested their judgment about the movie's obscenity on those answers, that should be the end of the matter.

When it decided the *Miller* case and announced the *Miller* standard, the Supreme Court believed that it had finally extricated itself from what the Court had itself described as "the intractable obscenity problem." By setting the threshold of "quality" very low—only expression that, as a whole, *lacks* serious literary, artistic, political, or scientific value could be obscene—the factual findings of the jury could be made conclusively reliable, or at least nearly enough so that the Court would no longer have to review every jury decision and watch every dirty film. After all, even if juries cannot be trusted to make refined judgments about *how much* value a work has, or what *kind* of value it possesses, juries can surely be trusted to identify those works that "lack" value, even "serious" value.

So the Court thought, at least. With the value conundrum thus disposed of, the jury could be trusted to administer justice wisely, judging not a work's "value," itself, but its "lack" of seriousness. And the justices would thus be able to extricate themselves from their unseemly judicial gatherings before a small screen in the darkened basement room of the majestic Supreme Court Building, judging what they saw by their collective judicial sense of value. The small viewing room in the Supreme Court had been put out of business forever.

The difficulty that the *Carnal Knowledge* case posed for the Court's new test was not, however, the obvious one. It was not, in other words, that the Albany jury had set out to defy the critics, doing so by applying a standard of quality that was different from and greater than the minimum "lacks serious . . . value" criterion. While there can be little doubt that this was the *result* of the jury's decision—*Carnal Knowledge* was, after all, a critically acclaimed movie with an audience of twenty million people—it cannot be said that defiance of the critics was the reason for the jury's decision, because the Albany jury rested its judgment on the film alone, not on the critics' opinions of which, we must assume, the jury was unaware. More basically, the Court had made it clear in its *Miller* opinion that the larger context afforded by a film's national audience and critical acclaim could not serve as a ground for reversing the jury's decision, for evidence of such matters did not have to be presented to the jury, and in any event the jury was free to apply *its own* standards growing out of *its own* community.

Instead, the difficulty posed by the *Carnal Knowledge* case was that the Court had only a narrow frame in which to judge the film's obscenity. The question was not whether *this* jury had simply reached the wrong qualitative judgment but whether *a* jury, apprised of sufficient evidence (the film itself, in this case) and applying the three *Miller* standards, *could possibly* conclude that *Carnal Knowledge* lacked serious value. On *this* question the *Miller* definition had left the Court with no artillery at all, for the Court had not said that the question of value is one of law for the Court to decide, nor had the Court stated *any* criteria, except for the jury's three factual conclusions, by which such a question might be answered.

In view of this very limited, and highly abstracted, frame for decision, it is not surprising that the lawyers defending the film on appeal were so anxious to supply an answer to the "quality" question; it can be found, they said, in the budget, the producer, the actors, the audience, and, most troublingly, the critics. But the Supreme Court knew that to accept this answer was to reject the *Miller* test itself; to substitute the critics for the regular jury; to get itself once again into the obscenity business, this time applying not its own aesthetic judgment but its judgment about the aesthetic judgment of the film critics. To take this step would be to make a bad situation even worse by placing government judgments, troubling as they are under the First Amendment, in private hands.

The fact of the matter was that there were no standards by which the Court could override the Albany jury's decision about "value." If, as the Court had undeniably said in its long and agonizing line of decisions, movie to movie, over the course of its "moviegoing" days in the Supreme Court theater, the First Amendment forecloses making any distinctions based on the relative "quality" of *Carnal Knowledge* and *Sex Kittens*, both of which can be said to be commentaries on or representations of social disorder or the human condition, then how could the Court deny the possibility that a jury might reach the opposite result — that the "claimed" quality as a social commentary or cultural representation just wasn't there? Can it be that the First Amendment beknights the critics but not the members of the jury?

The *Carnal Knowledge* case had thus "cornered" the Court. The *qualitative* judgment implicit in the Albany jury's decision was essentially unreviewable. This is the reason Justice Rehnquist had such difficulty formulating an opinion for the Court. And this explains why, when he did finally issue his opinion, *nothing* was said about "quality" or "value" or even the wrongness of the jury's judgment on these questions.

But the Court could not escape the deeper problem of quality — the one going to the film's *meaning*, not to its goodness or badness — for it was firmly entrenched in the case. Indeed, it was embedded in the very function assigned to the jury in free speech cases, for quality is, fundamentally, a function of meaning, and *meaning* is assigned by the Court's *Miller* standard to the jury. Just as one cannot judge the quality of a photograph without seeing the photographic image, as opposed to witnessing the scene the photographer captured, so also one cannot judge the quality of a film without "seeing" it. And "seeing" a film, as opposed to simply viewing it, is an act of interpretation, of extracting meaning, significance, and perception from what is otherwise simply a descriptive and inchoate two-dimensional representation.

The danger presented by the jury's control over the fate of *Carnal Knowledge* was not, really, the jury's ability to decide whether the film was "good" or "bad" theater but, rather, the jury's ability to determine its *meaning*. Quality, in the sense of the film's goodness or badness, is utterly dependent on what the film is "seen" to be — its meaning. In Jenkins's case the jury was permitted by the *Miller* test, indeed practically required by it, to decide what the film meant in the community and culture of Albany, Georgia. And the jury served up a direct and unambiguous — *and practically unreviewable* — answer.

Quality as a Function of Meaning

And now look again, and see what will naturally follow if the prisoners are released and disabused of their error. At first, when any of them is liberated and compelled suddenly to stand up and turn his neck round and walk and look toward the light, he will suffer sharp pains; the glare will distress him, and he will be unable to see the realities of which in his former state he had seen the shadows; and then conceive some one saying to him, that what he saw before was an illusion, but that now, when he is approaching nearer to being and his eye is turned toward more real existence, he has a clearer vision — what will be his reply? And you may further imagine that his instructor is pointing to the objects as they pass and requiring him to name them — will he not be perplexed? Will he not fancy that the shadows which he formerly saw are truer than the objects which are now shown to him?

Far truer.

And if he is compelled to look straight at the light, will he not have a pain in his eyes which will make him turn away to take refuge in the objects of vision which he can see, and which he will conceive to be in reality clearer than the things which are now being shown to him?

True, he said.

And suppose once more, that he is reluctantly dragged up a steep and rugged ascent, and held fast until he is forced into the presence of the sun himself, is he not likely to be pained and irritated? When he approaches the light his eyes will be dazzled, and he will not be able to see anything at all of what are now called realities.

Not all in a moment, he said.

He will require to grow accustomed to the sight of the upper world. And first he will see the shadows best, next the reflections of men and other objects in the water, and then the objects themselves; then he will gaze upon the light of the moon and the stars and the spangled heaven; and he will see the sky and the stars by night better than the sun or the light of the sun by day?

Certainly.

Last of all he will be able to see the sun, and not mere reflections of him in the water, but he will see him in his own proper place, and not in another; and he will contemplate him as he is.

Certainly.

He will then proceed to argue that this is he who gives the season and the years, and is the guardian of all that is in the visible world, and in a certain way the cause of all things which he and his fellows have been accustomed to behold?

Clearly, he said, he would first see the sun and then reason about him.

And when he remembered his old habitation, and the wisdom of the den and his fellow-prisoners, do you not suppose that he would felicitate himself on the change, and pity them?

Certainly, he would.

And if they were in the habit of conferring honors among themselves on those who were quickest to observe the passing shadows and to remark which of them went before, and which followed after, and which were together; and who were therefore best able to draw conclusions as to the future, do you think that he would care for such honors and glories, or envy the possessors of them? Would he not say with Homer, "Better to be the poor servant of a poor master," and to endure anything, rather than think as they do and live after their manner?

Yes, he said, I think that he would rather suffer anything than entertain these false notions and live in this miserable manner.

—Plato, *The Myth of the Cave*

To summarize what has been said so far about the *Carnal Knowledge* case, we can state two relatively clear propositions. (1) Quality is not an admissible factor in the free speech equation. "One man's vulgarity," as Justice Harlan had aptly said in *Cohen v. California*, must be presumed for constitutional purposes to be "another man's lyric." (2) Meaning, however, is an altogether different thing than quality. It relates not to a film's goodness or badness but, rather, to its very identity, to what is seen or perceived.

Meaning is thus a precondition to the interpretive judgments of quality, for quality can be judged only in terms of the message conveyed, as Plato suggested, and identifying what message is conveyed is a question of *meaning*. Meaning, the Supreme Court implies, is to be judged in the polity, by the jury, and not in the elite sanctuary of the movie critic's review or the judge's chamber.

At first blush the two propositions about quality and meaning seem logically inconsistent. Quality and meaning, being interdependent, cannot be so easily isolated from one another. But perhaps on further reflection the logical problem can be solved. Quality is, the Court implies, a function of meaning, but not vice versa. Meaning, in other words, can first be assigned, and by so doing a smaller universe of possible interpretation is defined within which questions of quality can be judged (or not, as the case may be).

In some instances, then, "one man's vulgarity" *cannot be* "another man's lyric." The adage holds true only if both men are reading from the same script; if, that is, they are both reflecting on the quality of the same message. If not, if one sees a bird and the other a car, the "lyric" stems not from a different interpretation of the "vulgarity's" quality but from an altogether different message that contains no vulgarity. In such cases, differences of opinion are not based on different standards of taste but on the fact that altogether different scripts are being read, one in shadow, one in light.

This is precisely what happened in the *Carnal Knowledge* case — with the Court's blessing. Upon hearing the evidence and viewing the film, the jury was instructed, in effect, to "see" the film — to interpret it and give it meaning. The standard the jury was to bring to this task was that of the "community," which we can take to mean either (1) the values, habits, and culture of Albany, Georgia, or (2) the shared values, habits, and culture of the members of the jury, drawn from Albany.

The jury was instructed to "see" the film *Carnal Knowledge* through the standards of the community, to assign its *meaning* by superimposing the template of Albany's community standards and culture and value upon the screen, extracting the message, or meaning, from that which filtered through. The jury's template might, of course, have allowed a message of despair and meaningless of a life dominated by sex without love to show through. It might have revealed the same meaning when applied to *Sex Kittens*, as well.

But a different template of community standards, perhaps the one actually used by the *Carnal Knowledge* jury, may have been more constricting, allowing much less to be "seen" and thus narrowing the jury's range of possible interpretation. Such a template might have yielded a very different meaning, one that revealed little more than the excitement of sexual lust (punctuated, though without significance, by representations or spoken lines about despair); or one that legitimated sexual promiscuity (even though at the risk of boredom); or one that contained a message of male domination and female sexual subordination. This is the template, perhaps, of the community that had not been lifted from the cave to confront, and thus to "know," the new image revealed by the light of the sun.

With the meaning thus revealed by the template, the *Carnal Knowledge* jury was left to judge, *in light of its assigned meaning*, whether the film, *taken as a whole*, appealed to the prurient interest; whether it depicted in a patently offensive way sexual conduct specifically defined by Georgia law; and whether the film, *taken as a whole*, lacked *serious* literary, artistic, political, or scientific value. If for the Albany jury that judged *Carnal Knowledge* the template revealed a meaning equivalent to that conveyed by *Sex Kittens*, it is hardly surprising that *Carnal Knowledge* was judged to be obscene. More important, it would be virtually impossible to reverse the jury's decision without the Court's once again going into the movie business.

The Supreme Court was able to avoid this result and reverse Jenkins's conviction only by relying on a technicality. Obscenity, the Court said, must in all cases involve the depiction of sexual conduct, a term that the Court drew from the specific language of the *Miller* test and then took literally. In *Carnal Knowledge* much and varied sexual conduct was implied. Its concrete imagination could not be escaped. But the act of sexual intercourse, to state but one possible example, was not *literally* and explicitly depicted on the screen. No matter how powerful the film's evocation, how prurient its appeal, how offensive its content, how lacking its value, no film that stops short — just short, as we know from experience — of actual depiction of intercourse, the Court said, is obscene.

This is, surely, a technicality only, and an unconvincing one. It bears no sensible relationship to the community's standards or to the presence or absence of serious literary, artistic, political, or scientific value. It yields the incongruous — obscene seems a more fitting word, actually — result that *Sex Kittens*, if craftily filmed to avoid any frames showing the physical act of penetration, must be allowed to play in Albany, but *Carnal Knowledge*, if it contains but one such graphic sequence, need not. This peculiar result flies in the face of the very purpose of the *Miller* test. For this reason, if no other, it is small wonder that Justice Rehnquist had such apparent difficulty crafting the Court's opinion.

But if we set the technicality of the *Carnal Knowledge* opinion aside, the more basic questions raised by the Court's community-standards approach are clearly revealed. Why, we should ask, ought the question of *meaning* be left to the community? Are there no limits that can be practically enforced on the range of meanings that a community's template reveals?

The first question has many answers. Communities *do* have different standards born of different cultures, histories, aspirations, and values. Albany, Georgia, is very different from Albany, New York. Times Square is even different from Wall Street. Must the maintenance or destruction of those differences, many of which are valuable, be left only to market forces? Times Square wouldn't sell on Wall Street, which is why the two places are different. But if a foolish entrepreneur wants to try a little Times Square in Wall Street, must we let him do it?

We know from our experience that the same message often means different things in different places and to different people. Thus a rule that flatly protects all sexually explicit speech, for example, would not in fact be equal in its consequences. A rule that prohibited talk of fornication, for example, would affect a religious community differently than it would affect a community devoted to sexual liberation. Likewise, a rule that permitted all uses of a racial epithet would yield uneven results depending on who expressed it, how it was expressed, or whether it was used in a community of white supremacists, in an integrated community, or in the targeted racial community by members of that community toward one another.

No rule, in short, can be crafted in a way that assigns only one meaning, or even a range of meanings, unless exceptions to it are allowed.
Given this, the issue of the appropriate role of the jury, if any, boils down
to whether we must simply accept, in the name of the First Amendment,
a rule that all speech is absolutely protected notwithstanding the unfortunate but necessary fact that some of its meanings will surely produce
harm; or whether room may instead be left for exceptions in light of the
certainty of harm flowing from different meanings.

The first alternative, absolute protection for all speech, has never been
accepted by the Supreme Court, and it isn't likely to be adopted in the
foreseeable future. It is not, after all, a violation of the Constitution to
use zoning to keep adult movie theaters from setting up shop in residen-
tial neighborhoods; nor is government prohibited from restricting public
school classroom activities to education or from regulating the time and
manner of telemarketing in the interest of preserving our solitude. Even
Justice Hugo Black, the First Amendment "absolutist," left room for
government to regulate the speech activities that could take place in public libraries, or around courthouses, or in courtrooms.

So, absent a constitutional revolution we are left with the second
alternative: that some exceptions to the freedom to speak can be made in
recognition, among other things, of the differential harms that a given
instance of speech may produce in different times or places or communities. And this alternative leads us, finally, to the Court's solution in the
obscenity arena, for if exceptions can be made in recognition of differences in meaning and harm, we must ask: "Who will be assigned the
task of making them?"

The Court's answer in *Miller* was that exceptions should be crafted by
the jury and the community, not by the legislature, not by the judges, not
by the speakers, not by the invisible hand of the free market, and *certainly
not by the critics.* And the common-sense reason for selecting the jury
flows naturally from the recognition that harm, like quality, is a function
of meaning; that meaning is a product of interpretation; that only that
which can be seen can be interpreted; and that interpretation based on
shared values is preferable because it is more restrained than interpretation at the level of the individual, and in any event interpretation at the
community level is but a more finely tuned approximation of the exceptions that would be carved at the legislative, judicial, or executive levels.

If this be so—if, in other words, the Albany jury's decision was an
epistemological one, concerning what it saw and therefore knew, and

not a political one, concerning what it preferred—who but the jury and the community is better situated to judge the questions of meaning from which conclusions about value and harm spring? By what reasoning would we judge the Georgia legislature more able than a jury in Albany to ascertain the consequences *Carnal Knowledge* would produce in Albany, Georgia?

Surely the Supreme Court would not have reversed Billy Jenkins's conviction on a technicality if an alternative were available to it. But if we accept, as the Court did, the correctness of the jury's role in defining the template through which the film would be seen, we must confront the second question posed earlier: Is there any ground upon which the jury's range of discretion can be effectively limited?

At one level, of course, we know that there is. If the *Jenkins* case had involved *Ulysses* rather than *Carnal Knowledge*, few would doubt that the case involved something very different from *Sex Kittens*, and that a template yielding the same meaning for both is simply, because obviously, wrong, even in Albany, Georgia. This is the very point Mr. Nizer was making with his crude but effective charge of "cultural illiteracy." It is also the point that Justice Stewart made in 1964 in *Jacobellis v. Ohio* when he wrote, in obvious frustration, that while he couldn't define obscenity, "I know it when I see it"—to which he might have added with respect to *Carnal Knowledge*, as he did in *Jacobellis*, "and this case is not that!"

But knowing that the jury had gone too far, that the template was simply wrong, is an entirely different matter from explaining why that is so. The Supreme Court doesn't simply decide cases. It gives reasons for its decisions, reasons that relate to the purposes and principles of the Constitution, and reasons that provide guidance for the decision of future cases that might arise. So mere foot stomping won't do.

Some general limits that might be placed on the jury's authority are obvious. One of them is representativeness. If the jury is to make a value- and culture-based judgment for the community, it ought to reflect the community for which it speaks. The jury ought to know, also, whether the template it selects is being applied evenhandedly, and thus in pursuit of the community's standards, or whether the pattern of prosecution suggests selective enforcement. If the latter, something other than the community's values is at work, and the jury's template, no matter how appropriate, should not serve as a shield for other aims. These are enforceable, practical limits that could be judicially applied to limit the jury's power, but in the *Carnal Knowledge* case (where the second jury was all male, but racially diverse; and where the law enforcement effort was anything but discriminating or selective) they were of doubtful utility.

Another possibility for limiting the jury's discretion is to require that the jurors hear the judgment of the critics so that, even if they don't accept it, they are aware of the range of possible meanings the film has been given. Here, however, the problems are substantial. If the question is really one of the community's standards, how are the critics' interpretations relevant? If they are relevant only for comparative—for educational—purposes, can the jury's use of them be so limited? The danger, of course, is not that the jury will be swayed to the critics' view but exactly the opposite: that the jury's reaction to their testimony will cause a backlash, reinforcing the jurors' conviction that the everything-goes moral relativism of Times Square should at least be confined to Times Square and certainly not exported to Albany. This, of course, is the very reason that a defense lawyer in a case such as Jenkins's might decide that prudence is the better course. Nothing now prevents the defense from introducing such evidence, but requiring that it do so would be an unprecedented, and unwise, step.

So we are left with nothing more than "I know it when I see it . . . and this case is not that." There is precious little intellectual satisfaction in this ending. But it is the end of Billy Jenkins's story. His conviction was reversed, for which we can perhaps be grateful, but little was done in the course of his case about the still-intractable "obscenity problem."

Images

The Supreme Court has worked mightily to extricate itself from the movie business—from the rite of gathering together nine wise and well-educated men and women of the law in the darkened room in the basement of the Supreme Court. In this, at least, it seems to have succeeded, for the moment at least. The *Carnal Knowledge* case left the jury's power intact and virtually unreviewable, a necessary result if closing the Court's theater was the ultimate aim. But we are entitled to ask: "At what cost?"

Image One: Pornography as Subordination

Bellingham, Washington (Courtesy of the *New York Times,* November 26, 1995, sec. 1, p. 3):

Two decades after Justice Potter Stewart of the United States Supreme Court defined obscenity by saying, simply, "I know it when I see it," a pair of Washington shopkeepers will stand trial for seeing satire where prosecutors saw smut.

Ira Stohl, the owner of The Newsstand, a magazine shop and coffee bar here, and the shop's manager, Kristena Hjelsand, are scheduled for trial January 22 [1996] in Whatcom County Superior Court, charged with selling an issue of the alternative magazine "Answer Me," that graphically discussed rape. . . .

[T]he Whatcom County prosecutor, David S. McEachran, who brought the charges, said the rape issue of "Answer Me" was unacceptable to the majority of Bellingham's 20,000 citizens. He cited the issue of "Answer Me" that features stories of a rape from the rapist's perspective, a fictional account of a man torturing a girl with Down syndrome, photographs of decapitated crime victims and a pull-out section called "The Rape Game." . . .

The arrests have been a hot topic for nearly a year in this town, nestled between Mount Baker and Puget Sound [and home of Western Washington University]. . . .

[The] charges were born of an incident last January in which . . . an English major at Western Washington University . . . threatened a student boycott of The Newsstand unless its owners yanked the publication. The merchants did not budge. But when a criminal complaint was filed by the Women's Crisis Center—to which the students had also complained—and the case was referred to local prosecutors, the shop's owners stopped selling "Answer Me." In its place, they erected a shrine, of sorts, to free speech: a copy of the magazine bound in chains and padlock, with a sign that reads "not for sale." . . .

The case has . . . put feminist groups on the defensive and free speech activists in the spotlight.

Katy Casey, the executive director of the Whatcom County Women's Crisis Center, said: "It's not just offensive, it's destructive. It relates a glorified violence to sex. This magazine normalizes something we don't think is normal." . . .

Jim and Debbie Goad of Portland, Ore., who publish "Answer Me," say it is designed to shock. But rather than glorify violence, Mr. Goad said, the disputed issue of the magazine tried to offer as grisly a portrait of depravity as possible to underscore the horror of rape. "We present rape in all its ugliness," Mr. Goad said.

The magazine is described by its owners as having "a National Lampoon-style sensibility fused with a snuff-film esthetic."

Meaning is a function of culture, values, aspirations, and experience, derived through a process of interpretation. In "Foucault's Pendulum" Umberto Eco quotes (allegorically, I suspect) Elphias Levi, writing in 1856: "Allegory, mother of all dogmas, is the replacement of the seal by the hallmark, of reality by shadow; it is the falsehood of truth, and the truth of falsehood." Is there "truth" in the meaning of *Answer Me*? Is that truth, as Katy Casey would have it, "glorification of violence in sex"; the normalization of the abnormal; the representation of women and children as dominated sexual objects? Is the "truth," as Jim and Debbie Goad insist, the allegory itself, the depravity of satirizing "a grizzly portrait of . . . the horror of rape"? Is it the truth of falsehood, or the falsehood of truth? Or might both allegories be true because, for Katy Casey and for Jim and Debbie Goad, the true meaning of *Answer Me* is a function of what they see and therefore what they know?

If, in pondering these questions, we conclude that the only "truth" *is* allegory and that because there are many possible allegories, there are many truths, must we then also conclude that all allegories must be admitted to the marketplace? Or might we conclude instead that since there is no *real* truth but only allegory, we violate no truth by selecting the preferred allegory and rejecting the others?

The jury's template is its preferred allegory, grounded in the collective preferences and values and aspirations and norms of the community: Albany, Georgia; Bellingham, Washington; intellectuals; parents; feminists. Feminists do not see the pornographic representation of women as dominated sex objects as a political statement. They instead see pornography as an allegory, a template through which the values and aspirations of the audience are shaped, through which the community's preferred norms of family, decency, and equality are wrested from it. For them, the template that reveals women as dominated sex objects is not theirs or the community's. It is instead the knowledge that comes from being forced to see the light. The First Amendment, they argue, should not be read to prohibit the community's insistence on *its own* template, its own allegory, its own epistemology. The *political* fight about the rightness of the community's template — are we a community of dominance or peace, equality or violent submission—can take place in the open, free, and reasoned marketplace of argument. To consign the argument to allegory is unnecessary and, more important, dangerous.

For many, the feminists' view is little more than foolishness; an unprecedented division of freedom of speech into separate camps of reason and emotion, argument and allegory; and an unjustified fear of the power of stories to move us, unconsciously and therefore surreptitiously, to adopt attitudes that we would not, under the civilizing influence of reason, consciously embrace.

But for others, the feminists' view has the ring of truth to it: we raise our children on those allegories that teach the right lessons; we distinguish conduct, which is often emotion incarnate, from the more dispassionate and reasoned forms of speech; our institutions—schools, libraries, businesses, governments—are large allegories of civilization. Prohibiting *Answer Me* in Bellingham, Washington, or *Carnal Knowledge* in Albany, Georgia, is not an act of censorship but, instead, one of authority over the preferred allegory, a claim of right to the image we see rather than the image others would force us to see.

Many devotees of the First Amendment, of course, would view the matter very differently. For them, rejection of the Albany jury's verdict is a necessary step in the struggle against ignorance. After all, to borrow from Plato's allegory, wasn't it to *make* them "see the light" that people were forced from the cave? And after they were acclimated to the light and beheld its new wonders—after they saw the objects of which they had formerly seen only the shadows—didn't the people reflect on their fellows who were still in the cave, and "pity them," preferring "to endure anything, rather than think as they do and love after their manner"?

But Plato's allegory is neither as simple nor as comforting as this view of the First-Amendment-as-Light would have it, for it turns out that lightness and darkness are epistemologically the same, opposite sides of the same coin, so to speak, neither superior to the other. While revealing new images to the people who emerged from the cave, the light also blinded them to what they had seen before. For Plato, light and dark represent the falsehood of truth, and the truth of falsehood, a closed circle revealed at his *Myth of the Cave*'s end:

> Imagine once more, I said, such a one coming suddenly out of the sun to be replaced in his old situation; would he not be certain to have his eyes full of darkness?

To be sure, he said.

And if there were a contest, and he had to compete in measuring the shadows with the prisoners who had never moved out of the den, while his sight was still weak, and before his eyes had become steady (and the time which would be needed to acquire this new habit of sight might be very considerable), would he not be ridiculous? Men would say of him that up he went and down he came without his eyes; and that it was better not even to think of ascending; and if any one tried to loose another and lead him up to the light, let them only catch the offender, and they would put him to death.

No question, he said.

If we can understand the disturbing allegory of sexual violence and domination in Bellingham, Washington, and the felt need to block it out, is it such a stretch to understand the allegory of *Sex Kittens* in the jury's interpretation of *Carnal Knowledge*? If the template used by the jury in the *Carnal Knowledge* case is a true reflection of values of mannerliness, propriety, religiosity, and order, can we deny the good-faith intention of the jury in Albany, Georgia, to guard its template from subversion by a competing allegory the meaning of which *its* template would distort?

Perhaps not. Perhaps, when it comes to speech, templates should be inadmissible. But even if this is so, we can at least hope that the template used by the Albany jury was truly based on decency, respect, love, for if by 1972 this had become the preferred allegory in Albany, we might conclude that its soul had at last been transformed.

Image Two: The V-chip and Family Values

In January of 1996 President Clinton, with Vice President Gore at his side, stood in the Great Hall of the Library of Congress, a national symbol of free and open inquiry. On this elaborately staged occasion the president signed the Telecommunications Act of 1996, a central component of which is the V-chip, a small computer chip that had come to symbolize the family-and-cultural-values high ground.

The Telecommunications Act requires that V-chips be installed in every new television set, thus enabling parents (or anyone else, for that matter) to control in advance the kind of programming they will receive. According to the president, the V-chip will permit parents (with a little help from broadcasters and program producers, who must encode a rating for violence and sexual content in their programming) to regain control once again of their children's television viewing habits by impressing their own template of values and culture on the meanings that are admitted to their television screen. In this moment of political obeisance to family values, a strengthened commitment to community, and morality, the president's comments seemed eerily reminiscent of the sentiments expressed by the Supreme Court in *Miller.*

But the idea embodied in the V-chip is very different from that reflected in the Court's obscenity jurisprudence. It may at one and the same time be better *and* worse, for in successfully delegating authority over culture and value *beyond* the community, to the individual, it may jeopardize both the First Amendment and community.

For those who resist the very idea of obscenity out of faith in individual freedom and distrust of community standards, the V-chip signifies nothing less than another effort to introduce prejudice and narrow-mindedness into the First Amendment, to reinstall censorship but at an even lower and less visible level. Is legally sponsored private censorship better simply because it is hidden from view? Is it somehow not censorship because, being programmed in advance, the V-chip does not require the "censor" to choose what should be watched? Is the V-chip more benign because it is an epistemological rather than a political tool, reflecting the choice of those who remained in Plato's cave, "pitying" the one who was blinded by the light?

For those who support the Court's effort in the *Miller* case out of a belief that culture and meaning must be located in communities, the V-chip signifies something equally bad. Our society's problems, they would say, are cultural, not individual; only through cultural norms and values can our baser instincts be civilized. The V-chip, in profound contrast, rests on the oxymoronic assumption that culture can be atomized, preserved at the level of the individual. Such a view deprives the term "culture" of all meaning. To allow everyone the freedom to see the light and then return to the shadows in the cave would surely destroy the culture of the cave.

In the end, the V-chip represents nothing less than a legitimation of censorship, but at such a discrete and individualized level that its consequences approach libertarianism. Censorship and libertarianism are strange bedfellows, indeed.

The *New York Times* story also reported that Bellingham residents whose tastes run to "unabashedly hard-core" pornography need walk only two short blocks beyond The Newsstand to Great Northern Books, the local dirty-book store, where the smut is unsullied by avant-garde and intellectual fare.

Business is thriving.

They don't sell *Answer Me* there.

ADDITIONAL READING

Catharine A. MacKinnon, "Pornography, Civil Rights, and Speech," 20 *Harvard Civil Rights/Civil Liberties Law Review* 1 (1985).

Catharine A. MacKinnon, *Feminism Unmodified* (1987).

Report of the Attorney General's Commission on Pornography (1986).

Nadine Strossen, *Defending Pornography: Free Speech, Sex, and the Fight for Women's Rights* (1995).

Miller v. California, 413 U.S. 15 (1973).

PART 3

The Audience

Speech consists of three parts: a speaker, a message, and a receiver. We now turn our attention to the third part of the trilogy, the receiver. In this age of exploding forms of communication there is really no good, single term to describe the recipient of a communication — we read, we hear, we feel, we visualize, we imagine, singly and in every combination. Yet the term "receiver" seems both cumbersome and impersonal. So I will use the admittedly inaccurate but common term "audience" to describe the many roles in which we find ourselves on the receiving end of the communication process.

We will consider the relationship of the audience to the freedom of speech through two stories that deal with two aspects of the audience's role. In the first story, "The Pharmacist," we will explore the ways in which audiences give meaning and significance to speech; the ways in which audiences define the speech that is being received and bring it to life through their resulting action. As we will see, the audience's interpretation of speech can often be surprising, even to the speaker. Audiences can be obstinate, as anyone in the advertising business will freely admit. What role, if any, should the audience play in deciding whether speech has taken place, especially when the audience's interpretation follows a script different from that intended by the speaker? Should the First Amendment protect the advertiser as a speaker, or the audience as a frustratingly independent receiver of speech?

In the second, "The Medium and the Message," we will probe the mysteries of mediums of speech, the various channels through which audiences receive speech. Many of us are still creatures of the print-based culture; we indulge the old-fashioned habit of reading books and magazines and poetry and newspapers. The more modern of us increasingly rely on the newer counterparts of print, such as e-mail, Internet "conversations," and "surfing" for text-based information on the new "superhighway."

Whether the medium is the book, the poem, the newspaper, or e-mail, however, the exercise is fundamentally the same, based in the abstract yet, as Marshall McLuhan observed, also "cool" and more personal medium of text. In the print medium the author is an abstraction whom we neither see nor know. As readers, therefore, our job is to break down the message as it is given us in its stark, single-sensory form and then to fill in the gaps, to internalize it, transforming it from the work of another to our own work. We, as readers, become the author, infusing the text with our experiences, our analysis, our emotion, our imagination, and ultimately our passion. We thus transform the most apparently dispassionate medium into the most personal and passionate medium. This personal involvement and transformation is what McLuhan meant when he called a medium "cool."

Today, however, we increasingly communicate through many, not just one or two, senses; through combinations of aural, visual, and tactile stimuli. We communicate in "high definition" with pictures and words and sound rather than with words alone; with photographic image rather than abstract representation—we lack, in other words, the gaps or voids that we fill with our own experiences, perceptions, imagination, and passion. And we communicate in "real time," without the opportunity to gain perspective and frames of personal reference that the dimensions of time and space have traditionally afforded us in the largely after-the-fact mediums of the printed word, the photograph, or, earlier, the oral tradition.

In this multisensory world of television and cable and satellite and instant communication we become less the judge than the participant, less the object than the subject and the verb. We have more data yet less capacity for understanding. In this world, ironically, we are at once more impassioned yet less passionate, more physically and emotionally involved yet our relation to what we see is strangely impersonal. The *events* in which we participate become the author, not us. This is what McLuhan described as a "hot" medium, a place where by involving ourselves we give up our self.

The new media engage our senses and erase space and time from our comprehension, making us participate in rather than reflect upon and internalize what we see and hear and feel, spectators connected to events in strangely abstract and impersonal ways, as if in an out-of-body experience. Do these kinds of changes in the way we communicate transform our understanding of speech? Do they make the ideas of speakers and

speech deeply ambiguous? Is the speaker the producer, the camera operator, the organization that constructs the medium in sensory and time
and space ways, or even the event itself? Do these changes alter also the
influence and role of the audience, requiring that we greet with considerable skepticism the claim that the audience is a significant actor in the
speech transaction?

These are complex and subtle, perhaps also unanswerable, questions.
But as we enter what many have called the new telecommunication age
with its marvels of technology, its threatening uncertainties, and its risks
of monopolization and control of the channels of communication, where
the power of a medium may be as important as the content of a message,
they are important questions that must be asked, if not fully answered.

We begin the inquiry with a discussion of the mysteries of advertising
in "The Pharmacist." It was through advertising, after all, that the
power of medium was first discovered.

The Pharmacist: Speech and Its Consumers

(Virginia State Board of Pharmacy v. Virginia Citizens Consumer Council, 425 U.S. 748 (1976))

Introductory Note

The role of the audience under the First Amendment is a subject that has already been touched upon but not directly confronted in many of the earlier stories. It was raised in a glancing way in the first story, "The Jacket," where Justice Harlan addressed the conflict between Paul Cohen's right to wear a jacket in the courthouse emblazoned with the words "Fuck the Draft," on the one hand, and the offense the message could engender in those who saw the jacket, on the other. The role of the audience was raised more directly, although narrowly, in "The Author," where we surmised that, especially with fiction, meaning and characters come to life largely, and often idiosyncratically, in the mind of the reader, not in the mind of the author or in the text. And in "The Artist" we explored the nature of "meaning" as supplied by the Albany, Georgia, jury for the movie *Carnal Knowledge* and by the Whatcom County Women's Crisis Center for the magazine *Answer Me.*

We now turn our attention directly to the role played by the audience—the readers, listeners, viewers, bystanders—under the First Amendment. The audience's role is a critical one, for speech is a process, not an isolated act. Speech involves a *speaker*, a *message*, and an *audience* to which the speaker's message is transmitted. Without the audience the idea of speech would be stillborn, for the text would have no interpersonal or social significance.

It is this interpersonal and social significance of speech that will occupy us as we explore the function played by the audience under the First Amendment. We will ask two questions:

First, should the meaning and significance given to speech by the audience be the controlling one, even when the audience's interpretation differs from the speaker's or even from the "plain" meaning of the text? If, for example, I hold out a tin cup to beg for money because I need it, but those who see me find in my plea a message of social despair, is my act of begging one of speaking, and if so what message should I be understood to be communicating for purposes of the First Amendment? Just who, in short, is doing the speaking?

Second, what role should the interpersonal and social function of my speech play in measuring the amount of First Amendment protection that should be accorded it? If, for example, the interpersonal and social value of begging is judged to be minimal and thus warrants little protection under the First Amendment, but the message of social despair reflected in my act is judged to be of great value to a free, compassionate, and self-governing people and thus to be entitled to substantial protection under the First Amendment, do we elect to use but one, or both, values in our constitutional calculus?

There are many fascinating stories that could be used to explore these important questions, stories about burning draft cards, desecrating flags, camping out in Lafayette Square across from the White House. Our story, however, involves the more universal and peculiarly American figure of the "Ad Man." When the Ad Man speaks, who is in control, the Ad Man or we? This is a question, the Supreme Court tells us, of First Amendment protection for "commercial speech"—speech that does no more than propose a commercial transaction.

The Pharmacist

Do consumers have a constitutional right to price advertising?

The question arose in the early 1970s when a public interest organization, the Virginia Citizens Consumer Council, challenged a rule of the Virginia State Board of Pharmacy that prohibited pharmacists from advertising the price of prescription drugs and thus engaging in price competition. Most of the pharmacists, we may safely assume, were happy with the rule against price advertising, especially the local pharmacists who undoubtedly feared competition from the larger discount pharmacies. For them life was comfortable and profitable, in a market defined solely by convenience, service, and the personal touch, unimpeded by the distorting influence of price competition.

The Virginia Citizens Consumer Council, of course, disagreed, believing that price advertising and competition would drive prices down and thus serve the consumers' pocketbook interests. In a forerunner of the wars now ongoing with Wal-Mart in cities throughout the country, the Consumer Council brought a lawsuit, arguing that lower prices were not inconsistent with personal service, and that in any event if personal service were important to the consumer, he or she would be willing *knowingly* to pay a higher price for it.

When the *Virginia Pharmacy* case arrived at the Supreme Court, it took the form of a First Amendment claim. In an interesting twist of irony, the claim was that the pharmacists, most of whom preferred not to advertise, had a First Amendment right — possibly even an obligation — to do so. The pharmacists, in short, were left to argue *against* their own freedom. But they could not even do this, for they were nowhere to be found in the case. It was the consumers' case, and the pharmacists were not parties to it.

Perhaps because of this ironic twist, the First Amendment focus quickly shifted to the audience — to the consumers of prescription drugs who claimed a constitutional interest in receiving the speech that was to be communicated by the unrepresented and not altogether willing pharmacists. It shifted, in other words, to the audience; to its interpretation and use of a message, and to when, if ever, a message's value to an audience can transform a speaker's different and inconsequential message into something of much greater constitutional significance. Is "a rose by any other name but a rose," for purposes of the First Amendment, or can it be more?

The story will be told through the edited transcript of oral argument in the case, elaborated at points with discussion of the issues and controversies that emerge in the course of the colloquies among the justices and with the lawyers. The oral argument, as we shall see, involved much higher stakes than price advertising for prescription drugs in Virginia.

But first, some necessary background.

The tradition of government regulation of advertising and other competitive practices by pharmacists, like opticians, doctors, lawyers, accountants, and a host of other professions and businesses, can be traced at least to the Progressive Era at the turn of the century. Beginning then and continuing to this day such regulation has been enacted pervasively at both the state and federal levels. This is, after all, the "stuff" of modern government, ranging from antitrust regulation, truth in advertising, occupational safety, consumer safety, environmental protection, affirmative action, harassment in the workplace, and on and on.

For a time at the dawn of this new era the Supreme Court attempted to curb the progressive appetite for intrusive regulation of the economy. It did so under the mantle of the due process clauses of the Fifth and Fourteenth Amendments, reasoning that private enterprise must be granted the liberty to use its own devices to achieve productive economic results, even if those devices included excessive hours and unhealthy working conditions, child labor, even monopoly.

But all of that came to an abrupt end after the Great Depression, when the Court switched course, concluding that the Constitution of the United States, as Justice Oliver Wendell Holmes, Jr., put it in his famous 1905 dissent in *Lochner v. New York*, "does not enact Mr. Herbert Spencer's Social Statics." The Court thus freed governments, state and federal alike, from the heavy constraints of the due process clauses, allowing government pervasively to regulate the economy in pursuit of new visions of the public interest — and to do so even for reasons that might be widely thought to be silly and to border on the irrational. Due process no longer functioned as any real constraint on the insatiable appetite for regulation.

It was in this new and freer environment that the State of Virginia, like most others, enacted a broad range of regulations limiting working hours, prohibiting child labor, setting minimum wages, and controlling monopolistic and anticompetitive practices. Along with these commendable advances in the role of government in the economy came some others that might not be seen in such a positive light. Virginia's limitation on price advertising of prescription drugs is an example. It was enacted in 1969 as part of a regulatory scheme that licensed, and thus controlled entry into, the pharmacy business, and that might be said to protect the "club" of pharmacists as much, if not more, than the consumer.

Without price competition, profits could be assured and business could be easy. Of course, such a comfortable and profitable life could be endangered if too many people caught on and decided to become pharmacists. But this risk was disposed of by the power to license, and therefore limit, those who could practice the trade. Virginia decided to place this power squarely in hands that could best wield it to their advantage: the pharmacists themselves.

One might describe Virginia's regulatory scheme for pharmacists as bad public policy, silly economics, even as pure protectionism cynically cloaked in the garb of the "public interest," but none of these descriptions, even if wholly accurate and provable, made it unconstitutional. Silliness and untoward motives, the Supreme Court had firmly concluded, were the exclusive province of the elected democratic process. As Justice Holmes put it in his *Lochner* dissent, "a constitution is not intended to embody a particular economic theory, whether of paternalism and the organic relation of citizen to the State or of laissez faire. It is made for people of fundamentally differing views."

In view of the Supreme Court's wholesale retreat from judging the constitutionality of state legislation under the due process guarantees, the Virginia Consumer Council was obliged to rest its challenge to the pharmacist advertising ban on different constitutional grounds. It picked the First Amendment. This was not an obvious choice, for the Court had said in 1942 in *Valentine v. Chrestensen*, during the course of its wholesale retreat from judging the constitutionality of state economic regulation, that the First Amendment placed no "restraint on government as respects purely commercial advertising." And there could be little doubt that advertising the price of prescription drugs was, for pharmacists, "wholly commercial advertising." But that earlier case was old, it was virtually the Court's only statement on the subject, and much water had passed over the First Amendment dam in the intervening years.

The Consumer Council's First Amendment theory faced two major obstacles. First, the Court had to be convinced that its earlier, 1942 decision could be distinguished from the Virginia case, or that it should be overruled. In this the council had been helped by a case decided just one year earlier and that also arose in Virginia. That case, *Bigelow v. Virginia*, involved a Virginia law that prohibited the publication of advertisements for abortions performed in other states where abortion was legal. The Supreme Court declared the Virginia statute unconstitutional, even though abortion was illegal in Virginia at the time, because it restricted speech protected by the First Amendment.

The speech that Virginia had attempted to regulate in the *Bigelow* case was clearly advertising, and thus the Virginia Consumer Council could take some comfort in the Court's earlier decision as it planned its challenge to the pharmacy law. But the *Bigelow* case had been decided on the heels of the Court's abortion decision in *Roe v. Wade*, and the abortion problem was then, as it remains today, unique. Whether the First Amendment's protection for a legal abortion advertisement, which clearly involved a matter of considerable public importance and controversy, would carry over to "purely commercial advertising" of drug prices by pharmacists was far from obvious.

The second obstacle faced by the Consumer Council was more funda-mental, going to the heart of the First Amendment speech guarantee: just whose speech was to be protected? If the speech claim rested on the pharmacist's freedom of expression the case might fall apart, for no pharmacist was claiming any right to speak. And even if a pharmacist could be found to make such a claim, the claim would rest on an asserted First Amendment freedom to do no more than propose a com-mercial transaction — to advance purely economic interests by undercut-ting the price of other competitors in the commercial marketplace. This was hardly the lofty stuff of the First Amendment. There was, after all, more than a grain of truth in the Court's earlier statement that "purely commercial advertising" possesses little of value for purposes of the First Amendment.

In any event, the council's interest was in the consumers — the audi-ence for the advertisement — and *their* freedom to have and make use of the price information as *they* saw fit. This interest, of course, had little if anything to do with the pharmacist's motive in advertising. More funda-mentally, if the council based its First Amendment claim on the "rights" of the consumers, not the pharmacist — on the rights of the audience, not the speaker — where did that leave the pharmacist, who after all *was* the one speaking and on whose speech the interests of the audience depended?

Were the First Amendment tables to be turned from the *Cohen v. Cal-ifornia* case decided just four years earlier? Was the audience, not the speaker, to be placed in control, with the speaker becoming little more than an instrument for the needs and preferences of the audience? Was the audience to be placed in control of the message itself (the price advertisement is no longer simply one means of commercial competition but now useful information upon which people can base their economic decisions in the free market); in control of its value (not higher sales but greater public choice); and ultimately in control of the speaker? If the audience has a First Amendment right to information, can it not claim a right to force someone to provide the information, even if he or she does not want to give it?

The audience, it seems, poses some serious problems for the First Amend-ment if it is brought fully into the speech equation. And these problems were not lost on the Supreme Court, as oral argument in the *Virginia Pharmacy* case revealed.

The Court that gathered for oral argument on Tuesday afternoon, November 11, 1975, was not much changed from the Court that decided Paul Cohen's case just four years earlier. But while few in number, the changes were notable.

Justice Harlan, who had written the *Cohen* opinion, had retired in 1971 and died shortly thereafter. Justice Hugo Black, the First Amendment absolutist ("No law means *No* Law!"), had also retired and died the same year. These two great justices had been replaced by Lewis F. Powell and William H. Rehnquist. Powell was a Virginian and a patrician who would come to be compared with Justice Harlan for the craftsmanship and balance of his decisions, and who would often cast the deciding vote on a divided Court for the next twenty or so years. Rehnquist had been appointed from within the Nixon administration. His conservative credentials had been won in Arizona politics. He was a man of conservative beliefs and considerable kindness and humanity. By and large, however, he reserved his humanity for after-work hours, for his job was not to evoke Scripture but to interpret the Constitution, a decidedly dispassionate and utilitarian text with a very specific history and a limited range of meaning. Rehnquist, of course, was to become chief justice some ten years later.

This was a Court now firmly in transition. A conservative block of justices was forming, but it would be more than twenty years before it became dominant. In the meantime the Court would remain divided (and occasionally divisive), with shifting coalitions holding the Court firmly to the middle path. But this Court was not incapable of breaking from the past, setting out in new and important constitutional directions. The *Virginia Pharmacy* case would prove that.

The lawyers who stood at the front of the Court beneath the *banc* as the justices entered were both able and experienced advocates. Anthony F. Troy, of Richmond, was the chief deputy attorney general of Virginia. His duty was to defend the Virginia rule prohibiting price advertising by pharmacists. Alan B. Morrison was a public interest lawyer from Washington, D.C. He had argued before the Supreme Court on many occasions, representing the clients and causes his public interest law organization supported. Troy and Morrison were both aware that the Virginia case was very important and potentially groundbreaking—and that the issues the case presented were difficult, complex, subtle, and far-reaching.

At precisely 1:27 P.M. Troy rose and approached the podium beneath the *banc*, surveying the nine justices before him behind the elevated bench.

> *Mr. Chief Justice Burger:* We will hear arguments next in No. 74-895, Virginia State Board of Pharmacy against Virginia Citizens Consumer Council, et al. Mr. Troy.
>
> *Mr. Troy:* Mr. Chief Justice and may it please the Court. It has been traditional that the practice of professions are to be above the morals of the marketplace. This case presents the question of whether the practice of pharmacy and the disposing of drugs should be subject to the morals of the marketplace.
>
> Should prescription drugs be advertised?
>
> The concerns of this case, however, are not only in the professional pharmacy but, rather, in each and every profession: law, medicine, optometry, dentistry, and any other profession controlled by the State.
>
> The true question, then, is the ability of a legislature to regulate these professionals within the economic and social policies deemed provident.
>
> *Question:* Mr. Troy, let me get this straight out. How do you define a profession?
>
> *Mr. Troy:* Your Honor, the General Assembly has defined this profession. It has defined it within the framework of what has traditionally been defined as a profession: a learned profession, a requirement of a degree, a requirement of some protection to the health, safety, and welfare of the people. And in this case it has been shown, not only by the statute but in the record itself [evidence presented at trial], that the pharmacist is the last professional who interposes himself between a patient and a drug.
>
> He has a vital role in the medical health team.
>
> A pharmacist, in dispensing drugs, is doing more than I, as a layman, would comprehend. The entire educational training of a pharmacist is geared to impart to him a knowledge greater than a physician as relates to drugs, their chemical composition and their reactions, contraindications or synergistic effects of such chemical elements.
>
> *Question:* Well, if that is the case, why doesn't he write prescriptions?
>
> *Mr. Troy:* I'm sorry, your Honor?

Question: If that is the case, why doesn't he write prescriptions?

Mr. Troy: The reason that he doesn't write prescriptions, of course, is that his education is to the extent of knowing the chemical elements of drugs and their contraindications.

The doctor, of course, is the one that knows what the therapeutic effect of these drugs is for the particular disease.

Question: And their contraindications.

Mr. Troy: And their contraindications in some cases.

Question: In some cases?

Mr. Troy: In some cases, yes, your Honor, because . . . pharmacists do keep medical profile records containing a patient's allergies, sensitivities, or reactions to drugs.

Question: What happens if somebody gives a prescription to their butler and tells him to go over and get it filled?

Mr. Troy: Under the medical profile records that a pharmacist would have, your Honor, the prescription, of course, would be written in the name of the individual, the record would be in the name of the individual. The pharmacist, by looking at the record and comparing the prescription about to be filled, could tell if there would be any side effects.

Question: Mr. Troy, you have mentioned the importance of druggists compounding drugs. As I understand [it], 95 percent of the drugs dispensed do not require compounding by the druggist.

Mr. Troy: That is exactly correct, your Honor, and it could be even a little more, but the point is . . . that today as compared to prior years when druggists used to compound drugs, today we are talking about drugs that have a benefit of curing rather than just a palliative effect. . . . While they have the benefit of curing, [they] also have the ability to do great harm.

In his opening statement and his early responses, Troy had succeeded in doing two things. First, he cast the Virginia advertising restriction as part of a general scheme for regulating the profession of pharmacy; he emphasized the important role played by the pharmacist, and, most important, he portrayed the regulation as but one aspect of the state's admitted power to regulate economic activities in the interest of the health, safety, and welfare of citizens. It was this broad power that the Supreme Court had largely abdicated to state governments in the post-depression era, and Troy wanted the Court to see the Virginia case as one that would require the

Court, were it to strike the regulation down, to reverse its course once again and entertain challenges to all measure of state regulation of business and economic activity. This, of course, the Court would not do.

Second, Troy succeeded in upping the stakes in the *Virginia Pharmacy* case by placing the challenged regulation alongside those imposed on the other professions. Deciding this case in favor the of the Consumer Council, in other words, would open a Pandora's box of challenges to the licensing and conduct, including advertising, of lawyers, doctors, dentists, optometrists—even opticians, veterinarians, barbers and beauticians, and so on and so on.

Troy, of course, knew that this strategy, as important as it was for placing the case in a perspective, would not succeed for long in diverting the Court's attention from the First Amendment. And it didn't.

> *Question:* Mr. Troy, may I ask, I don't quite understand how this argument addresses the question that you presented, whether or not . . . the prohibition of price advertising is a violation of the First Amendment. Is that the issue we have?
>
> I thought the question you gave us was whether or not commercial advertising had First Amendment protection.
>
> *Mr. Troy:* Yes, your Honor, and this is the connection. The statute here is a measure addressed to the public health. It is, as Mr. Justice Stewart [said in an earlier due process opinion] "within the most traditional concept of what is compendiously known as the [state's] police power" [the power to regulate economic activity in the interests of public health, safety and welfare].
>
> The lower court paid lip service only to the [Court's due process decisions] and found that this was not a [due process] case but rather, was a First Amendment case because it violated the consumers' right to know.
>
> *Question:* And you disagree with that?
>
> *Mr. Troy:* Yes, your Honor, for this reason. . . . Somehow [the lower court] reasoned that approaching this case from a consumer viewpoint would not be an intrusion upon the State's regulation of pharmacists.
>
> I suggest that the court's decision is analytically unsound. It has set at war the First and Fourteenth Amendments.
>
> How can there be a constitutional right to receive information which the State has a legitimate and constitutional right under the

Fourteenth Amendment in prohibiting the dissemination of that very same information?

There can only be two answers. One, that the right to know is a concomitant right. It is not an independent right which would allow access to any information, commercial or otherwise, which perhaps has an economic impact on the consuming public.

The second answer is that an independent constitutional right would exist and consequently, if so, [this Court's due process cases granting the state broad authority to regulate economic and business affairs] must be overruled.

The two are diametrically opposed and cannot stand together.

Now, this Court has not granted a right to know where there has not been a concomitant First Amendment right to speak.

Troy had done an admirable job of defining the issue in the case as a conflict between the state's generous powers of regulation, on the one hand, and the First Amendment, on the other. A decision favoring the First Amendment would breach the dam of the Fourteenth Amendment and immerse the Court once more in detailed supervision of the wisdom and fairness of state economic regulation. To be sure, the supervision would be carried out under the mantle of freedom of speech rather than due process, but it would carry similar consequences and a similar risk that the Court might attempt again to enact "Mr. Herbert Spencer's Social Statics" under the guise of constitutional law.

But Troy still faced a Court skeptical of the value of Virginia's price advertising ban—perhaps even doubtful of whether its true purpose was public health or instead economic protectionism for pharmacists.

Question (by Justice White): What is the State's interest in prohibiting the advertising? To forbid—to do away with competition, or what?

Mr. Troy: No, your Honor, it is a health matter.

Justice White: Well, I know, but how does it protect health?

Mr. Troy: As I have indicated—let me answer this directly . . . consumers could put the needs of their pocketbooks above their remedial needs.

Justice White: So if you advertised price—so-called "price cutting," you think it might lead everyone to cut prices, which lowers profits which would put the druggist in a poorer position to do his job. Is that it?

166 | *The Pharmacist*

Mr. Troy: The General Assembly [of Virginia] in its wisdom has decided that the delivery of a prescription drug is part and parcel entwined with the health care that must be given.

Justice White: All right. Now, how does advertising impinge on that?

Mr. Troy: The advertising, of course, would induce consumers to think of this as a mere commodity and would be deceptive in and of itself because they would not realize what. . . .

Question: Well, the General Assembly, in its wisdom, hasn't—doesn't fix prices on drugs and it doesn't prevent a druggist from cutting a price at the request of a consumer.

Mr. Troy: That is correct, your Honor. This has no effect on prices.

Question: And it wouldn't prevent, I suppose, consumers picketing a drugstore to say that the druggist was charging too high a price.

Mr. Troy: No, I don't think it would at all.

Question: And it wouldn't even prevent one druggist from picketing another.

Mr. Troy: Well, the statute—

Question: Would it? *Would it?*

Mr. Troy: —does not intend to regulate price.

Question: So if a druggist wants to sell the drugs more cheaply than his competitors, he may do so without interference.

Mr. Troy: That is correct.

Question (by Justice Rehnquist): Well, but doesn't—if you are talking about a Fourteenth Amendment type of analysis where [any rationale for the statute, whether right or wrong in fact, can be used to defend the state's law], don't you have to get back to Justice White's earlier question [and argue in support of the advertising ban] that if you have price advertising you are going to have price wars and if the pharmacist does have a responsible position the less he can charge for the unit the less time he is able to devote to supervising its distribution?

Mr. Troy: Well . . . that is perhaps an analysis, Justice Rehnquist.

Justice Rehnquist: Thank you.

(Laughter)

Mr. Troy: The—sorry—that just came out. What I meant to say is that, though we did not rely on that analysis *per se* in the lower court, what we felt was that this monitoring situation, if you have advertising, you are going to induce patrons, patients, to shop around—to shop from pharmacy to pharmacy and by not having price advertising, you are, in effect, creating a system whereby perhaps a physician-pharmacist relationship would exist.

    The General Assembly . . . found that there was a rational relationship between [the absence of price competition and] monitoring — between [no price advertising and] having patients go to the same pharmacist and consequently, on that basis, enacted the statute.

The Court's reservations about the advertising restriction were not to be resolved. There seemed little doubt that the General Assembly's assumptions — that with no price advertising consumers were more likely to remain with the same pharmacist, who would then have better information based on past experience with which to monitor the best drug or dosage and to avoid drugs that might cause unwanted side effects for the customer — were reasonable, though they were blunt-edged and exacted a significant cost. It was entirely possible, for example, that even with price advertising most customers would remain with the same pharmacist but would enjoy the added benefit of lower prices.

But further discussion of the rationality of the Virginia scheme would have to await Mr. Morrison's later argument on behalf of the Consumer Council. For the moment, the tide of questions instead turned to the more important and theoretical First Amendment problems presented in the case. Exactly who — or what — was the speaker in the case, and what, precisely, was the speech?

> *Question:* Is there any First Amendment interest [of] the druggist to take account of in this case?
>
> *Mr. Troy:* No, I don't think so. . . . In this case, what is advertised is commercial advertising in its purest sense. [Unlike the Court's decision last term in the *Bigelow v. Virginia* case, involving advertisements for legal, out-of-state abortions,] phrases such as "compare, save, pay less, or dial-a-discount" do not . . . convey information of interest regarding the form, the subject matter of the law in another state, or advertised activity which pertains to a constitutional interest, abortion. Such phrases do no more than simply propose a commercial transaction. They are entitled to little, if any, constitutional weight.
>
>   Now, as I have said, those phrases would create, perhaps, a retail incentive for price competition, but where is the constitutional right to the lowest price possible?

If a balancing of whatever First Amendment interests are involved must be made, then . . . it should be done in light of this Court's recognition for over 40 years of the inherent interests of the State through its police power to regulate the various professions. [The Virginia price advertising ban] has been found, by [the] district court . . . , to have . . . a rational and reasonable basis.

The Virginia statute, wise or foolish, economically sound or improvident, should be sustained. By doing so, this Court will be sustaining the constitutional framework that legislative bodies, not courts, must decide the wisdom of economic and social policies.

Chief Justice Burger: Thank you, Mr. Troy.

Mr. Troy's time was up and he returned to his seat at the counsel table behind the podium. As he did so, he was no doubt reflecting on the oral argument that had just transpired, perhaps with satisfaction.

On the one hand, he seemed to have succeeded in keeping the Court's attention focused on the importance of preserving the state's regulatory authority over the professions, and to have emphasized effectively the danger of the Court's enmeshing itself once again in judging the wisdom of the economic and social policies adopted through the democratic legislative process at the state level. To decide the case in favor of the Consumer Council, in other words, the Court would have to surmount two imposing obstacles: its long-established history of deference to state social and economic policy choices; and the well-entrenched tradition of pervasive state regulation of the professions.

Troy had also responded directly and clearly to the First Amendment questions posed by the Court. The questions had been phrased in precisely the way he wished: "What are the First Amendment rights of the pharmacist?" This phrasing allowed Troy to assert, accurately, that the pharmacist's claim was for the right to do no more than propose a commercial transaction—"dial-a-discount," as Troy deftly put it. It was thus, inferentially, simply a claim by the discounters and big chains to invade the settled territory of local pharmacists, who provided valuable continuity of care and attention to their customers, a claim that could not easily be distinguished from that of a used-car dealer. The right to engage in price competition by means of speech contributed little of value to the larger First Amendment ends of individual freedom of thought and conscience and democratic self-government, and it was clearly different from the speech (though in advertisement form) about the availability of legal abortions that was at issue in the Court's earlier decision in the *Bigelow* case.

But Troy might also have entertained a doubt or two about the course that oral argument had taken. The First Amendment issue was, after all, hardly touched upon by the Court, yet the issue was at the center of the case and involved difficult and subtle questions that the Court had not seen fit to press upon him. That the First Amendment issue could be so easily dismissed on the basis of the pharmacist's relatively weak interest without mention of the interests of the consumers, the audience, was too good to be true. The Court had, after all, agreed to set the case down for briefing and oral argument, and with specific reference to the First Amendment claim.

Yet in its limited questioning, the Court had not given Troy much chance to engage the Court in oral argument on the significant theoretical and practical problems posed by a First Amendment theory premised not on the speaker's claim of right but on the audience's. If the freedom of an advertisement depends on its value to the audience, how do we judge the audience, and how do we determine its selection of "value"? Is the audience's First Amendment interest simply one of utility, so that information that can be usefully employed is thereby protected? Or is the audience's interest grounded somehow in the constitutional liberty of the members of the audience?

If, for example, an individual reads an advertisement announcing the price of a used car, is the First Amendment's protection for the ad based on its usefulness to that individual as a potential buyer of a used car? Or can we distinguish, for purposes of the First Amendment, the utility of used-car prices from the utility of prescription drug prices, prescription drugs being more important to the individual's well-being or, perhaps, a more basic necessity of life? If such distinctions are to be drawn, how can we find a principled basis for drawing them in the First Amendment? Aren't such distinctions the very questions of indeterminate social policy that are best left to the elected branches of government, and not to the courts?

Couching the interest in used-car prices in terms of liberty rather than the information's utility doesn't in the end change the analysis. The liberty to buy prescription drugs rather than a used car, after all, isn't more easily distinguishable than the utility interest in one versus the other. Are prescription drugs somehow more central to liberty than a used car? If so, isn't that because, for a specific member of the audience, drugs are more important, and the liberty interest lies in *that individual's* ability to make that trade-off, not the government's (or the First Amendment's)? But admitting this, what connection does an individual's personal preference for used cars rather than prescription drugs have to do with the First Amendment, which deals with expression?

To be sure, the First Amendment deals with speech; speech includes information as well as ideas; and information enables individuals who receive it to know more, to further develop their thoughts and beliefs, and to act in a more independent, autonomous way. In this sense speech inevitably tends toward greater freedom in others, which in turn tends toward new belief and insight and ultimately to new speech, which begins the circle again. But if this is what the First Amendment is about, we must account for the many unanticipated, and even bizarre, results it yields. The same "circle of enlightenment" argument applies not just to information and ideas received by a person from the speech act of another person. It applies, as well, to virtually all stimuli: the song of a bird, the crash of thunder, the felt texture of a rug, the experience of pain or disease, the perception of time and space, indeed everything that assaults the senses and consciousness, perhaps even the unconscious. All of these contribute to our thoughts and beliefs, to our sense of self, and thus to our independence, autonomy, and ultimately to our speech.

The First Amendment could, of course, be interpreted to protect all of these things: to foreclose government from denying us the bird's song, the experience of nature; to safeguard our right to experience pain and disease. But such a First Amendment would be radically different from the one we know, and from the much more limited one the Supreme Court has enforced. Under such a First Amendment, we wouldn't need the Endangered Species Act, for by permitting logging of the federally owned habitat of the spotted owl the government would be denying our First Amendment right to hear and see the owl, denying us the information thus to be gathered, assimilated, and reflected in newly expressed ideas and beliefs.

This would be a silly result, Troy might have argued, that could be avoided only by drawing lines, by distinguishing among stimuli or among types of information, based on their value in the hands of the audience. So whether we are talking about a bird's song or prescription drug prices, the First Amendment question when viewed from the perspective of the audience's interest, not the speaker's freedom, comes down to a line-drawing question. And as such, it requires the Court to engage in the very same inquiry into value or utility that an approach based on the pharmacist's freedom to speak required.

Is information about used-car prices distinguishable, in principle, from information about prescription drug prices? If there *is* a distinction between them, is it not unavoidably a distinction based on expedient and temporal considerations of wise social policy or naked democratic preference best left to the elected branches of government? If courts must rest their actions on the text of the Constitution or at least on general principles of constitutional origin that transcend the outcome reached in the case at hand, where in the First Amendment, which reads "Congress shall make no law . . . abridging the freedom of speech," can such a principle be discovered?

This is the argument Troy might have made had he been given the chance. The argument, to be sure, is not without its weaknesses (if no principle can be judicially crafted, for example, how can the distinction between "purely commercial speech" and other forms of speech be defended), but it is a powerful one that goes deeply to the *real* problem in the case.

Mr. Troy was not allowed to make the argument. It was instead left to the justices to make it in the form of the questions posed to Mr. Morrison, who was arguing, ultimately, on behalf of the audience. As Morrison rose and stepped to the podium, he may also have been reflecting on these very questions. In any event, he surely knew what was coming.

> *Mr. Morrison:* Mr. Chief Justice and may it please the Court.
>
> This is a First Amendment case. There is only one question and that is the constitutionality of the Virginia statute which prohibits the advertising of the price of prescription drugs.
>
> The Pharmacy Board [and the State of Virginia] rely on . . . the proposition that commercial advertising is entitled to no protection under the First Amendment.
>
> Now, whatever the merits of that position may have been before June 16th of last year when this Court decided *Bigelow* [the abortion advertisement case], that position simply has no merit today.
>
> *Bigelow* clearly and unmistakably forecloses any . . . argument . . . that all commercial advertising is outside the First Amendment.
>
> *Bigelow* said you have got to look at the information being conveyed . . . and find a clear relationship between the prohibition [of the information] and the goals of the State.

Whichever way you strike the balance, the scale tips so heavily in favor of public disclosure of this information under the First Amendment that under even the most relaxed rational relationship test the plaintiffs will prevail.

[This case involves] the interest that the consumers have in finding out . . . how much they are going to pay for drugs that may save their lives. . . .

Mr. Morrison's opening statement, interrupted by a few technical questions about the scope of the drug price ban that have not been included here, succeeded in placing the case in the most favorable light to him. The First Amendment, he asserted, required that the drug-price-advertising ban bear a reasonable relationship to the ends it was designed to achieve — improved quality of pharmaceutical services to the customer. As the discussion with Mr. Troy had revealed, this relationship was tenuous at best, and the specter of protectionism for local pharmacists was ever-present in the statute's operation. Tenuous reasoning might be enough under the due process clause, but the First Amendment clearly required more. Once firmly planted on First Amendment ground, therefore, Morrison's argument was nearly open and shut.

The problem in the case, of course, was getting to and holding the First Amendment ground. Here Morrison had managed to skate over virtually all of the difficult terrain, choosing instead to plant his feet strongly on the Court's earlier *Bigelow* decision. He did so, to his credit, with decisiveness and aplomb.

But not with success, for Justice Rehnquist quickly sensed the sleight of hand that had been attempted in Morrison's statement — not argument — that the case involved the "consumers' . . . interest in finding out how much they are going to have to pay for drugs that may save their lives."

Justice Rehnquist: Is that a constitutional interest that you are talking about?

Mr. Morrison: Yes it is, Mr. Justice Rehnquist. It is the right to receive information under the First Amendment and the concomitant right on the part of the pharmacist to speak freely and while the pharmacist is subject to regulation under the Fourteenth Amendment, there are still specific First Amendment prohibitions that cannot be overruled.

We might accuse Morrison of dissembling just a bit in his answer. He starts out clearly enough: "It is the right to receive information under the First Amendment. . . ." The First Amendment right, in other words, belongs to the audience; it consists of the receipt of information, not its production.

But Morrison then turns, as perhaps he must, to the pharmacist, for the audience cannot have a right to receive information that is not given (unless, of course, the First Amendment is interpreted to force someone to give it, much as a constitutional right of access would do). He describes the pharmacist's right as a "concomitant right . . . to speak freely." With this seemingly innocuous phrase Morrison has executed a clever sleight of hand. If the pharmacist's right is a "concomitant" one, of what is it concomitant? Morrison asserts that it is concomitant with, and implicitly dependent on, the audience's right to receive information from the pharmacist. He thus manages in a short phrase to turn the First Amendment upside down: a speaker's freedom flows from the audience's right to hear, rather than the other way around.

Traditional First Amendment theory, in contrast, makes the speaker's freedom primary and the audience's secondary. The audience's elucidation, in other words, is a by-product of the speaker's liberty; a happy and important one, to be sure, but a by-product nevertheless. If things were put the other way around, the First Amendment would protect, in effect, only those ideas that an audience wished to hear, a result that would seriously undermine the First Amendment's commitment to protecting dissent and safeguarding the opportunity for ideas believed false to compete with conventional "wisdom."

Mr. Morrison was saved from having to confront this problem, at least for the moment, by the next question, which shifted the focus to another difficult problem that Mr. Troy had planted in the Court's mind: must lawyers, too, be allowed to advertise?

> *Question:* But what about your—if your argument is applied to the legal profession . . . is the state bar regulation prohibiting lawyers from advertising a violation of the First Amendment?
>
> *Mr. Morrison:* Well, I want to answer that question directly because it is something that has been alluded to a number of times.
>
> *Question:* That is your next case.
>
> *Mr. Morrison:* The first point I want to make is that the mode of analysis employed in *Bigelow* . . . requiring the recognition of a

First Amendment right and requiring the balancing of the two kinds of interests, that is, the interest . . . in obtaining the . . . specific items of information . . . against the interest that the state has in precluding the dissemination of that information, that kind of balancing test would most definitely have to be engaged in a case similar to the one that you suggested.

I can see a wide distinction, for instance, between information about what a lawyer charges on a specific per-hour basis, on the one hand, and a lawyer who stipulated to make the same kind of guarantees that the dentist did in a similar case, saying "I guarantee no pain,"—whatever the legal equivalent of that may be— "and I guarantee satisfaction." Those are two different kinds of questions and they would have to be looked at differently. . . .

Similarly, we don't know and we don't have a record, as we have here, on what specific justifications the Bar would put forth. Here, we have the monitoring justification.

[With lawyers] the state has an interest in seeing that professionals do not engage in what we call overreaching activities and it may very well be that in the context of analyzing what professionals— who, after all, are licensed by the state, given an imprimatur of going out to the public and say, you are a professional—the state may well—and I don't suggest that there is a definite answer—but may well be able to say: "Hold on. You can't say the same thing as soap makers."

Morrison had danced with sprightly ambiguity through the lawyer minefield, but in the end it didn't really matter much. The justices were perfectly aware of the fact that their decision in this case would have clear implications for other licensed professional settings . . . and that among the first such claims to arrive at the Court would be claims by lawyers. Morrison knew this, too.

But what Morrison may not have anticipated was the coming twist in the road, for his statement that the state bar might be able to limit what lawyers can say in advertisements to saying less than the "soap makers" brought Morrison into a head-on collision with the rights of the speaker. It was Justice Brennan, this time, who quickly jumped in.

Justice Brennan: But you can't do that, I gather, from what you are suggesting here. Your next step is going to be that you can't do that as to the consumer.

Mr. Morrison: Well, the—
Justice Brennan: If they are evaluating the conduct of the professionals themselves, that is one thing, but here you are talking about
whether the consumer is entitled to this information.
Mr. Morrison: No, I would say, Justice Brennan, that both of those
interests can properly be focused. We can focus on the entire transaction.
Justice Brennan: Right.
Mr. Morrison: And I do not mean to suggest that the state could not
focus on it.
Justice Brennan: All right.
Mr. Morrison: Indeed, I think there are very many important interests
that can be protected against by deceptive and fraudulent advertising. All I am suggesting is that in the context of a particular case
with regard to the regulations of a particular profession, we have
to look at the particular information under the kind of analysis we
are suggesting here. . . .

Justice Brennan had, surprisingly, let the issue slip away, and then
Morrison had managed to bury it further in a fog of ambiguity coupled
with an irrelevant diversion into deceptive and fraudulent advertising.
How, Justice Brennan had asked, could the state's denial of information
about lawyers be justified at all if, as Morrison had asserted, the primary First Amendment right is the audience's right to receive the information, making whatever use of it it chose? Morrison's talk of
balancing interests in the contexts of particular cases is mere diversion,
for it is not responsive. And his talk of preventing fraud and deceit is
beside the point, for neither the lawyer advertising example nor the *Virginia Pharmacy* case involved any element of fraud or deceit. Morrison
could, of course, have made the argument that all lawyer advertising is
inherently deceptive, but he didn't make that argument, and he didn't
want to.
So we are left to wonder why Justice Brennan let Morrison off the
hook. It was not until a later point in the argument that Justice Blackmun returned to the issue.

Justice Blackmun: Mr. Morrison, let me ask you this and I hope it
isn't irrelevant. I think that drugs by trade names generally are
more expensive than drugs by their basic chemical—
Mr. Morrison: Generic names.

Justice Blackmun: —or generic names. Suppose Virginia had a statute requiring physicians to prescribe in the generic name. Would this be unconstitutional, do you think?

The question posed by Justice Blackmun wasn't, of course, irrelevant. It was in fact very crafty, for it would flush Morrison out on the issue of exactly whose rights were at stake in the case, the pharmacists' or the audience's. Morrison, of course, elected the audience, and thus found himself right back where Justice Brennan had inexplicably left off.

Mr. Morrison: Well, I would first say that I—my first offhand reaction is that that would not be a First Amendment issue. I would think that the state would have a legitimate interest if it made a factual determination that pills are pharmacologically identical, to be able to say to the doctor, "You must prescribe that unless there is some medical reason for doing so."

Question: Would you think, in further answer to Justice Blackmun's question, that a physician had a First Amendment right not to prescribe in the generic name and you would then balance the state's interest to see whether he would prevail or the state?

Mr. Morrison: Well, I don't see the speech element of the First Amendment coming in.

Question: Well, why shouldn't the doctor be able to prescribe a certain proprietary drug if he just thinks it is better or he just wants his customers to use that drug?

Mr. Morrison [seeming a bit confused by the turn the question has taken]: Well, my—

Question: I mean, why isn't it at least a First Amendment issue?

Mr. Morrison: Well, it might be. As I say, I haven't focused on it. It would seem to me that it is not a traditional kind of expression issue.

Morrison *should* have focused on the issue. After all, is the doctor's claimed right to prescribe a proprietary drug all that different from the pharmacist's right to advertise the price of the drug? Both could be seen to be speaking. And in both cases the audience (patient) would receive information that would be useful and that the state was attempting to prohibit.

But Morrison's surprising uncertainty was only a prelude to what would come as Justice Stewart turned the focus once again to lawyers and, more important, to the basis for Morrison's "right to know."

Justice Stewart: Mr. Morrison, before you go on . . . , I'll try to put a
fairly straightforward factual situation.

As you know, most lawyers have an hourly rate, at least for
internal record purposes, and the first step in most legal charge
computations is to look at one's record and see how many hours
have been devoted to the representation.

Let's assume a desire on the part of lawyers — or assume that
the issue were whether or not lawyers would be allowed to advertise that their hourly rate for non-litigation advice was $25 an hour
or whatever it might be. What would your reaction to that be?

Mr. Morrison: Well, my first reaction would be that that is certainly
an item of information that consumers would want to know.

Justice Stewart: Right.

Mr. Morrison: That the lawyer would want to be able to disseminate
that, either because he wants to be sure the people he is attracting
can pay the fee or because he thinks that he will get people to come
in at that rate because he thinks it is a good, competitive rate.

Now, on the assumption that we are talking about a dignified
notice . . . I would see no interest of the state of the kind that I
would think would be sufficient to overturn it, but . . . before we
prejudge a case . . . the state ought . . . to have an opportunity to
present whatever justification, the equivalent of monitoring or
whatever, the state has to put forth. . . . My own judgment would
be . . . that there is no sufficient interest of the state involved. . . .

Justice Stewart: Well, even if there were, according to your submission, as I understand it, the First Amendment of the Constitution
would override it.

Mr. Morrison: Well, the First Amendment —

Justice Stewart: If there is a right to know. If there is, as you submit, a
constitutional right to know on the part of potential clients or
potential customers of pharmacists.

Mr. Morrison: Well, in every case, of course, there would be a strong
presumption that the right to know would be —

Justice Stewart: Well, if he has a right to know.

Mr. Morrison: Yes. But there could — there is always engaged in the
permissible balancing test that there are certain kinds of cases —

[Here Morrison is not waffling but is rather observing that there
are no absolute rights or absolute answers in constitutional law —
even his "right to know" would countenance exceptions if the

state's interest, such as the interest in preventing fraud, were sufficiently great.]

Justice Stewart: Well, some people think so, but others don't.

Mr. Morrison: That is right.

Justice Stewart: Others think if there is a clear constitutional right,
that is the end of it and any state statute that impedes or interferes
with that right is invalid.

Mr. Morrison: I think that is correct, Mr. Justice Stewart.

Justice Stewart: That is not your submission, as I understand it. Your
submission is that in this instance, the state interest does not override the right to know. Isn't that it?

Mr. Morrison: I think that is right.

Justice Stewart: First of all, on an absolutist view or any other view,
you have to look at the Constitution, don't you?

Mr. Morrison: That is correct.

Justice Stewart: And where do you find in the Constitution any right
to know?

Mr. Morrison: Well, it's the correlative—

Justice Stewart: Particularly if you were an absolutist.

Mr. Morrison: It is the correlative, I would say, of the right to speak—
freedom of speech that I think Justice Brennan said that the marketplace [of ideas] would be a barren place indeed if we had only
sellers and no buyers and we have recognized the right to receive
information specifically in a number of contexts, [including the]
Lamont case [which involved postal restrictions on what people
could receive in the mail].

Justice Brennan: I don't think anyone joined in saying that, though,
did they? Wasn't I alone?

Mr. Morrison: Yes. [But] you were concurring.

We are now at the heart of the matter: Is there a "right to know" possessed by the audience under the First Amendment; and is the right independent of the right of the speaker to speak? Morrison had earlier
implied that the right to know—the audience's right to receive information—was freestanding, not dependent on the speaker's primary right.
In his exchange with Justices Stewart and Brennan he had shifted
ground, saying that the right to know was correlative of—and therefore
impliedly secondary to—the right to speak. This ambiguity, which Morrison may have wished to maintain, disguised the problem that lay at the

center of his case, for the pharmacists who would claim a First Amendment right to speak were nowhere to be found. This fact presented in stark relief a fundamental question of First Amendment interpretation: Just whose right are we talking about?

But if maintaining ambiguity was Morrison's aim, the Court would have none of it.

Question: One may fully accept [the audience's critical role in speech] and still say that the Constitution protects the right to know by guaranteeing the right to speak or the right to a free press, and that those were the constitutional guarantees and anything else is derivative and is not protected directly by the Constitution.

Mr. Morrison: Well, we would certainly say that to the extent that there is a direct right to speak, that would plainly support the right to receive the information, but there have been a couple of cases in which the right to speak has not been at issue. . . .

Question: Well, you are not suggesting, are you, that the consumers have a right to know even though the pharmacists don't have a right to speak?

Mr. Morrison: Well, I think the pharmacists do have a right to speak in this case.

Question: But they are not here.

Mr. Morrison: But they are not here and I do say that there have been cases in this Court and I simply make the observation, I think that the rights [of the speaker and the audience] are equal and the same and that when you view the entire transaction together considering all of the rights involved, that you do have a constitutional right to have this information disseminated and received in this case.

What I am saying is that there have been a couple of cases where the right to receive has seemingly been elevated above the right that the person who was making the statement had under our Constitution.

Justice Blackmun: Mr. Morrison, maybe this is why I, for one, anyway, am always a little uneasy about using a phrase such as the right to know.

I think I [would rather say] something like the free flow of information. It puts a little less emphasis on "right to know" on one party and the "right to speak" on the other, and we have restricted them here a little bit. I am groping, obviously.

"Groping" may well be the right term. Resolving the constitutional tension between the individual's right to speak and the audience's right to receive, or to "know," by the phrase "free flow of information" does little more than euphemize the ambiguity. To be sure, in most cases there will be no conflict between the speaker's right and the audience's right, for both are ordinarily willing participants. But in some cases—and the pharmacists' case may be one—the tension will be inescapable: if the speaker does not want to speak, does the audience's right to know nevertheless compel the speaker to do so? If a politician has a secret that the public wants to know, must he or she disgorge it?

For the moment, Morrison grasps frantically at the "free flow of information" straw that Blackmun has tendered.

> *Mr. Morrison:* I agree with you, one hundred percent, Mr. Justice Blackmun. I don't think—and I read my brief again with that specifically in mind—that we specifically adopted the "right to know" phraseology in this Court. . . .
>
> *Question:* But you don't suggest that the First Amendment, the right of free speech, means that you must have something to say, do you?

This is a very good question. If the First Amendment rests on a right to know, then something worth knowing must be said. If, on the other hand, the First Amendment protects the individual's liberty to speak, the "worthiness" of what is spoken is irrelevant, for it is the individual's liberty to express himself or herself that is protected.

> *Mr. Morrison:* No, I don't.
>
> *Question:* Then, if you—
>
> *Mr. Morrison:* Something meaningful to say?
>
> *Question:* Yes. Then if you are going to measure [the First Amendment] by the free flow of information, information presumably meaning "something to say," you have put a limit on the First Amendment, haven't you?
>
> *Mr. Morrison:* Well, I don't think so. I am only talking about—
>
> *Question:* A person has the same right to speak or to write even if what he is speaking or writing is utterly foolish, doesn't he?
>
> *Mr. Morrison:* That is absolutely correct. I am only talking about those cases in which a state is claiming that some interest in prohibiting

certain kinds of information may be raised and in those cases I think that it is proper to take a look at the kind of information that we are talking about.

That was my only point.

Question: Well, if we are only speaking of information.

Mr. Morrison: Yes. Yes.

At this point, Chief Justice Burger thanked Mr. Morrison for his argument and invited him to resume his seat behind the counsel table. Morrison's time was up. He was thus saved from further questioning and allowed to leave the "right to know" issue in the clouded ambiguity of the "free flow of information."

The First Amendment was thus left in logical limbo. Three alternative — and radically different — views of the First Amendment had emerged in the course of the oral argument.

The first alternative is a First Amendment that rests primarily on the right of the individual to speak, with the freedom of the speech to "flow" and the audience "to know" *deriving from* the speaker's liberty and, more important, depending on it. It was this view that underlay Justice Harlan's opinion in Paul Cohen's case, discussed in "The Jacket." Under this view the pharmacists' right to speak would be paramount.

The second alternative is a First Amendment that protects the *speech and its flow*, with the speaker's right to speak and the audience's right to "know" deriving from the *speech's* liberty, on the theory that the marketplace of speech — the "flow" of speech — would be "a barren place indeed if we had [no] sellers and no buyers." This is the view tentatively expressed by Justice Blackmun and Morrison at the close of the oral argument. It is also, notably, a view that would rest on a "balancing" of the value of the speech against the state's regulatory interest.

The balancing approach, ironically, was precisely the argument Troy had made on behalf of Virginia. If a distinction between the value of used-car prices and prescription drug prices is to be made, the democratically elected branches of government should make it. Courts are ill-equipped to formulate such broad social policy preferences.

The third and final alternative is a First Amendment that protects the audience's "right to know," with the freedom of the speech to "flow" and the individual's right to speak deriving from (and therefore being subservient to) the audience's elucidation. This, when all is said and done, was Morrison's theory in the *Virginia Pharmacy* case, though he was careful not to press it too far, preferring to disguise it in Justice Blackmun's "free flow of information" metaphor.

The Supreme Court's problem lay in crafting an opinion based on one of these three very different views of the First Amendment. The State of Virginia would be happy with either of the first two alternatives. If the First Amendment rests on the right of the speaker to speak, the absence of the pharmacists in the case could cripple the Consumer Council's case. If the First Amendment protects speech and its flow, Virginia would argue that a balancing of interests was therefore required and that deference should be paid by the Court to the state's power to formulate basic social policy free of intrusive judicial supervision. Viewed this way, the case was little different from Virginia's preference for generic rather than brand-name drugs, or to draw on a more contemporary example, the federal government's desire to limit tobacco advertising. Only the last alternative, which elevated the audience's interest to dominance under the First Amendment, would provide a clear path to victory for Morrison and the Virginia Consumer Council.

Perhaps the difficulty of reasoning to a conclusion in the case on the basis of one of these three very different First Amendment theories explains the Court's delay in issuing an opinion. Oral argument had been held on November 11, 1975, but the Court's opinion was not announced until May 24, 1976, nearly six months later. But when the opinion was finally released, the Court seemed surprisingly united. The opinion was written by Justice Blackmun, who had authored the opinion one year earlier in the *Bigelow* case. Blackmun's opinion was joined by the chief justice and Justices Brennan, Stewart, White, Marshall, and Powell. Justice Douglas had retired from the Court, and shortly thereafter had died. He was replaced by Justice Stevens, who did not participate in the decision. The sole dissenter was Justice Rehnquist.

Justice Blackmun's opinion for the Court, it should first be said, attempted to avoid a clear choice among the three competing First Amendment views expressed above. Language can be found in the opinion to support each view. "Freedom of speech," Blackmun began, "presupposes a willing speaker. But where a speaker exists . . . , the protection afforded is to the communication, to its source and to its recipients both." This was the judicial equivalent of a "hat trick."

But in the end the logic of his opinion rested on the right of the audience:

As to the particular consumer's interest in the free flow of commercial information, that interest may be as keen, if not keener by far, than his interest in the day's most urgent political debate. . . .

Generalizing, society also may have a strong interest in the free flow of commercial information. Even an individual advertisement, though entirely "commercial," may be of general public interest. . . . Advertising, however tasteless and excessive it sometimes may seem, is nonetheless dissemination of information as to who is producing and selling what product, for what reason, at what price. So long as we preserve a predominantly free enterprise economy, the allocation of our resources in large measure will be made through numerous private economic decisions. It is a matter of public interest that those decisions, in the aggregate, be intelligent and well informed. . . .

Virginia is free to require whatever professional standards it wishes of pharmacists; it may subsidize them or protect them from competition in other ways. But it may not do so by keeping the public in ignorance. . . .

There is no escaping the conclusion that it was the audience's interest in the price information, its value to them and the use that they could make of it, that accounted for the First Amendment protection. And it was likewise the state's conscious design to keep the information from the consumers—to keep them in ignorance—and *not* the restriction of the pharmacists' freedom to take out ads, that explained the law's unconstitutionality. "In this sense," Justice Blackmun declared, "the justifications Virginia has offered for suppressing the flow of prescription drug price information, far from persuading us that the flow is not protected by the First Amendment, have reinforced our view that it is. We so hold."

The Court's reliance on the audience's First Amendment rights was not lost, of course, on Justice Rehnquist, who was left to object in lone dissent:

The issue on the merits is not, as the Court phrases it, whether "[o]ur pharmacist" may communicate the fact that he "will sell you the X prescription drug at the Y price." No pharmacist is asserting any such claim to so communicate. The issue is rather whether . . . consumers may override the legislative determination that pharmacists should not advertise even though the pharmacists themselves do not object. . . .

Here the rights of the [consumers] seem to me to be marginal at best. . . . On the other hand, the societal interest against the promotion of drug use

184 | *The Pharmacist*

for every ill, real or imaginary, seems to be extremely strong. I do not believe that the First Amendment mandates the Court's "open door policy" toward such commercial advertising.

Notwithstanding Justice Rehnquist's dissent, the die had been cast. In the years that followed the *Virginia Pharmacy* case, the Court's new "commercial speech doctrine" flourished, and lawyers, physicians, dentists, optometrists, accountants, and even beer companies and gambling casinos walked through the Court's open door.

But Mr. Morrison's victory was not complete.

As the years passed and the true and virtually limitless scope of the open door became evident, the Court began cutting back, placing limits on the insatiable appetite of audience claims—claims *now* brought, of course, by *purveyors* in the name of an audience that, like the pharmacists, was not present. Thus when in 1989 purveyors of Tupperware claimed First Amendment protection for the college-student audience's right to have Tupperware parties in a college dormitory, the Court put a stop to it. It can safely be said that the students were not picketing for Tupperware, and Tupperware parties hardly seemed a fitting occasion for celebrating the First Amendment. It was perfectly reasonable, the Court said, for the university to keep commerce out of the dormitories, even if in so doing ignorance was bred.

But in calling a halt in the Tupperware case the Court stopped well short of a counterrevolution. Commercial speech is still protected by the First Amendment, even if no longer as stringently. The Court thus managed to sidestep, as it had since the *Virginia Pharmacy* decision, the perplexing questions that lay beneath the surface of the commercial speech cases: who, exactly, constitutes "the audience": And how do we measure the speech's value through the audience's eyes? Are some subjects of advertisements, such as the qualifications of political candidates, more important than others, such as whether to buy a used car? Indeed, notwithstanding Justice Blackmun's opinion in the *Virginia Pharmacy* case, there remains considerable uncertainty about the most basic question: Just who—or what—is the First Amendment protecting here, anyway?

In another respect, too, Morrison's victory was not complete. Shortly after Justice Blackmun's opinion was announced, there was a wave of excitement in First Amendment circles about a coming revolution in the First Amendment. This was not an unwarranted reaction, for if the idea that the audience is the principal possessor of rights under the First Amendment had spread, a wholesale and fundamental transformation in First Amendment law would indeed have taken place.

Newspapers, representing *their* audiences, would have been able to claim a right of access to all sorts of information even though the parties possessing it were unwilling to divulge it. Newspapers might also, of course, have been made more responsible to their audience, and thus compelled in the interest of providing full and accurate information to be fair and to admit and correct their errors. After all, radio and television had been made to do just that, and the requirement had been upheld against First Amendment challenge on precisely the same ground as the *Virginia Pharmacy* majority had rested its decision: the rights of the audience are paramount under the Constitution, and when those rights conflict with the broadcasters' claimed liberty, their liberty must give way to government-imposed rules designed to assure fair and accurate and important information for the public.

Perhaps more fundamental, audiences might have been placed more firmly in control of the meaning to be given speech, and of its value. The Court's problematic approach to obscenity, which left the questions of meaning and value to the jury *as audience* would have spread, with the risk that in all speech settings a speaker's words would be made subject to the audience's interpretation of them, and thus the speaker's freedom would be placed in the hands of others.

None of this, of course, has transpired, and it is not likely to do so. The reason is that the commercial speech door has been confined to commercial speech only. The rights of the audience continue to live, but only when the speech at issue is "pure commercial speech" that does no more than propose a commercial transaction. The audience's independent First Amendment claims are safely confined, marooned and isolated on the tight little island of commercial speech.

Perhaps that is for the best. There, at least, the audience gets no more than it asks for, indeed what it *already* believes. In his 1991 book, *Promotional Culture: Advertising, Ideology, and Symbolic Expression*, Andrew Wernick claims that "the point of advertising is to identify the product with what targeted consumers are known already to cherish and desire." Advertising is thus "a kind of inert gas," reinforcing, not challenging or adding to, what audiences know and believe. As one Ad Man put it: "What we're doing is wrapping up your emotions and selling them back to you."

With advertising, at least, this is the picture we have come to expect. But just think what the consequences would be if this were the picture of political speech.

ADDITIONAL READING

Ronald Collins and David Skover, "Commerce and Communication," 71 *Texas Law Review* 697 (1993).

Thomas Jackson and John Jeffries, "Commercial Speech: Economic Due Process and the First Amendment," 65 *Virginia Law Review* 1 (1979).

Alex Kozinski and Stuart Banner, "Who's Afraid of Commercial Speech?" 76 *Virginia Law Review* 627 (1990).

Red Lion Broadcasting Co. v. Federal Communications Commission, 395 U.S. 367 (1969).

Story Seven

The Burning Flag: The Medium and the Message

(Texas v. Johnson, 491 U.S. 397 (1989))

In part 1 we explored the relationship between speech and its author through the story of Margaret McIntyre and her anonymous leaflet. In the story about the Michigan Chamber of Commerce and corporate political speech, we explored the closely related question of the need for an author (whether identified or not) as a precondition to First Amendment protection of speech in the name of liberty or freedom. In both cases we came to understand the importance of an author, someone speaking his or her own mind, to the protected act of speaking.

But there is more that should be said on the subject, for the demand that speech have *an* author also involves stakes that are infinitely greater than those involved in McIntyre's anonymous leaflet, or even the political or commercial speech offered by the Michigan State Chamber of Commerce or by General Motors.

It was Marshall McLuhan who coined the phrase, well before its time, that "the medium *is* the message." His dictum suggests that for some speech, the source of meaning may be neither an individual nor an organization but the medium itself; that television, for example, projects a different meaning simply because it is television. In today's world of new communication technologies, we can perhaps better appreciate his foresight—and the challenges its poses for the First Amendment.

In a growing crescendo of alarm, scholars have begun to express concern over the impact of new communication technologies. Computers, telecommunications, and related technologies have removed space and time from the communication process, permitting instantaneous worldwide transmission of information. More important, this new real-time communication takes the form not of printed letters or analytically dispassionate words—codes that require the deconstruction and reconstruction of messages in a linear and print-based form—but of multisensory visual and aural images that place the viewer *in* the events being portrayed, not outside them. It is different, so the argument goes, to read about an attempted coup in Russia than to watch it unfold as it happens.

This is not a new insight. The law has for decades distinguished sharply between a written account of an execution and the televising of it. But the stakes may now be higher. Because of technology, we now are able (perhaps even forced) simultaneously to see, hear, feel, and participate in communication in ways unimaginable in the earlier ages of oral (often face-to-face) and written communication. With the multisensory and real-time stimuli characteristic of the new forms of communication, we feel and know but may not think and understand; because we are made participants in what we are being told, we have no context, we are afforded no perspective, for events, when lived, cannot provide them.

It is understandable that in this real-time, visual, participatory communication setting, the distinction between speech and conduct, a relic of the oral and print ages, is made less relevant, for what we communicate is representation not of words or language but of conduct. A live broadcast of a child falling to his death from atop an apartment building blurs any distinction between speech and conduct. Were we witnesses at the scene, we would hardly call the tragedy "speech." If, instead, technology allows us to "be there," what, exactly, accounts for its First Amendment transformation into "speech"?

Conduct, then, is understandably a more central part of multisensory, real-time communication; indeed, it is how we communicate. We have seen this for many years in advertising, which has been ahead of the game all along. The advertiser, armed with the multisensory power of communication, knows that the coldly rational and print-based idea of giving people information upon which to make reasoned decisions is anachronistic. People's behavior *and beliefs* can be better influenced by appeal to image, by direct encouragement of conduct (buy an Infiniti and realize your imagination).

The advertisement, in this view, can make consumers feel their conduct, thus circumventing reason, analysis, rational and self-interested choice. Interpretation, in short, is made as close to a purely emotional and physical act—and as distant from a thinking act—as possible. What is important about this is the role of medium, not (at least in the rational way we think about the term) message. The government's futile efforts to require inclusion of a message—facts about price, health risk, and about "truth" in what is claimed—are effectively lost in the dominant multisensory, subliminal force of emotion that effective advertisements convey. And it is medium, not content itself, that contributes the multisensory "message."

If, then, medium is as important as (perhaps more important than) message, we must think about medium, itself, as communication. And one way to think about "medium" is to ask whether *it* has an author. Can a medium sometimes "speak for itself"? Can its power transform meaning even when *no one* intends it? Should we not ask the same questions about the origin of the medium's message when the medium is the emotional force of multisensory image as we ask when the medium is the consciously chosen word "Fuck" written on the back of Paul Cohen's jacket, or a burning cross? And shouldn't we make those who control and manipulate messages through a medium defend their claim to liberty—justify their act as speech and not conduct—just as we demanded that Paul Cohen and Robert Viktora defend theirs?

We will explore these questions in the story that follows. It is not a story about high technology, about the Internet, cable television, or other new mediums of communication. It is instead about burning a flag—*the* flag, in fact. Flag burning, of course, is an act often engaged in to express a view. But the flag is a medium in which the act occurs; much like the printed word, film, photographs, or words or pictures broadcast through the airwaves are mediums of speaking.

The question that will occupy us is whether, just as the medium of a live picture of an event contributes some distinct meaning to the event being portrayed, the flag itself contributes something distinct to the meaning or message being conveyed by an act of desecration. Does the flag itself, as a medium through which the communicative act occurs, have a meaning or contribute a message of its own? Or is the flag a content-free-medium, like a stick that might be set afire and waved before a crowd, adding force, perhaps, but not new meaning to a message? Is it a bit of both, adding meaning and also transforming meaning at one and the same time, much as a film of a lynching gives new meaning to lynching itself and also brings it to life in a new way undisclosed by written accounts?

The American flag will help us better to understand and to ponder the significance for the First Amendment of McLuhan's dictum "the medium *is* the message." The question presented by the flag-burning case, ultimately, is whether the relationship between speech and conduct, which we have previously explored, is really one between medium and message.

The year 1984 was the year of the Reagan landslide. President Ronald Reagan was completing his first term; inflation was down and the economy was expanding; and America was in the midst of a remarkable military buildup that would, in the view of many, soon result in the breakup of the Soviet Union, Reagan's "evil empire."

The Republican Party held its 1984 National Convention in Dallas, Texas. Dallas was, generally, friendly country for the Republicans. Texas was the home state of Vice President George Bush. But even in Dallas there were demonstrations against the military policies of the Reagan administration and against the corporate interests that benefited from them.

A series of such demonstrations was planned for the streets of Dallas on August 22, 1984, during the course of the convention. Dubbed the "Republican War Chest Tour," the demonstrations consisted of protests, "die-ins," and related events at a series of corporate and government offices in downtown Dallas, with the participants marching from site to site, ending in a demonstration and speeches in front of City Hall.

The demonstration, as it turned out, was not large, consisting of only a hundred or so people. One of the protesters was Gregory Lee Johnson. Johnson and his fellow demonstrators marched through the streets, stopped to stage "die-ins" at some corporate offices, spray-painted slogans on the side of a few buildings, and proceeded ultimately to City Hall.

The demonstrators were accompanied by Dallas police officers. One of the officers testified at trial that when the demonstrators arrived at the Mercantile Bank Building, "several of the protesters bent a flagpole" in front of the building and "removed an American flag." The flag was then handed to Johnson, who "wadded it up and stuck it under his T-shirt."

The demonstrators then moved on to other downtown sites. "When they got to City Hall," the officer "saw Mr. Johnson remove the flag from under his shirt. He tried to light it with a cigarette lighter. It would not light. Someone from the crowd then handed him the can of lighter fluid. He soaked it, ignited it, and the flag burned." As the flag burned, the group chanted "America, the red, white, and blue, we spit on you."

The flag burning was the demonstration's catharsis. Shortly after it occurred, the demonstration ended and the protesters, including Johnson, left the area in front of City Hall.

As the demonstrators disbursed, a man who had witnessed the flag burning quietly walked to the place where Johnson had ignited the flag. He proceeded carefully, even reverentially, to collect the ashes and remains from the ground, took them home, and buried them in his yard.

Within a half hour or so of the flag burning Johnson was arrested, along with a number of other protesters. Johnson, alone, was charged with a crime. The charge was desecration of a venerated object, in this case the American flag, a Class A misdemeanor. Johnson was tried, convicted, and sentenced to a year in jail and a $2,000 fine.

After one unsuccessful appeal to the Texas District Court of Appeals, Johnson succeeded in having his conviction overturned in the Texas Court of Criminal Appeals. The State of Texas then brought an appeal to the United States Supreme Court, arguing that the First Amendment to the United States Constitution did not give Johnson the right to desecrate the American flag by publicly burning it as part of a protest against the government of the United States.

At one level the Johnson case presented a pretty simple and straightforward question for the justices of the Supreme Court to decide. Johnson was clearly expressing his political views at the time he burned the flag, and the flag-burning was indisputably part of his expression. Speech protected by the First Amendment, in other words, was clearly taking place.

But at another level the case posed a difficult problem. The State of Texas agreed that Johnson was exercising his freedom to speak, but claimed that he was not arrested for speaking but, instead, for burning the flag. The question thus posed was what relation the act of setting the flag afire had to Johnson's speech. This question, it turns out, was *not* a simple and straightforward one. Was the flag, itself, speech because of its symbolic meaning? Or was the flag the medium through which Johnson's protest message against nuclear war was expressed? If it was the medium, what contribution did it make to the speech, and what amount of protection, if any, should it have *as a medium* under the First Amendment?

In its argument before the United States Supreme Court, the State of Texas took the position that burning the flag, even as part of Johnson's effort to communicate his sentiments about the Reagan military buildup and the threat of nuclear war, was not protected by the First Amendment. The state's position was presented—*very* ably, it should be said—by Kathi Alyce Drew, an assistant district attorney for Dallas County, in the oral argument that was held before the Supreme Court at 2:00 P.M. on Tuesday, March 21, 1989.

> *Ms. Drew:* The issue before this Court is whether the public burning of an American flag which occurred as part of a demonstration with political overtones is entitled to First Amendment protection. We believe that preservation of the flag as a symbol of nationhood and national unity is a compelling and valid state interest. We feel certain that Congress has the power to both adopt a national symbol and to . . . prevent the destruction of that symbol.
>
> *Question from the Court:* Now, why does—why did [Johnson's] actions destroy the symbol? His actions would have been useless unless the flag was a very good symbol for what he intended to show contempt for. His action does not make it any less a symbol.
>
> *Ms. Drew:* Your Honor, we believe that if a symbol over a period of time is ignored or abused, it can, in fact, lose its symbolic effect.
>
> *Question:* I think not at all. I think . . . when somebody does that to the flag, the flag becomes even more a symbol of the country. It seems to me you're running quite a different argument: not that [Johnson] was destroying its symbolic character, but that he was showing *disrespect* for it; that you want not just a symbol, but you want a venerated symbol. But I don't see how you can argue that he's making it any less of a symbol than it was.
>
> *Ms. Drew:* Your Honor, I'm forced to disagree with you.
>
> Texas is not suggesting that we can insist on respect. We are suggesting that we have the right to preserve the physical integrity of the flag so that it may serve as a symbol [and that] its symbolic effect is diluted by certain flagrant public acts of flag desecration.
>
> All Texas is suggesting . . . is that we have got to preserve the symbol by preserving the flag itself because there really is no other way to do it.

The argument Drew is making is subtle but crucial. She is not arguing that Texas can compel people to respect the flag, for this would be just another way of requiring people to be patriotic and to hold patriotic beliefs. Freedom of speech and thought would clearly be violated by such a law.

Nor is Drew arguing that Johnson was arrested and charged because of the particular political sentiments that he was expressing through the symbolic medium of the flag, for this would mean that we can use the flag in furtherance of only certain, patriotic, views. It couldn't matter, for Drew's argument, whether Johnson was pro-Reagan or anti-Reagan. Indeed, it couldn't matter whether Johnson was lighting the flag to make a point or to start a charcoal fire on which to roast hot dogs.

The state, she claimed, was neither trying to enforce respect for a message nor censor belief. Instead, it was simply trying to preserve the flag, which exists in a physical *and* a symbolic form. Both dimensions of the flag's existence are utterly interdependent, much as the physical walls of a building are inextricably bound to its architecture, or aesthetic effect. To prohibit spray-painting on the walls of a building is not to enforce respect for, or agreement with, an aesthetic idea or architectural style but simply to preserve that architecture, whatever one thinks of it.

The difficulty with this argument, however, is that the symbolic effect, or meaning, of the flag is not neutral, like architecture, but is itself political. Patriotism, nationhood, national unity, are the symbolic meanings the flag represents — indeed, they are the messages the flag itself emits as a symbol, just as nature and harmony are the messages emitted by a Frank Lloyd Wright house.

The fact that with the flag the symbolic meaning corresponds with a political idea complicated Drew's argument. It is too easy to respond by arguing that preserving a symbol with a specific *political* meaning is a very different matter under the First Amendment from preserving cubism in art, or modernism in architecture, or historical integrity in old structures; too easy, but also incorrect. This is because Drew's point had nothing to do with the flag's particular message or meaning but, rather, with its quality as a symbol, as a medium through which Johnson's expression took place.

If a medium of communication has significance independently of that which is being communicated through the medium, should the *medium* be deemed speech protected under the First Amendment? Should the State of Texas be prohibited from protecting the integrity of the flag, in other words, because the flag *itself* has a meaning (patriotism)? Does a requirement that the flag be preserved amount to an effort by government to legislate one idea—patriotism—and prohibit the expression of another? Is the state prohibited, in effect, from censoring *the flag*?

The Supreme Court's answer would be yes. The flag, the Court would ultimately conclude in Johnson's case, has a meaning, as if it were speaking its own message. To restrict use of the flag in ways that are inconsistent with that meaning, in ways that conflict with the flag's expression of its message, is censorship, because it amounts to a law preferring the flag's message over competing ones.

At first blush this seems to be a sensible and persuasive basis for the Court's decision to reverse Johnson's conviction and prohibit the enforcement of flag desecration laws against people, like Johnson, who would use the flag as a medium for expressing beliefs that are not consistent with those symbolic meanings the flag itself expresses. But the question whether a *medium's* message is itself "speech" protected by the First Amendment is a bit trickier than that.

Take, for example, the problem of violence. Many thoughtful students of media and culture conclude that the depiction of violence on today's high-definition television—McLuhan's "hot," emotional, tribalizing medium—has a different effect than its depiction in print, print being a "cooler," more dispassionate, and rational medium. The medium of television, in other words, might with depictions of violence have a meaning *of its own*, a message of legitimacy and compulsion (rather than patriotism and unity) that can be traced to the medium itself, to its symbolic effect. Should any government efforts to regulate or control the impact of the medium of television itself on violence be flatly prohibited as censorship, just as Texas's attempt to control the impact, or symbolic effect, of the flag was also foreclosed?

What about public-school dress codes, another fad of late? Clothes, it might be said, are simply that: clothes. But for most, if not all of us, clothes are symbols with meaning; mediums that reflect ideas such as seriousness, conformity, discipline, obedience. In this respect they are indistinguishable from the flag, which symbolizes patriotism and unity. Clothes thus "speak" just as the flag speaks. And requiring certain clothes in school in order to preserve their symbolic meaning in that place is likewise an attempt to impose that meaning, that referent, and thus, by the Supreme Court's logic, to violate the First Amendment.

And what about cigarette advertising and the Marlboro Man? The freedom and independence symbolized by the Marlboro Man in a TV advertisement are certainly evocative. If the symbol had no meaning, and if the television medium had no message, we would presumably still find such ads on the airwaves. Yet Congress chose to outlaw them many years ago, and no objection has been voiced by the Supreme Court.

Advertising, it has been said, consists mainly of packaging our own emotions and selling them back to us. In this sense medium is everything in the advertising business, not because the message is unimportant but, rather, because the medium *is* the message. When R. J. Reynolds Tobacco Company produces a TV advertisement using the Marlboro Man, there is little doubt that R. J. Reynolds is speaking, just as Johnson was speaking when he burned the flag. But it is equally clear that the Marlboro Man is speaking, too, for the Marlboro Man is a symbol with meaning of its own.

Should the First Amendment protect, as speech, the Marlboro Man's meaning as if "he" were speaking? The law permits R. J. Reynolds to control the symbolic meaning of the Marlboro Man, preventing others from using it or altering it. It does so under the heading of trademark and copyright protection. Is the law inconsistent with the First Amendment because it restricts what the Marlboro Man can say, just like Texas was trying to restrict what the flag would say?

Just as virtually all things have symbolic meaning in our social and political culture, so also one might assert that all mediums, whether objects such as flags or clothes or cars or houses, or processes such as print or television or film or cable or satellite, or characteristics such as delayed versus live broadcast or head shot versus panorama, have meaning too. This is the message of the medium. It is the medium's speech, not the speech of the person who speaks through it, whether the person be Johnson speaking through the flag, R. J. Reynolds speaking through the Marlboro Man, or Ted Turner speaking through CNN.

This was the essence of Texas's argument as Drew expressed it in Johnson's case. Johnson was free to express his views, whether they concerned President Reagan or the meaning of the flag. But he was not making a point about the flag. He was instead using the flag as a medium through which to make a point about the president, foreign policy, and nuclear war. In prohibiting Johnson from burning the flag as a means of expressing those views, the state was regulating the medium through which Johnson spoke, not the ideas he was expressing.

Drew recognized that mediums "speak" in the sense that they contribute meaning or impact of their own—they evoke images and emotions and consequences—but she argued that they are not by virtue of that fact "speaking" for purposes of the First Amendment. Government can regulate the meaning and impact of the American flag as a symbol when used as a medium, just as it can choose not to fly the Confederate flag over the state capitol, just as it can regulate school attire, and just as it can regulate the mediums of television, radio, cable, or satellite broadcasting, at least with respect to the impact they have as mediums independently of the ideas expressed through them.

Drew had defined her argument with great care and subtlety. Perhaps too much subtlety for the Supreme Court on that day.

> *Question from the Court:* Ms. Drew, you begin by saying that [the flag is] a symbol and by acknowledging, at least in this part of your argument, that what [Johnson] did was speech, is that correct?
>
> *Ms. Drew:* We are assuming that [Johnson was engaged in First Amendment speech] for purposes of [this argument].
>
> *Question:* All right. At this point. What is the [rule] you are asking us to adopt in order to say we can punish this kind of speech? Just an exception for flags? It's just a—there's just a flag exception to the First Amendment?
>
> *Ms. Drew:* Your Honor, I think Texas . . . has made a judgment that certain items are entitled to more protection.
>
> *Question:* I understand that. But up to now we have never allowed such an item to be declared a national symbol and to be usable symbolically only in one direction, which is essentially what you are arguing. You can honor it all you like, but you can't dishonor it as a sign of disrespect for the country.
>
> *Ms. Drew:* No, Your Honor. We are not arguing that at all.
>
> *Question:* Oh?
>
> *Ms. Drew:* Not at all. We are in no way arguing that one cannot dishonor the flag or that one cannot demonstrate disrespect for the flag. Individuals have that right.
>
>   What we are arguing is that you may not publicly desecrate a flag regardless of the motivation for your action.
>
> *Question:* Well, one hardly desecrates it in order to honor it. I mean, you only desecrate it in order to show your disagreement with what it stands for, isn't that right? So, it's sort of a one-way statute.
>
> *Ms. Drew:* I don't think that it is exactly, Your Honor, because . . . there are other forms of conduct which are equally prohibited. Let me put it this way. The same conduct is prohibited regardless of the motive of the actor.

Question: Will you give me an example where . . . somebody dese-
crates the flag in order to show that he agrees with the policies of
the United States?
(Laughter)
Ms. Drew: I think it is possible . . . that an individual could burn a
flag as an honor for all the individuals who died in Vietnam. This
is their most prized possession. They are going to take it in front of
the Dallas City Hall in the midst of a hundred people in the middle
of the afternoon, they are going to soak it with lighter fluid, and
they are going to ignite it, and they are doing this to honor the
Americans who died in Vietnam.
Question: Your statute would cover that example . . . ?
Ms. Drew: Yes it would, Your Honor, because it does not go to the
motive of the actor. If a vandal takes a flag . . . in front of Dallas City
Hall, soaks it with lighter fluid, sets it on fire, [the vandal] is . . .
liable under this statute. [He] has desecrated the flag, [though] with
no intent to dishonor the country . . . [or] to dishonor the flag. [He]
has no intent to do anything except, oh . . . vandal[ize].

In this exchange, Drew is emphasizing her argument that it is the flag
as a symbol with its own meaning that is being protected under the
Texas law. The Texas law is not directed against Gregory Lee Johnson's
ideas or even his act of speaking; it doesn't matter under the law
whether the desecration takes place during the course of someone's
speech. Instead, the Texas law functions, under Drew's theory, almost
like a First Amendment protection *for* the flag: it protects the flag's ability to carry its symbolic message without interference with that message
by others.

This is a tricky position for Drew, for while the Texas statute does, in
fact, protect the flag's message, it also assigns that message to the flag.
The Texas statute thus assumes that the flag can have a message, but
that it cannot be a speaker for purposes of the First Amendment. The
flag's message of patriotism, in other words, is not speech protected by
the First Amendment. The state can therefore act to prevent interference
with that message.

The argument is ingenious, however, for it effectively shifts the burden of persuasion to Johnson, who must argue that the flag's message *is*
speech, and that the *flag* is therefore, in some metaphysical way, at least,
"speaking" for purposes of the First Amendment. This is where the

questions from the Court would now turn, although it is not clear that the justices are fully aware of the complexity of the issue they are addressing.

> *Question from the Court:* If [your] theory alone is enough to support the statute, I suppose you could have such statutes for Stars of David and crosses and maybe—I don't know—Salmon Rushdie's book or whatever, whatever might incite people. . . .
> *Ms. Drew:* Your Honor, again, there are other sections of this statute where other items are protected, specifically public monuments, places of burial and worship. I don't believe that anyone could suggest that one may paint swastikas on the Alamo in San Antonio. That is desecration of the Alamo.
> *Question:* But that . . . but that's because it's public property—
> *Ms. Drew:* True.
> *Question:* —and unless you want to say that the flag is somehow public property of us all and ignore traditional distinctions of property, then your example just doesn't work.

That, of course, is precisely what Drew must, and does, argue. The flag is public property—in its capacity as a national symbol and as a medium through which that symbolic meaning is communicated. This doesn't mean that the State of Texas claims physical ownership of all flags; it means instead that Texas claims ownership of the symbolic message. The flag is the medium, and the medium is the message.

And mediums aren't the same as messages under the First Amendment: they don't speak.

> *Ms. Drew:* Your Honor, I believe that [my Alamo example] does work. I believe it does. The brief filed on behalf of Mr. Johnson in this case by the American Civil Liberties Union confesses that there is no First Amendment interest in protecting desecrations of either public monuments, or places of worship or burial, because they are "Someone else's cherished property."
> I think the flag is this nation's cherished property, that every individual has a certain interest [in it.] The government may maintain a residual interest, but so do the people. And you protect the flag because it is such an important symbol of national unity.

Question: If we say so, it becomes so. But it certainly isn't self-evi-
dent that—I never thought that the flag I owned is your flag. I
mean. . . .
  (Laughter)
Ms. Drew: Many Justices of this Court have held that the flag is a
national property.

On that note, Drew returned to her seat, having acquitted herself
extremely well in a subtle and complex argument. If her argument failed,
it was perhaps the justices' failure to comprehend it—or their conscious
decision to ignore its nettlesome implications.

Johnson was represented by William Kunstler, a well-known lawyer
from New York who had been associated with liberal and radical causes
throughout his entire career. His argument, which needs no recounting
here, was bombastic and often wandering, even hard to follow. It
focused on a central assertion: that Johnson had been arrested and convicted for what he said, not what he did, and more specifically that he
had been arrested and convicted because the ideas he expressed through
the flag-burning offended onlookers. Johnson, in short, was punished
for his ideas because those ideas gave offense to others. Such a view of
the case would compel reversal of Johnson's conviction under the First
Amendment.

This is precisely why Drew had worked so hard to structure her argument around the state's interest in preserving the symbolic meaning of
the flag as a medium, an interest that had nothing to do with what ideas
Johnson was expressing—indeed with whether he was expressing any
ideas at all—or with whether any persons witnessing the flag burning
were in fact offended.

Kunstler's argument thus passed Drew's argument as if they were two
ships in the night, neither engaging nor even acknowledging the other.
But Kunstler's view of the case had an important advantage: it would
allow the Court to reverse Johnson's conviction while at the same time
avoiding the issues raised by Drew. Kunstler thus provided a convenient
means of escape, and the Supreme Court took it.

The Supreme Court's opinion in Gregory Johnson's case was not issued
until near the end of the Court's Term, some three months after oral
argument. On June 21, 1989, the 5-4 decision in favor of Johnson was

announced. Justice Brennan wrote the opinion for the majority, which consisted of himself and Justices Marshall, Blackmun, Scalia, and Kennedy. The dissenting justices were Chief Justice Rehnquist and Justices White, O'Connor, and Stevens.

The majority opinion addresses Drew's argument directly and rejects it explicitly, though perhaps without full appreciation of the implications of doing so:

> If we were to hold that a State may forbid flag burning wherever it is likely to endanger the flag's symbolic role, but allow it wherever burning a flag promotes that role—as where, for example, a person ceremoniously burns a dirty flag—we would be saying that when it comes to impairing the flag's physical integrity, the flag itself may be used as a symbol—as a substitute for the written or spoken word or a "short cut from mind to mind"—only in one direction. . . .
>
> We never before have held that the Government may ensure that a symbol be used to express only one view of that symbol or its referents. . . .
>
> To conclude that the government may permit designated symbols to be used to communicate only a limited set of messages would be to enter territory having no discernible or defensible boundaries. Could the government, on this theory, prohibit the burning of state flags? Of copies of the Presidential seal? Of the Constitution? [To] decide which symbols were sufficiently special . . . , we would be forced to consult our own political preferences, and impose them on the citizenry, in the very way that the First Amendment forbids.

The dissenting opinions of Chief Justice Rehnquist and Justice Stevens were equally to the point, and saw the case in dramatically different terms. Rehnquist wrote:

> Only two Terms ago the Court held that Congress could grant exclusive use of the word "Olympic" to the United States Olympic Committee. The Court thought that this "restriction on expressive speech properly [was] characterized as incidental to the primary congressional purpose of encouraging and rewarding the USOC's activities." As the Court stated, "when a word [or symbol] acquires value as the result of organization and the expenditure of labor, skill, and money by an entity, that entity constitutionally may obtain a limited property right in the word [or symbol]." Surely Congress or the States may recognize a similar interest in the flag. . . .
>
> [T]he First Amendment does not guarantee the right to employ every conceivable method [or medium] of communication at all times and in all places. The Texas statute deprived Johnson of only one rather inarticulate

symbolic form of protest . . . and left him with a full panoply of other symbols and every conceivable form of verbal expression to express his deep disapproval of national policy. Thus, in no way can it be said that Texas is punishing him because his hearers—or any other group of people—were profoundly opposed to the message that he sought to convey. . . . It was Johnson's use of this particular symbol, and not the idea that he sought to convey by it, for which he was punished.

Justice Stevens was even more pointed in his dissenting opinion:

The Court is . . . quite wrong in blandly asserting that respondent "was prosecuted for his expression of dissatisfaction with the policies of this country, expression situated at the core of our First Amendment values." Respondent was prosecuted because of the method he chose to express his dissatisfaction with those policies. Had he chosen to spray-paint—or perhaps convey with a motion picture projector—his message of dissatisfaction on the facade of the Lincoln Memorial, there would be no question about the power of the Government to prohibit his means of expression. The prohibition would be supported by the legitimate interest in preserving the quality of an important national asset. Though the asset in this case is intangible, given its unique value, the same interest supports a prohibition on the desecration of the American flag.

In the end Texas lost its case; Johnson won his. The flag can be burned with impunity. *Its* message is protected speech; the flag is a speaker, even as it burns; and its final gasp of speech, at whoever's hands, must be permitted even if the gasp is a wail of protest at the use to which it is being put. The message of the flag, its message as a medium, is fully protected by the First Amendment and cannot be proscribed or limited by government.

What, exactly, does the Supreme Court's decision in Johnson's case mean for other mediums of expression and the government's ability to regulate them? Some mediums are like the flag, they have one or a limited number of "messages" in the form of symbolic meanings: the Lincoln Memorial, as Justice Stevens suggested in his dissent; or the Marlboro Man, whom the government may no longer, after the Johnson case, be able to keep off the airwaves; a school dress code; a graduation exercise; a prize or award. Johnson's case clearly means that the government's ability to preserve their meaning, their ceremonial symbolism, will be severely limited.

But there are other mediums that also have messages, though they are messages of a somewhat different sort, and the Johnson case will surely have implications for government's ability to regulate them, as well. The classic "medium with a message" is television. Television, unlike print, is a multisensory, visual and aural, medium. Our involvement with the television medium is intense and participatory, not dispassionate; emotional rather than rational; yet at the same time television makes us feel strangely indifferent rather than mentally engaged. Television and other multisensory, participatory, electronic mediums, Marshall McLuhan predicted, would "restore . . . a tribal pattern of intense involvement. The nonspecialist electronic technology retribalizes," he said, shifting arrangements from large group to small, from group to individual, breeding attitudes of alienation, isolation, and insecurity.

"The meaning of a message," Kenneth Boulding said in 1956 in "The Image: Knowledge in Life and Society," "is the change which it produces in the image." The meaning of television as a medium—its message—is the change it produces in the viewer's image of what is being broadcast or the viewer's understanding of its significance. This is the message of television as a medium: passion; indifference; isolation; individualism; tribalization. These are the equivalent messages, for television, of the messages of patriotism and national unity for the flag.

In his recent book, *The Roar of the Crowd*, Michael O'Neill offers us a compelling description:

> What sets television apart from all other forms of communication ever invented is its ability to transmit human experiences in real time over great distances with a visual power and motion that mimics life itself—that, indeed, can so intensify experience through the manipulation and repetition of images that the real world often suffers by comparison. . . . The printing press . . . promoted the standardization, preservation, and proliferation of knowledge. . . . Television uniquely sweeps knowledge across the barriers of literacy, transforming all of life into moving images and sensory stimuli. It creates impressions instead of ideas and emotions instead of thought. . . .
>
> [With print] time and distance intervene; the event must be re-created . . . and your reactions reconstructed out of remembered associations and emotions. Inevitably, the effect is attenuated by an element of detachment. . . . The separation of language from senses is more congenial to deliberative thought and the reasoning process. [Language, the stuff of words,] is linear. . . .

"There is nothing linear or sequential about the total field of awareness that exists in any moment of consciousness," McLuhan observed. "Consciousness is not a verbal process." The actual sensory world, in other words, is more closely approximated by TV images than by writing.

"When sensations dominate thought and feelings substitute for deliberation," O'Neill concludes, "they deny wisdom its place in both personal and public affairs. When the process of knowing is altered by the medium of knowing, then life itself is changed because knowledge is its mold."

To many people, such sentiments are gross oversimplifications, the last gasps of protest by relics of the print era. But there is likely some, perhaps even much, truth in what McLuhan, Boulding, and O'Neill are saying. The dispute centers on whether the changes they describe are for the better or the worse.

The important point for present purposes, however, is not the rightness or the wrongness, the better or the worse, of the argument. It is instead what we draw from it. Mediums like television *do* have messages—symbolic and perceptual effects that are distinct from the particular subject matter being carried on the set, whether that be *COPS* or *Nightline* or *Charlie Rose*—just as a flag has a message that is distinct from the ideas any given individual uses the flag to express.

Are those effects significant enough to warrant our serious attention? Is the First Amendment an obstacle to our doing anything about them?

Of late, concerns have begun to be expressed about the impact of the newest medium of communication, the Internet. The concerns are in many respects closely related to those presented by television. Some individuals claim that information is provided on the Internet in vast quantities, in multisensory forms, and in ways that compel participation, emotion, and reaction, but not detachment, reason, and reflection. Space and time no longer serve as gatekeepers or filters for communications; instead, unrelieved immediacy is the normal fare. Exposure to vast amounts of information provided at retail, unfiltered and without perspective and distance, and often anonymously, may change the meaning and value of information itself. With no effective controls on the accuracy or significance of information, nothing may be believed.

Culture and individual character, moreover, are shaped by the common language of experience. What we know and believe are affected, if not determined, by what we see and hear. If there are no effective ways to control what can be experienced — seen and heard — on the Internet because the medium, by technological definition, is beyond control, the cultural effect, the symbolic meaning and message, of the Internet as a medium will surely transcend the particular items of information found there.

This is, of course, what the V-chip is all about, a technological device to place a measure of control over *exposure to content* back in the hands of the user. It is also the basis for efforts to prohibit indecency on the Internet, such as the recently enacted federal Telecommunications Act, or efforts to implant filters in computer chips that will screen out certain types of material.

But does the First Amendment permit such steps to be taken, even when they are directed not at censoring what someone wants to say but at regulating the quite distinct and implicit (and therefore arguably insidious) message of the medium through which they choose to say it? Might the State of Texas, drawing on the V-chip example, enact a law that permits flag-burning, but only after those who might unknowingly witness it are informed of it in advance so that they can refrain from seeing that which offends them? The statute might read:

> *Flag Desecration.* No person may desecrate a flag by burning it unless that person has provided reasonable notice that the desecration will occur in advance of the desecration and in such a manner as to permit others to avoid witnessing it.

Or might a law be enacted prohibiting flag burning in certain places, places where significant numbers of unwitting and unwilling witnesses would be present and thus forced to experience the *medium's* message or *its* desecration?

Or do these examples about flag desecration laws suggest something else? Do they suggest that the Supreme Court's decision in Gregory Lee Johnson's case went further than it should have, even than it needed to, and as a consequence it threatens, in the name of the First Amendment, to foreclose government from enacting such measures as the V-chip? Do the examples make it clear that in protecting the right to burn the flag the Court went too far, extending First Amendment protection not only to the ideas we express but to the mediums in which we express them, and most disturbingly to the messages *those mediums convey*, be they symbolic, metaphorical, perceptual, or cultural? At a time when the buying and selling of mediums — cable television; movie production properties; multimedia distribution networks; Internet access — is one of the biggest businesses in America, have we found ourselves strangely unable distinguish the First Amendment interest in AT&T's Internet connection, or Disney's vertical integration, from an individual's right to hold and express his or her beliefs?

Is it really necessary in order to safeguard our liberty of speech that schools be prohibited from enforcing dress codes because to permit states to do so would be to permit states to promote the messages of order and obedience that are implicit in the prescribed clothing practices? Must the First Amendment be interpreted to require that the arrest of a protester who spray-paints the Lincoln Memorial be based only on the government's interest as a "property owner" (harmed to the tune of the cost of paint removal only) rather than on a collective interest in preserving the symbolic message of the memorial?

Is it possible that out of a fear that any distinctions that might be made (such as between flags and the Marlboro Man, or between the broadcast and the print mediums) would be imperfect, we have arrived at a point at which none may be permitted at all?

Can we afford that luxury, even in the name of the First Amendment, especially when what is at stake is our collective cultural interest in regulating the messages of our mediums, not our minds?

ADDITIONAL READING

M. Ethan Katsch, "Rights, Camera, Action: Cyberspatial Settings and the First Amendment in Cyberspace," 104 *Yale Law Journal* 1681 (1995).

Michael J. O'Neill, *The Roar of the Crowd* (1993).

Marshall McLuhan, *Understanding the Media* (1964).

Federal Communications Commission v. Pacifica Foundation, 438 U.S. 726 (1978).

Reno v. ACLU, 117 S.Ct. 2329 (1997).

Reminiscences

Reflections on Enduring First Amendment Questions

October of 1995 marked the start of a new Term of the Supreme Court. It had been twenty-five years exactly since the Court took up the case of *Cohen v. California*, the case that, Justice Harlan observed, "may seem at first blush too inconsequential to find its way into our books" but that presented an issue "of no small constitutional significance." And it was a new Supreme Court, too, for by 1995 none of the justices who had been present at the argument of *Cohen v. California* remained on the Court.

On October 7, 1995, the first Monday in October, the Supreme Court justices gathered together, as they always do, to begin the new Term of the Court. It would be the 1995 Term, running from October of 1995 to the end of June 1996. The justices gathered shortly before 10:00 A.M. in the robing room just behind the Supreme Court chamber, or courtroom. They put on their robes, exchanged pleasantries, shook one anothers' hands, and proceeded across the hall to an area behind the high purple curtain that separated them from the imposing courtroom. In the courtroom the clerk of the Supreme Court announced their entrance, calling, "Oyez, Oyez, Oyez, all rise. . . ." In order of seniority, with the chief justice first, they parted the curtain, entered the courtroom from behind the elevated bench, and proceeded to take their seats behind the bench, again in order of seniority.

Thus the 1995 Term of the United States Supreme Court began.

The Court that assembled on that first Monday of October 1995 was very different from the Court that had assembled in 1970 to hear arguments in Paul Robert Cohen's case. In most respects other than the absence of Chief Justice Earl Warren, that earlier Court had remained the Warren Court. It was an activist Court that focused much of its energy on the parts of the Constitution that guaranteed the individual rights of fair trial, freedom from self-incrimination, the right to counsel, equality before the law, and, of course, the right of free expression.

Twenty-five years later, the faces of the justices were all new. The chief justice was not Earl Warren but William Rehnquist, an extremely able, thoughtful, and generous man, a conservative appointed to the Court in 1971 by President Nixon who had risen now to the position of chief justice, "first among equals," as the justices described the post, and who was also the most senior member of the Court. Following him in order of seniority were Justice John Paul Stevens, a moderate and often unpredictable justice from Illinois, who was President Ford's sole appointment to the Court; Justice Sandra Day O'Connor, the first woman justice, who was generally conservative, appointed from Arizona by President Reagan; and Justice Antonin E. Scalia, an ardently conservative judge and former law professor appointed also by President Reagan. These four were followed by Justice Anthony Kennedy, also a former law professor and judge from California, appointed by President Reagan; Justice David Souter of New Hampshire, a former state court judge appointed by President Bush after the nomination of Robert Bork had been waylaid in the Senate; and Justice Clarence Thomas, also appointed by President Bush, and the second African American to serve on the Court. The Court's two newest justices, and the only justices appointed by a Democrat, came last, occupying the two seats at the end of the bench. These were President Clinton's appointees: Ruth Bader Ginsburg, a federal judge and former law professor, and the second woman justice to serve on the Court; and Stephen Breyer, a well-respected and moderate federal judge and also a former law professor.

With the new faces on the Court had come new approaches to interpreting the Constitution. The Warren Court had been solicitous of individual rights and often suspicious of government action, especially laws enacted by the states. The Constitution stood as a firm restraint on the power of both the state and federal legislatures. The Rehnquist Court, in contrast, was more skeptical about claims of individual rights and more solicitous of the decisions of the democratically elected branches of the state and federal governments. In the early 1990s the Rehnquist Court had manifested a renewed confidence in the laws enacted by legislatures and a growing concern about the Court's power, as an unelected branch of government, to set aside the product of legislative bodies, even if the laws they enacted were often confused, messy, and inconsistent. Such qualities, after all, were characteristic of the special interests and shifting coalitions that governed the making of laws by the legislative and executive branches.

But the Rehnquist Court did not follow this path unwaveringly. There were exceptions to a rule of restraint and deference by courts, and the First Amendment seemed, often, to be just such an exception. As Justice Holmes had said decades before, in his 1919 dissent in *Abrams*, "Persecution for the expression of opinions seems to me perfectly logical. If you have no doubt of your premises or your power and want a certain result with all your heart you naturally express your wishes in law and sweep away all opposition. . . . But when men have realized that time has upset many fighting faiths, they may come to believe even more than they believe the very foundations of their own conduct that the ultimate good desired is better reached by free trade in ideas — that the best test of truth is the power of thought to get itself accepted in the competition of the market. . . ." Thus the Rehnquist Court, devoted with as much activism as the Warren Court to the opposite goal of judicial restraint with respect to state as well as federal legislation, approached the 1995 Term and the 1996 Term that would follow it also with an activist commitment to freedom of speech guaranteed by the First Amendment.

The Court's docket for the 1995 Term would include a broad range of free speech cases, some of which had already been accepted for review by the first Monday in October, others of which would be accepted as the Term unfolded. The cases included one from Colorado challenging the constitutionality of a restriction on the freedom of political parties to speak through advertisements on behalf of its candidates. Another Colorado case involved a cable company's right to decide whether indecent programming would be carried on its public access and leased channels. A case from Rhode Island challenged a state law that barred liquor stores from advertising the price of beer on the theory that price competition would encourage consumption. Finally, a group of cases from Chicago raised the question whether political patronage — in these cases the awarding of contracts to private companies — could turn on the political views of the contractors seeking the public contracts. What else, one might ask, *is* patronage?

In many of these cases the Court would be closely divided. In all of them there would be ardent dissents from some of the justices. In a few of them the Court's opinions would be muddled and confused, even purposely ambiguous. And the issues posed in each of the cases would find their roots, interestingly enough, in the stories we have told.

The Colorado case that challenged the right of political parties to advertise in support of the party's candidates turned on the role and function of organized political parties. Like the Michigan State Chamber of Commerce's advertisement on behalf of Richard Bandstra, the case ultimately would turn on whether political parties were sufficiently coherent in their political views that the party's speech could be said to represent the views of the members. Are the Republican or Democratic parties, in short, more like the ACLU and the NAACP, or like General Motors and the Michigan State Chamber of Commerce?

The liquor-price advertising case from Rhode Island saw the Court visiting, once again, the perplexing question of whether commercial advertising should be treated as speech fully protected by the First Amendment. Like the *Virginia Pharmacy* case, the question lurking beneath the surface of the Rhode Island case was simple but fundamental: Whose interests, the speaker's or the consumers', are protected by the First Amendment? Is free speech protection accorded to the liquor store's liberty interest in advertising for customers, or to the utility that price information has for the purchaser?

The patronage cases would spawn deep divisions on the Court. The right to do the public's business by winning a trash-hauling contract, some justices would say, is too far removed from the act of speaking one's mind that the First Amendment protects; moreover, a government's decision to award a contract, or not to do so, is more akin to conduct, and the bidder's political allegiances should not immunize the bidder from the traditional practices that the patronage system has engaged in from time immemorial. Should Robert Viktora's political views about race immunize him from the law's command that private property be respected and that race-based acts of vandalism, such as the burning of a cross in the front yard of a black family in the neighborhood, must be punished? Was the private company seeking the public contract "speaking" through its application, any more than Viktora, in his drunken and drug-induced stupor, was "speaking" as he conspired to ignite the cross?

Perhaps the most interesting case, however, was the Colorado case that involved the cable operator's right to screen out programming with indecent content, just as a newspaper might decide to reject (or edit) an article that failed to comport with its standards of decency, or news, or even with the views the newspaper preferred to express. Is the cable operator, like the newspaper editor, a speaker entitled to virtually complete freedom to decide what to publish? Or does cable television, as one of the new technologies of communication, present an entirely different and additional set of problems? Is cable television, in short, a medium that carries not only the messages of others but also a message of its own, a message of intrusiveness, of communicative power different from print's, of immediacy, of appeal to emotion and passion rather than reason and dispassion? Is the message of this new medium, as Texas had argued in the flag case, a dimension that warrants a degree of governmental oversight that would not be permitted in the more familiar and domesticated world of print journalism?

And if the qualities of power, immediacy, emotion, passion, and intrusiveness do, in fact, warrant a measure of government regulation of cable and the other new technologies of communication, what place in the new First Amendment equation do we give Justice Harlan's opinion in Paul Cohen's case, for it was Harlan who justified First Amendment protection for the painted lettering "Fuck the Draft" on Cohen's jacket because of its "emotive" force. Free speech, he said, is not limited to the realm of reasoned discourse but, instead, involves passion, emotion, and affront, each of which, we might say, were a product not of Cohen's message but of its medium.

The Supreme Court would be deeply divided in the Colorado cable television case, permitting the government, not the cable company, to make judgments about decency. The Court's opinion was as narrowly couched as possible, deciding only those questions that could not be escaped, and then doing so in the most limited way. The Court candidly acknowledged deep uncertainty, a reluctance to tread where no one had before, and a recognition of the fundamentally conflicting directions in which the Court's prior decisions, including the Michigan State Chamber of Commerce case (who is a speaker under the First Amendment?) and Paul Robert Cohen's case (when is emotion and the force of communication speech, itself?), pulled.

During the next Term of Court, the 1996 Term running from mid-1996 to mid-1997, the same Court would address fewer free speech cases, but the cases would present even more fundamental First Amendment questions. The first of the cases involved a claim by an Arizona state employee that an Arizona law requiring her to speak only in English while on the job violated her freedom of speech. The case thus presented a difficult question about government control of employee speech, and more basically about whether our liberty to speak freely depends on the capacity in which we speak—as a private person or as an employee—much like the R.A.V. cross-burning case involved the capacity (inebriation and aimless immature antics) in which the boys burned and "got crazy," or like the Michigan Chamber of Commerce case involved the capacity in which a corporation and its "agents," be they advertisers or executives, purport to speak. These questions the Court managed effectively to avoid, however, by dismissing the Arizona case without addressing them because the state employee had left her public job by the time the case was argued in the Supreme Court, and therefore the case was "moot."

Two other cases decided during the 1996 Term involved technology and its implications for First Amendment freedoms. The first involved a claim by Turner Broadcasting Corporation that the government's requirement that Turner's cable companies carry local over-the-air channels in the communities Turner serves violated Turner's right to free speech. Turner, in other words, claimed the right to speak only *its own* views. To require it to carry the speech of local broadcasters rather than, for instance, MTV or C-Span, would be the equivalent of the State of Texas requiring that the flag be treated with respect.

To make such a claim, however, Turner would have to argue that in deciding on the channels it would carry it was acting as a full-fledged speaker with First Amendment rights equivalent to yours or mine, or to a newspaper reporter's or editor's. The argument was made, but failed. Turner Broadcasting is a corporation making business decisions about who else's speech to carry on its cable channels; it is not making decisions about speech of its own making. The Supreme Court thus viewed Turner as more like the Michigan Chamber of Commerce or General Motors rather than like you or me or even the ACLU or the NAACP. The government's requirement that local channels be carried was upheld, and Turner's First Amendment claim was rejected.

Perhaps the most interesting and potentially far-reaching case the Court decided in the 1996 Term was the Internet case, entitled *Reno v. ACLU.* The case involved a challenge by Internet users to a 1996 federal law that restricted indecent and sexually explicit material from being placed on the Internet if children could get access to it. The case thus presented a raw clash between the most fundamental liberty interests of the individual, on the one hand, and the power of technology and the impact of medium, on the other. It was a clash between Paul Cohen's right to wear a jacket emblazoned with "Fuck the Draft" in a public place and Texas's interest in regulating the "medium" (not the message) of the flag. Liberty won and the 1996 law was stricken, but the decision was narrow and confined to voluntary transmission of indecent material. For this, the Internet worked just like a postal system, though an efficient and reliable one, unlike the alternative.

The moral of the Court's 1995 and 1996 Terms, and the moral of the stories we have considered here, is twofold. The first is that the mysteries of the First Amendment, the mysteries of the meaning of speech, of speaking, and of the power of language and image in the human imagination, still continue to plague the Court's efforts to establish a theoretical system in which the goals of the Constitution's inscrutable text—"Congress shall make no *law abridging* the *freedom* of *speech*"—can be identified and, then, well served.

The second moral is that the questions presented by these stories will continue to persist without any clear resolution, at least so long as human imagination and ingenuity exist. There are, as Justice Holmes suggested, no pat answers, but only interesting questions. But that is as it should be. "Truth," Holmes said in his essay *Natural Law*, is but "the system of my (intellectual) limitations." To reduce "truth" to law, especially First Amendment law, would be to "radiate constitutional doctrine without avowing it."

We should wish, therefore, not for answers from the Supreme Court but, instead, for continuing struggle and disagreement, messy as that seems at times. This is the nature of constitutional law: uncertain, adaptive, intellectually stimulating, constantly shifting and changing. Just like the human condition upon which it rests.

Index

About the Author

Randall Bezanson is a professor of law at the University of Iowa. A graduate of Northwestern University and the Iowa Law School, he served as a law clerk to Justice Harry A. Blackmun of the United States Supreme Court during the 1973 Term. In addition to teaching and writing in the fields of constitutional law and freedom of expression, Professor Bezanson has served as a vice president of the University of Iowa and as Dean of the Washington & Lee University School of Law in Lexington, Virginia. His books include the award-winning *Libel Law and the Press*, coauthored with Gilbert Cranberg and John Soloski, and *Taxes on Knowledge in America: Exactions on the Press from Colonial Times to the Present.*

Professor Bezanson lives in Iowa City, Iowa, and Clam Lake, Wisconsin, with his wife Elaine, and their two dogs. They have two grown children, Melissa and Peter.

www.ingramcontent.com/pod-product-compliance
Lightning Source LLC
Chambersburg PA
CBHW032134020426
42334CB00016B/1155